EDUCATING CULTURALLY RESPONSIVE TEACHERS

SUNY series, Teacher Preparation and Development
Alan R. Tom, editor

EDUCATING CULTURALLY RESPONSIVE TEACHERS

A Coherent Approach

ANA MARÍA VILLEGAS

TAMARA LUCAS

State University
of New York
Press

KH

Published by
State University of New York Press, Albany

For information, address State University of New York Press,
90 State Street, Suite 700, Albany, NY 12207

Production by Susan Geraghty
Marketing by Jennifer Giovanni

Library of Congress Cataloging-in-Publication Data

Villegas, Ana María.
    Educating culturally responsive teachers : a coherent approach / Ana María Villegas,
Tamara Lucas.
        p. cm. — (SUNY series, teacher preparation and development)
    Includes bibliographical references (p.   ) and index.
    ISBN 0-7914-5239-5 (alk. paper) — ISBN 0-7914-5240-9 (pbk. : alk. paper)
        1. Multicultural education—United States. 2. Teachers—Training of—United States. I.
Lucas, Tamara, 1951– II. Title. III. SUNY series in teacher preparation and development.

LC1099.3 .V55 2001
370.117—dc21
                                                                            2001020813

10 9 8 7 6 5 4 3 2 1

10|25|04

CONTENTS

LIST OF FIGURES

ACKNOWLEDGMENTS

As those who know us can attest, the writing of this book consumed us for longer than we imagined it would. Along the way, we received encouragement and support from friends, colleagues, and family members that sustained us through the book's completion. Our colleagues at Montclair State University read drafts, made suggestions, and worked with us to apply many of the concepts and practices we discuss in the book. Chief among them are Tina Jacobowitz, Cindy Onore, Nicholas Michelli (now at the City University of New York), Ada Beth Cutler, and Jennifer Robinson. Ken Zeichner, University of Wisconsin, and Estela Bensimon, University of Southern California, also offered helpful recommendations and encouragement at important stages in the process. Tamara's sister, April Bolton, an editor at the St. Anthony Messenger Press in Cincinnati, and Nancy Laurel Peterson, literacy instructor at Bronx Community College, used their expert editorial skills to help us fine-tune the writing. Alan R. Tom, University of North Carolina and editor of the SUNY series Teacher Preparation and Development, was supportive of our work throughout the process. We also want to acknowledge the comments of three anonymous reviewers, whose suggestions for revisions strengthened the final product considerably. Finally, we are grateful to our families for their constant support—especially Ana María's mother and brother, Solfina and Jesus Villegas, and Tamara's sister, April Bolton.

INTRODUCTION

The changing student population is one of the most critical factors in American education today. Currently, more than one of every three students enrolled in public elementary and secondary schools is of a racial or ethnic minority[1] background (National Center for Education Statistics [NCES], 2000), and by the year 2035 this group is expected to constitute a numerical majority of the K–12 student population (U.S. Department of Commerce, 1996). Presently, one in five children under eighteen years of age lives in poverty (Children's Defense Fund, 2000), and the proportion of poor children will most likely increase in the years to come as the safety net shrinks due to recent changes in welfare laws. More than one in seven children between the ages of five and seventeen speaks a language other than English at home; over one-third of them are of limited English proficiency (Federal Interagency Forum on Child and Family Statistics, 1999).[2] The number of language minority students is also expected to rise dramatically in the years ahead due largely to immigration trends. Clearly, it is increasingly imperative that tomorrow's teachers be prepared to deal responsibly with issues of race, ethnicity, class, and language.[3]

Historically, members of economically poor and minority groups have not succeeded in schools at rates comparable to those of their white, middle-class, standard English-speaking peers. While the achievement gap between minority and majority children narrowed somewhat after the 1960s, it began to widen again in the 1990s (Education Trust, 1996), and schools continue to distribute benefits inequitably among groups. Relative to white middle-class pupils, poor and minority students consistently attain lower scores on standardized achievement tests of reading, writing, mathematics, and science; are overrepresented in special education programs, in instructional groups designated as low-achieving, and in vocational curricular tracks; and drop out of high school at much higher rates and enroll in postsecondary education in much lower proportions (see Educational Testing Service [ETS], 1994; Ekstrom and Villegas, 1991; Meier, Stewart, and England, 1989; Oakes, 1985; NCES, 1997c, 1997d, 1999b, 1999c; Tomás Rivera Center [TRC], 1993). This pattern of inequitable education is unacceptable in a democratic society, especially one as affluent as that of the United States.

The educational system, including teacher education, must become more responsive to the needs of this growing segment of the student population. Not to do so would make a mockery of the espoused principles of this nation.

Adding to the complexity of the situation, the teaching force is growing more homogeneous as the student population becomes more diverse (Villegas, 1998). The proportional representation of minorities in teaching may drop even further unless active measures are taken to reverse this pattern (Hidalgo and Huling-Austin, 1993; Smith, 1992). Marked differences between the biographies of the overwhelming majority of teachers—who are white, middle-class, and English monolingual (Fuller, 1992; NCES, 1993a; Zimpher and Asburn, 1992)—and those of the growing numbers of poor, racial/ethnic, and linguistic minority students make it increasingly difficult for teachers to design instruction that capitalizes on the background experiences of their students (Cabello and Burnstein, 1995; Fuller, 1992; Noordhoff and Kleinfield, 1993; Reed, 1993; Shaw, 1991). The relative absence of teachers of color is also problematic in that it deprives students of color of vital "role models," "cultural brokers," and "advocates" in elementary and secondary schools (American Association of Colleges for Teacher Education [AACTE], 1989; Bass de Martinez, 1988; Cole, 1986; Foster, 1989; Irvine, 1990a; Mercer and Mercer, 1986; Stewart, Meier, La Follette, and England, 1989; Villegas, 1997).

RESPONSES TO DEMOGRAPHIC TRENDS

Clearly, preparing teachers who are culturally responsive is a pressing issue in teacher education. Immediate attention is needed on two fronts. First, everyone entering the teaching profession—regardless of background—must be prepared to teach a racially, ethnically, economically, and linguistically diverse student population. Second, teacher education programs must find ways to increase the number of minority teachers. Failure to act swiftly and decisively on these two fronts could have devastating consequences for the social and economic stability of this country (Banks, 1991a; Darling-Hammond, 1996; Hidalgo and Huling-Austin, 1993; National Commission on Teaching and America's Future, 1996; Rendón and Hope, 1996; Villegas, 1997; Zeichner, 1996b).

Despite the urgency of the situation, teacher education has been slow to respond to the shifting demographic landscape (Gomez, 1994, 1996; Grant, 1994b; Grant and Secada, 1990; Ladson-Billings, 1991; Tabachnick and Zeichner, 1993; Zeichner, 1993; Zeichner and Hoeft, 1996). Aside from a handful of initiatives to increase the number of minorities in the teaching profession, most teacher education programs have taken limited steps to address the growing racial/ethnic imbalance between the teaching force and the student body. Nor is there much evidence of serious work to address issues of race/ethnicity, class, and language in the teacher education curriculum (Martin, 1995b). Such lack of action helps to perpetuate the persistent achievement gap between white, middle-class, English-speaking children and their poor and minority peers.

Teacher education programs have typically responded to the growing diversity among K–12 students by adding a course or two on multicultural education but leaving the rest of the curriculum largely intact (Garibaldi, 1992; Goodwin, 1997a; Zimpher and Asburn, 1992). While separate courses on multicultural education play an important role in preparing teachers to teach students of diverse backgrounds, there is growing evidence that an add-on approach to diversity does not go far enough (Davis, 1995; Grant, 1994b; Larkin, 1995; McDiarmid and Price, 1990; Reed, 1993). For one thing, when special courses are designed to address racism, classism, and other issues associated with diversity, faculty members teaching other courses may assume that they are not responsible for addressing these issues. Further, because added courses are often optional, students can graduate from teacher education programs without receiving any preparation whatsoever in issues of diversity.

Solely adding a multicultural education course or two to the teacher education curriculum cannot prepare prospective teachers adequately for a changing student population. Nor can efforts of individual faculty members to redesign their own courses for diversity accomplish this goal, no matter how effective these courses are (Ahlquist, 1991; Gomez, 1996). In the absence of a broad vision for preparing culturally responsive teachers, such courses can be contradicted by the rest of the curriculum, marginalizing those individual efforts to address diversity issues.

But what are the alternatives? Many multicultural education advocates argue for an infusion strategy whereby issues of diversity are addressed not only in specialized multicultural education courses but throughout the entire teacher education curriculum (Brown, 1992; Grant, 1994a; Larke, 1990; Larkin, 1995; Martin, 1995b; Tabachnick and Zeichner, 1993; Zeichner and Hoeft, 1996). Although work in this area has begun, it is still not clear what this infusion might entail and how best to accomplish it. There is also a concern that, in practice, infusion will result in superficial attention to multicultural issues, especially since most of us who teach teachers are ourselves not adequately prepared to effectively integrate such issues into the curriculum (Banks, 1993b).

THE NEED FOR A COHERENT APPROACH TO EDUCATING CULTURALLY RESPONSIVE TEACHERS

To successfully move the field beyond the fragmented and superficial treatment of diversity that currently prevails, we teacher educators need to reconceptualize our approach to educating teachers. In this book, we present such a reconceptualization. A salient aspect of this work involves placing issues of diversity at the center of the teacher education curriculum. By *curriculum*, we mean the learning experiences offered to prospective teachers not only in education courses but also in arts and sciences courses and in field experiences and practica in communities and schools. We contend that without conceptual coherence across these learning experiences, derived from a common vision of teaching and learning in a multicultural society, prospective teachers may never see the relationships among key ideas or make the connections between theory and practice they will need to become effective teachers.

We present a curriculum proposal that builds on principles of social justice and advances a vision of the culturally responsive teacher. In our view, culturally responsive teachers are those who

- have sociocultural consciousness; that is, those who recognize that the ways people perceive the world, interact with one another, and approach learning, among other things, are deeply influenced by such factors as race/ethnicity, social class, and language. This understanding enables teachers to cross the cultural boundaries that separate them from their students.

- have affirming views of students from diverse backgrounds, seeing resources for learning in all students rather than viewing differences as problems to be solved.

- have a sense that they are both responsible for and capable of bringing about educational change that will make schooling more responsive to students from diverse backgrounds.

- embrace constructivist views of teaching and learning. That is, they see learning as an active process by which learners give meaning to new information, ideas, principles, and other stimuli; and they see teaching largely as a process of inducing change in students' knowledge and belief systems.

- are familiar with their students' prior knowledge and beliefs, derived from both personal and cultural experiences.

- design instruction that builds on what students already know while stretching them beyond the familiar.

It is this vision of the culturally responsive teacher that gives conceptual coherence to our curriculum proposal.

We have adopted a constructivist perspective because we think it is more consistent with principles of social justice than is a transmission-oriented view. As we explain in this book, a constructivist view is respectful of student diversity and recognizes the central role that individual and cultural differences play in the learning process. By giving students an active role in their own learning and by expecting them to learn for understanding, a constructivist education can also cultivate the sense of agency and the critical thinking skills they will need later in life to participate responsibly in the democratic process.

The reconceptualization of curriculum that we propose, while necessary, is not sufficient to adequately prepare culturally responsive teachers. Because teachers tend to teach in the ways they were taught (Floden, 1991; Feiman-Nemser and Melnick, 1992; Korthagen and Kessels, 1999; Howey, 1996; Tom, 1997), instructional practices used to carry out the reformed curriculum need to be aligned with the conceptions of teaching and learning promoted by that curriculum. Such alignment is the second dimension of the coherent approach to preparing culturally responsive teachers we advocate. Thus, arts and sciences faculty—with whom education students take the majority of their courses—and education faculty can contribute to the preparation of culturally responsive teachers by modeling responsive teaching practices for them. Similarly, elementary and secondary school educators who mentor prospective teachers during field experiences, including student teaching, can promote their developing skills in responsive teaching by exemplifying those practices themselves.

A conceptually coherent curriculum and instructional practices that are aligned with it, while essential to preparing culturally responsive teachers, are not likely to produce the desired results without an institutional infrastructure to support and sustain them. This institutional dimension has four salient elements:

1. *Ongoing work to make the college/university a multicultural community by actively seeking to recruit and retain students and faculty of color.* The intellectual diversity that derives from different perspectives and experiences enhances the quality of the learning environment for everyone involved. Prospective white teachers, in particular, stand to gain substantially from exposure to more peers and faculty of color, both in and outside education courses. By interacting with people different from themselves, they are more apt to develop the cultural sensitivity, interracial understanding, and sense of social responsibility needed to teach the changing student popu-

lation. A diverse institutional environment also provides prospective teachers of color with opportunities to learn about the experiences of people from different cultural groups, which they too need to become responsive educators.

2. *Use of multicultural criteria to recruit and select prospective teachers.* Haberman (1991), Haberman and Post (1998), and others have shown that those who enter teacher education with little or no sensitivity to diversity or with prejudicial attitudes—qualities that are antithetical to culturally responsive teaching—are not apt to change those views within the scope of preservice teacher education. Selection criteria, therefore, need to ensure that those admitted into teacher education are favorably disposed to diversity. The criteria also need to give priority to recruiting candidates of color, who bring to teaching cultural expertise that is currently lacking among both prospective and practicing teachers.

3. *Support for the establishment of structures and processes that foster collaboration among faculty in education, the arts and sciences, and the public schools—all of whom play critical roles in the preparation of teachers.* Without collaboration, there is likely to be little continuity in the learning experiences of prospective teachers across these three contexts.

4. *Strong investment in faculty development.* If the substance of our courses and our pedagogical practices are to promote responsive teaching in a multicultural society, those of us who teach teachers need to develop the dispositions, knowledge, and skills that characterize such teaching. To facilitate this development, institutions can support flexible, frequent, and varied learning opportunities, including workshops, retreats, seminars, study groups, team teaching, peer coaching, and curriculum development projects. To reach substantial numbers of faculty, the institution needs to make professional development central to its reward systems.

The coherent approach to preparing culturally responsive teachers that we advocate in this book cannot be accomplished overnight. It will take patience and hard work over an extended period. But now is the time to get down to the serious work of transforming teacher education for diversity. The changing demographics of the student population and of the country as a whole cannot be ignored, nor can the need for better preparation of teachers to teach this increasingly diverse population. In addition, it is expected that public schools will need to hire more than 2 million new teachers by the year 2008 (NCES, 1999d). Preservice teacher education programs can play a major role in determining the ability of these new teachers to responsively tackle the challenges they will face in schools. As educators of teachers, we have the opportunity to transform the capacity of the teaching force by transforming the quality of preservice teacher preparation. We cannot afford to let this opportunity pass us by.

BELIEFS AND ASSUMPTIONS GUIDING OUR VISION FOR EDUCATING CULTURALLY RESPONSIVE TEACHERS

Because it is a central premise of this book that knowledge never is and never can be neutral, we want to clearly expose the beliefs and assumptions that guide our vision for preparing culturally responsive teachers. These are derived from our reading of a large body of empirical and conceptual literature and from our professional and personal experiences. We have examined the literature on the central issues addressed in the book—including teacher education reform; preparing teachers for racial, ethnic, socioeconomic, and linguistic diversity; multicultural education; theories of teaching and learning; culturally responsive pedagogy in K–12 schools and in teacher education programs; and increasing the participation of people of color in teaching. Our professional experiences have included teaching in urban public schools and in teacher education programs at the undergraduate and graduate levels. We have conducted research on issues related to the education of students from subordinated groups in various U.S. public school contexts. More personally, we have been students in urban and small-town public schools and in public and private institutions of higher education. One of us is a Latina from a poor background who immigrated to the United States as a child from Cuba and who spoke no English when she first arrived in this country. The other is a woman of Scotch-Irish and English descent who grew up middle class in a small isolated town in Appalachia, her ancestors having immigrated to North Carolina several generations ago.

Our first assumption is that schools are intricately linked to the broader society and, therefore, can never be politically neutral. As institutions of society, schools mirror the culture, language, and values of those in power. The ways of talking, interacting, thinking, and behaving of the dominant group are the unacknowledged norm in teaching and evaluation practices. Therefore, schools place poor and minority children at a disadvantage in the learning process and systematically obstruct their development, whether intentionally or not. This bias legitimates the privileged position of the dominant group in society and produces the subordinate position of poor and minority groups (Bourdieu, 1986; Liston and Zeichner, 1991; Tabachnick and Zeichner, 1993; Villegas, 1988).

We further believe that although schools often function to maintain the advantage of the socially powerful, they can potentially serve as sites of social transformation (Bourdieu, 1986; Giroux, 1989). But altering the inequities that are deeply ingrained in the fabric of schools demands a cadre of teachers who understand the political nature of schools and teaching and who are adept at identifying inequalities in their own schools and classrooms, skilled in reconstructing the school and classroom culture in order to make it inclusive of all children, and committed to serving as change agents (Cochran-Smith, 1991; Giroux, 1989; Grant, 1991; Liston and Zeichner, 1991). This requires reflection and critical examination of common educational practices as well as of teachers' own social and educational principles (Beyer, 1996).

Like Goodlad (1990b), Tom (1984), and others, we believe that teachers are moral actors. Every classroom decision they make has consequences for children. They have the obligation to provide all children, not just some, with equal access to knowledge. Teachers who carry out this role responsibly are favorably predisposed toward diversity, believe all students capable of learning, and trust that they can make a difference in the lives of their students (Hilliard, 1989; Irvine, 1990a, 1990b, 1992). They also know their subject matter well, possess a broad repertoire of pedagogical strategies, and have a profound understanding of their students (Darling-Hammond, Wise, and Klein, 1995; Lucas, 1997; McDiarmid, 1991; Villegas, 1991; Zeichner, 1993).

Because students' strengths and needs vary widely and are constantly changing, teaching does not lend itself to the application of a prescription for effective teaching. The use of a decontextualized teaching formula assumes that children are so much alike that they will respond similarly and predictably to a common treatment. The formulaic approach to teaching ignores the needs of students who do not fit the mold on which the formula was based (Bartolomé, 1994; Cochran-Smith, 1995a; Reyes, 1992). Instead, teachers who are effective with a diverse student population make myriad decisions daily as they strive to tailor instruction to the students in their classes. This tailoring requires high levels of professional judgment and the ability to defend decisions on both pedagogical and ethical grounds.

We are aware that our emphasis on preparing teachers for elementary and secondary schools may suggest that we are placing an undue burden on them—both individually and collectively—to bring about educational and social change. We recognize that teachers cannot solve all the problems of the educational system. There are many complex social and political factors that impinge upon the success or failure of students, teachers, and the educational system as a whole. At the same time, we do believe that teachers are far more influential than they are usually acknowledged to be. We also know that the starting place for institutional and social change is the individual. Thus, while we do not believe that teachers are solely responsible for transforming the educational system, we do think they are responsible for playing a central role in such transformation.

We also believe that we as teacher educators have a similar responsibility. We agree with Liston and Zeichner (1991) that "every plan for teacher education, at least implicitly, takes a position on the current institutional form and social context of schooling. Teacher education programs can serve to integrate prospective teachers to the logic of the present social order or they can serve to promote a situation where future teachers can deal critically with that reality in order to improve it" (xvii). That is, no teacher education design is ever politically neutral. In recognition of this fact, our proposal for transforming teacher education invites teacher educators to take an active role in promoting a more equitable and participatory society by preparing future teachers with the dispositions, knowledge, and skills needed to interrupt inequitable policies and practices in schools and classrooms.

We see learning to teach as a process of conceptual change. To induce change in prospective teachers' thinking, teacher educators must first help them become aware of their own beliefs about the role of schools, the value of cultural diversity, and the nature of knowledge, teaching, and learning (Cochran-Smith, 1995b; Farber, 1995; Feiman-Nemser and Melnick, 1992; Feiman-Nemser and Remillard, 1996; Floden, 1991; Noordhoff and Kleinfield, 1993; Richardson, 1994; Rios, 1993). Because many teachers-to-be enter teacher education believing that schools are impartial institutions, that cultural diversity is problematic, that knowledge is objective and neutral, that learning consists of passively absorbing new information and repeating it by rote, and that teaching entails dispensing information, preparing them to be culturally responsive requires a complete resocialization (Feiman-Nemser, 1990; Zeichner and Hoeft, 1996). At the same time, most people want to become teachers so that they can make a difference in the lives of young people. This commitment to children is a resource teacher educators can draw on to facilitate the needed resocialization.

Our view of learning to teach as a process of conceptual change informs our perspective of how teacher education programs can best incorporate diverse teacher candidates. Both prospective white teachers and their minority peers need to critically examine entrenched views of schooling, knowledge, teaching, and learning as part of their preparation as teachers. They also need to learn about and examine their attitudes toward people who are different from themselves. However, key differences in the background experiences of these two groups are likely to play an important role in the preparation process. White teacher candidates, by and large, come from racially segregated, middle-class suburban communities and have attended predominantly white schools. As members of the dominant group in society, they have benefitted from the privilege accorded to the white, middle-class population. These experiences, unless examined critically, can limit their personal understanding of oppression based on race/ethnicity, class, language, and other factors, thereby reducing their insight into the lives of the growing number of poor and racial/ethnic minority students. As teacher educators, we can help them sharpen their insight by drawing out their preconceived notions about poor and minority students, cultural and linguistic differences, and the role of power in schools and society and by introducing alternative ways of thinking as appropriate (Cochran-Smith, 1991, 1995a; Floden, 1991; McDiarmid, 1991; Sleeter, 1995a; Tatum, 1992).

By contrast, prospective teachers of minority backgrounds are more likely either to live or to have lived in urban settings and to have attended urban schools. If they do not currently live in predominantly minority communities, they probably have family or friends who do. As members of racial, ethnic, and linguistic minority groups, they are likely to be conscious of having directly experienced racism and prejudice. As a result, they bring into teacher education a heightened awareness of the relationships among race, ethnicity, and economic status and an intimate familiarity with the language and way of life of minority students. This prior knowledge and experience, if skillfully tapped by teacher educators, can provide a solid foundation for understanding inequitable school practices and for developing responsive teaching strategies (Sleeter, 1992; Villegas, 1997). To ignore the wealth of knowledge and experiences that prospective teachers of color possess, as is current practice in most teacher education programs (Montecinos, 1995), is a serious mistake. Such neglect deprives the teacher education community of different perspectives on the education of students who are poor and of racial, ethnic, and linguistic minority backgrounds. It also undermines the goal of increasing the participation of minorities in the teaching profession by alienating minority teacher candidates from the learning process.

In sum, we view schools as social and political institutions and teaching as a social, political, and ethical activity. We see educators at all levels in the system as moral actors whose social and political values and actions shape the institution. Finally, we believe that learning to teach is not simply the acquisition of new knowledge and skills but rather a complex process of changing both one's ways of thinking and one's ability to change the social setting in which one lives and works with children. Even when we do not make them explicit, these principles guide our thinking throughout the book.

ABOUT THIS BOOK

In this book, we offer a coherent approach to preparing future teachers to be culturally responsive. We are writing primarily for teacher educators who, in most contexts, are faculty and administrators in colleges/schools of education whose work focuses on the preparation of teachers. But we consider faculty in arts and sciences and in K–12 schools who participate directly in the preparation of prospective teachers to be teacher educators as well. This book is of direct relevance to all these groups. Higher education leaders and administrators other than those in teacher education, whose actions have a profound influence on the education of teachers, will also find the book useful. Because of its comprehensiveness, we believe this book can be a helpful reference for anyone who is engaged in the work of transforming schools.

We have organized the chapters as follows. In the first chapter, we establish the urgent need to prepare future teachers to teach students of diverse backgrounds by reviewing current and projected demographic data for the K–12 student population and the teaching force. While bits and pieces of demographic data often appear in the education literature, the full impact of this information is most powerfully understood when the changing demographic landscape is examined holistically. In this chapter we also discuss why the disparity in the cultural and linguistic backgrounds of teachers and their students is problematic.

Chapters 2 and 3 detail our curriculum proposal. We have organized what we consider the essential dispositions, knowledge, and skills that future teachers need to be successful in our multicultural and multilingual society into six strands. We argue that these strands should be woven throughout the preservice teacher education curriculum to give conceptual coherence to the preparation of teachers. Chapter 2 elaborates upon the first three of these strands, which constitute the fundamental orientations to teaching diverse student populations: gaining sociocultural consciousness, cultivating affirming attitudes toward culturally and linguistically diverse learners, and developing the commitment and skills for becoming teachers who are change agents. Chapter 3, which presents the other three strands, defines culturally responsive teaching and grounds this powerful concept in constructivist views of knowledge, teaching, and learning. The chapter also describes strategies that prospective teachers can use to learn about their future students and to design instruction in ways that build on the students' strengths while simultaneously addressing their needs. In both of these chapters, we give examples of strategies that teacher educators can use to develop the desired dispositions, knowledge, and skills among prospective teachers. We also discuss ways in which the preparation of white and minority teacher candidates might differ.

In chapter 4, we contend that successful implementation of the curriculum we propose requires a change in the pedagogy typically used to teach future teachers. This change is needed both because a major goal of this curriculum is to modify beliefs and develop dispositions and because one role of teacher educators is to model culturally responsive practices. We argue for a move away from the transmission-of-knowledge approach to teaching that prevails in higher education to the construction-of-knowledge approach. We discuss various classroom-based practices that give students an active role in their own learning and facilitate conceptual change, including conducting inquiry projects, preparing action plans, engaging in authentic dialogues, writing reflectively, participating in simulations and games, and analyzing teaching cases. We also describe field experiences through which prospective teachers can learn about diverse communities and classrooms and can develop competence in culturally responsive teaching.

Chapter 5 examines salient aspects of the institutional infrastructure needed to support the curricular and pedagogical transformations we believe are necessary to prepare culturally responsive teachers. As we discussed above, these include committing substantial resources to creating a diverse college/university community; making it a priority to recruit and select students into teacher education who are favorably predisposed to diversity and are from diverse backgrounds; building collaborative relationships among faculty in education, arts and sciences, and the public schools; and investing in faculty development related to matters of diversity.

We have attempted to forge a new vision of teacher education by integrating and extending previous work in a number of areas. The book advances current thinking by recognizing that student diversity is central to the learning process and by placing this view of learning at the heart of teacher preparation. Without making such a view of learning the focal point of teacher preparation, diversity will continue to be treated as an add-on topic addressed largely through special courses or as a discrete subject examined in mainstream courses only superficially, if at all. We also offer a comprehensive approach to the preparation of teachers for diversity, considering curriculum, pedagogy, and institutional structures and processes. We give explicit attention to issues related to the preparation of a diverse teaching force, a topic that has been largely ignored by the teacher education literature. We make a case for the importance of diversifying the teaching force, moving the discussion beyond the "role model" function most frequently cited by educators. Finally, to make the book practical as well as conceptually grounded, we include exemplary practices that offer guidance for educators in their work of restructuring teacher education for diversity.

CHAPTER 1

The Shifting Demographic Landscape

The changes in teacher education that we envision in this book, like all educational change, will not come quickly or easily. In order to bring them about, those of us who are teacher educators must have the will to engage in the long and difficult process of reform. In this chapter, we will present what we believe is incontrovertible evidence of the urgent need for teachers who are well prepared to teach students of diverse backgrounds. In so doing, we hope to lay a strong foundation for our proposal for preparing culturally responsive teachers. First, we examine current and projected demographic data on race/ethnicity, English proficiency, socioeconomic status, and the academic underachievement of students of color. Then we describe the current and projected demographic profiles of the teaching force and discuss why the growing imbalance in the cultural backgrounds of teachers and their students is problematic.

While we present these data to support our argument that teacher education must be reconstructed, we recognize that, compelling as these numbers are, they do not inevitably lead to the conclusions we draw from them. For example, Herrnstein and Murray (1994) view data illustrating the persistent academic underachievement of students of color as evidence of their inherent inferiority. We view them, however, as evidence that our educational, social, economic, and political systems are not functioning properly. In a modern society that strives to be democratic and just, education should ensure (a) that all students develop advanced literacy and numeracy skills and facility with technology so that they can gain access to rapidly changing information; (b) that they acquire critical thinking skills, including the ability to analyze and interpret complex information, understand social problems, and envision potential solutions to those problems; (c) that they learn to respect and understand multiple perspectives and, at the same time, to evaluate the merit of different positions; and (d) that they become skilled at working collaboratively, making collective decisions, and communicating effectively in cross-cultural settings. Ultimately, it is the commitment to seeking social justice and the recognition that education is a political and inherently moral activity that will give us the will to make the changes in teacher education programs for which we are calling. Thus, while we believe that the shifting demographic landscape presented in this chapter gives a special urgency to the changes we espouse, we also believe that a just and democratic society must prepare its teachers to facilitate the development of these skills, perspectives, and knowledge by all students, regardless of the proportions of different demographic groups in the overall student population.

THE CHANGING K–12 STUDENT POPULATION

The United States is becoming more racially, ethnically, and linguistically diverse than ever, a trend that is expected to continue well into the twenty-first century. There are several reasons for this. For one thing, higher birth rates are projected for minority groups, especially among Latinos and African Americans.[1] Second, the differing age structure of each group will contribute to higher fertility rates and lower death rates among people of color, thereby increasing their share of the total population. Third, net immigration is expected to be considerably higher for nonwhite groups in the years to come. Combined, these factors will transform the makeup of the U.S. population over the next fifty years (U.S. Department of Commerce, 1996). Indeed, the future is already apparent in the school-age population.

Over the past thirty years, the elementary and secondary student population has grown increasingly diverse. This steady trend toward diversity is evident in figure 1.1, which presents the percentages of white students and students of color in K–12 public schools for selected years, beginning with 1972. In that year, students of color accounted for a little more than one-fifth (or 22 percent) of the total enrollment in the public schools. Fourteen years later, their share of enrollment had grown to three-tenths (or 30 percent). By 1998, they constituted over one-third (37 percent) of the student population. Much of this growth was among Latinos and Asians. Already, students of color make up the majority of the K–12 enrollment in five states—California, Hawaii, Mississippi, New Mexico, and Texas—as well as in the District of Columbia; and they account for half of the student population in Louisiana (NCES, 1998). Similarly, they constitute a majority in all but two of the nation's twenty-five largest school districts (NCES, 1997a). While children of color are largely concentrated in urban schools, their numbers are increasing in suburban settings as well, particularly in districts located near large cities (Lucas and Villegas, 1996; Villegas and Young, 1997).

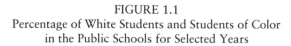

FIGURE 1.1
Percentage of White Students and Students of Color
in the Public Schools for Selected Years

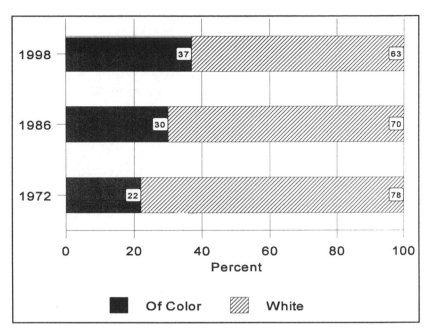

Sources: NCES, 1999a, 2000

No longer can we afford to ignore issues of diversity in the preparation of teachers, even when they are being prepared to teach in suburban schools.

According to the U.S. Department of Commerce (1996), during the first half of the twenty-first century, the K–12 student population is expected to grow substantially. If estimates hold, the number of five to nineteen year olds will increase from 56.2 million in 1995 to 79.6 million by 2050. This increase, however, will be distributed differentially between the white population and the population of color, as shown in figure 1.2. While children of color constituted about one-third of the student population in 1995, they are expected to become the numerical majority by 2035. This change will render the expression "minority students" statistically inaccurate. By 2050, so-called minorities will collectively account for nearly 57 percent of the student population.

Figure 1.3 presents the projected growth of the school-age population through the year 2050 for each major racial/ethnic group. Black Americans, the current largest student group of color, accounted for

FIGURE 1.2
Projections for Five to Nineteen Year Olds in the United States through 2050:
White Youth and Youth of Color

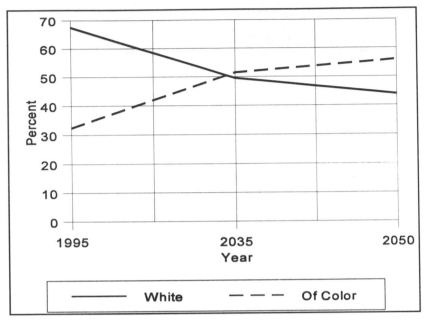

Source: U.S. Department of Commerce, 1996

14.7 percent of all five to nineteen year olds in 1995. By 2050, their representation is expected to rise to 16 percent, a relatively small proportional increase in the total share, but an important one given the sizeable growth projected for the K–12 student population. The American Indian student population will hold steady at about 1 percent over this time period. The proportions of young people of Hispanic and Asian backgrounds will increase significantly, however. As we reach 2050, Hispanics will constitute over 30 percent of the entire school-age population, up from about 13 percent in 1995. By 2010, Hispanic students will become the largest minority group in U.S. schools. Asians will also more than double their portion of the five to nineteen year old population, going from 3.6 percent in 1995 to nearly 9 percent by 2050. The biggest gains for both Hispanic and Asian groups are expected to occur by 2035. The growth among Hispanic and Asian students signals an increase in the number of young people who speak languages other than English at home, a fact that will have a significant impact on schools.

FIGURE 1.3

Current and Projected Distributions for Five to Nineteen Year Olds in the United States by Race/Ethnicity

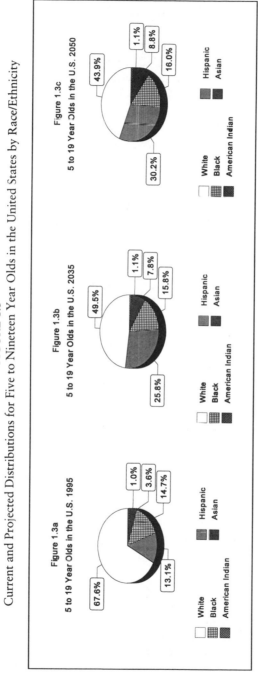

Figure 1.3a
5 to 19 Year Olds in the U.S. 1995

67.6%
1.0%
3.6%
14.7%
13.1%

White
Black
American Indian
Hispanic
Asian

Figure 1.3b
5 to 19 Year Olds in the U.S. 2035

49.5%
1.1%
7.8%
15.8%
25.8%

White
Black
American Indian
Hispanic
Asian

Figure 1.3c
5 to 19 Year Olds in the U.S. 2050

43.9%
1.1%
8.8%
16.0%
30.2%

White
Black
American Indian
Hispanic
Asian

Source: U.S. Department of Commerce, 1996. Calculations by authors.

Existing racial/ethnic categories downplay the reality of the variation that characterizes different groups. Cultural differences within Hispanic, Asian, American Indian, Pacific Island, and Alaska Native groups abound. For instance, more than 300 separate tribes are included in the Census Bureau's definition of the American Indian, Eskimo, and Aleut population (Educational Research Service [ERS], 1995), and numerous other tribes have not been officially recognized. Each of these tribes represents a different culture and language. Hispanics speak Spanish, but they come from many different countries, each with its own national heritage. The many groups that are considered "Asian" not only represent vastly different cultures but also speak many different languages. While many within this broadly encompassing group have done relatively well in this country educationally and economically, others—especially those from Southeast Asia—have fared less well in our society.

Linguistically, the K–12 student population has also grown more diverse in the recent past. Estimates of the actual number of limited-English-proficient students in U.S. schools over the past two decades have varied widely. Several factors have made it impossible to determine the exact number of English language learners in U.S. schools. There is no generally accepted definition of limited-English-proficiency and no standard for collecting information about limited-English-proficient populations, so data collectors and analysts have used different criteria to identify the populations they study. Further complicating matters, students may come from homes where a language other than English is spoken, but they may be fluent in English, thus complicating survey data collection. There is also the question of whether to consider only oral proficiency in population surveys or to include written proficiency as well. In addition, the attitudes toward immigration and the use of languages other than English in school and society are politically charged, making it difficult to judge the accuracy of survey responses. Nevertheless, in the early 1990s, estimates of LEP students ranged from about 2.5 million (Hopstock and Bucaro, 1993) to 3.7 million (Chapa and Valencia, 1993).

While we cannot be certain of the exact numbers of LEP students in the United States, we can be sure that their numbers have increased dramatically in recent years (Hopstock and Bucaro, 1993; McArthur, 1993; National Clearinghouse for Bilingual Education [NCBE], 1998). This trend is evident in figure 1.4, which summarizes estimates of the LEP student population provided by State Education Agencies (SEA) across the nation for the years between 1985–86 and 1995–96, as reported by Hopstock and Bucaro (1993) and the National Clearinghouse for Bilingual Education (1998). As shown, these data indicate a gain of 1.76 million LEP students in elementary and secondary schools during this

FIGURE 1.4
Estimates of LEP Student Population by
State Education Agencies in Millions, 1986–95

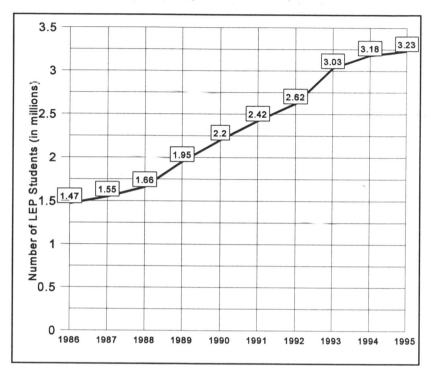

Sources: Hopstock and Bucaro, 1993 (for 1986–89);
NCBE, 1998 (for 1990–95)

period, with estimates rising to 3.23 million in 1995 from 1.47 million
nine years earlier.[2] Thus, between 1986–87 and 1995–96, a 120 percent
increase in the number of LEP students was reported by the SEAs.

Spanish has consistently been the language spoken by the overwhelming majority of students identified as LEP. In 1987, it was esti-
mated that 72.5 percent of LEP students spoke Spanish, and in 1991
that proportion was 72.9 percent (Fleischman and Hopstock, 1993;
Hopstock and Bucaro, 1993). While many people assume that all Spanish-speaking students are immigrants, this is not the case. In fact, in
1991, 39 percent of Spanish-speaking LEP students were born in the
United States (Fleischman and Hopstock, 1993). Partly accounting for
this phenomenon is the history of segregation of immigrant groups from
the white, English-speaking U.S. population, especially immigrant

groups of color. The second most common language is Vietnamese (3.9 percent of LEP students), followed by Hmong (1.8 percent), Cantonese (1.7 percent), Cambodian (1.6 percent), and Korean (1.6 percent). Despite the preponderance of Spanish, many school districts serve students who speak a kaleidoscope of languages, complicating the task of communicating with them and of designing curricula that meet their varied needs while simultaneously building on their strengths.

The sharp rise in immigration experienced by the United States over the past two decades has accelerated the racial/ethnic and linguistic diversification of the K–12 student population. In 1990, for instance, more than 2.2 million foreign-born children enrolled in the nation's elementary and secondary schools, accounting for 5 percent of the student population that year (American Council on Education, 1994). The immigrant student population includes a wide range of languages, cultures, and experiences. Unlike their predecessors, who came largely from Europe, immigrant students today are mostly from Latin America (Mexico, El Salvador, Guatemala, Nicaragua, Honduras), Asia (Vietnam, the Philippines, China, India, Korea), and the Caribbean (the Dominican Republic, Cuba, Jamaica, Haiti). Increasing numbers of immigrants are also arriving from Eastern European countries with previously little representation in the United States (U.S. Immigration and Naturalization Service, 1995). While many of these students have attended schools in their native country, a relatively large number—especially those from war-ridden countries and rural areas—have had little or no schooling prior to their arrival in this country (Chang, 1990; Gibson, 1987). Some of the children are literate in their native language, but many are not. A small proportion of them have attained some level of English-language fluency before entering U.S. schools, but the overwhelming majority speak little or no English (Chang, 1990). A sizeable number of these students were victims of extreme poverty in their native countries, and many continue to live below the poverty level in the United States. Some of the new immigrants have suffered the traumas of war, including the loss of or separation from their immediate families (National Coalition of Advocates for Students [NCAS], 1991). This wide range of experiences poses a major challenge to U.S. school systems, many of which find themselves unprepared to respond effectively to such diversity in backgrounds and needs (Villegas and Young, 1997).

The socioeconomic makeup of the student population is also undergoing a significant shift. Because a student's academic achievement is highly correlated with his or her socioeconomic status, the recent growth in poverty among children is of serious concern to educators. A review of recent trends is instructive. In 1965, the first year that the War on Poverty programs took effect, 14.7 million children—or 21 percent of everyone under the age of eighteen in the United States—lived in poverty. By 1973, that number fell sharply to 10 million, or 14.4 percent of all children in this country. As social programs experienced financial cuts during the 1980s, the poverty rate climbed again. By 1995, the number of poor children was back up to 14.7 million—or 20.8 percent of the population eighteen years of age or younger (Kilborn, 1996). Compared to other advanced nations in the world, the United States currently has one of the highest rates of children living in poverty (Children's Defense Fund, 2000).

In addition to reductions in government programs, marked changes in family structure to more one-parent homes—primarily single-mother homes—have contributed to the rise in poverty rates observed during the past two decades in the United States. In 1995, for instance, over 41 percent of all families with children headed by a single female were poor, compared to about 19 percent of families headed by a single male and 7 percent of two-parent homes (U.S. Census Bureau, 1999b). A decline in real wages for individuals with limited education is another salient factor related to poverty increases (ERS, 1995; Freeman, 1999).

Although the numerical majority of poor children in the United States is white, poverty is far more pervasive among racial/ethnic minority groups, as illustrated in figure 1.5. In 1995, for example, 16 percent of all white children lived in poverty, compared to 42 percent and 40 percent of black and Hispanic children, respectively (Kilborn, 1996). A survey in the early 1990s showed that 77 percent of limited-English-proficient students were eligible for free or reduced-price school lunches, a proximal indicator of poverty, compared with eligibility for only 38 percent of all students in the same schools (Fleischman and Hopstock, 1993). Thus, as the numbers of students of racial/ethnic and linguistic minority groups grow in the years ahead, the poverty rate within the student population is likely to rise. Making matters worse, a provision in the welfare law approved by the U.S. Congress and signed by the president in 1996 eliminated federal cash assistance for the nation's poorest children; this change threatens to push many more young people, both white and of color, into poverty in the future.

As this review of trend data shows, the number of students who are poor and of racial/ethnic and language minority groups is on the rise. Unfortunately, schools have historically served these populations inadequately. The consistent gap between racial/ethnic minority and poor students and their white, middle-class peers in scores on standardized tests is indicative of the inability of the educational system to effectively teach students of color as schools have traditionally been structured. Recent data from the National Assessment of Educational Progress (NAEP) illustrate this gap.

FIGURE 1.5
Percentage of White, Black, and Hispanic Children
in the United States Living in Poverty in 1995

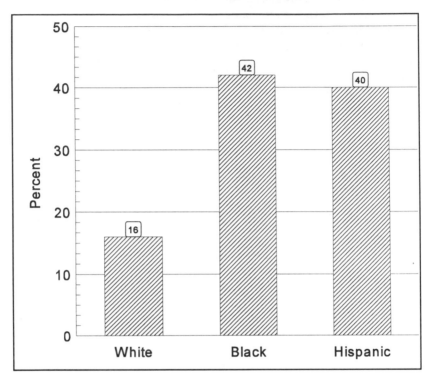

Source: Kilborn, 1996

Figure 1.6 compares the achievement levels of white, black, and Hispanic students in fourth and twelfth grades on the 1996 mathematics
assessment.[3] Of the fourth graders taking the test, 68 percent of black students and 59 percent of Hispanic students scored below basic, compared
to 24 percent of white students.[4] That is, these students did not show even
"partial mastery of prerequisite knowledge and skills." The figure also
illustrates that while students achieved at higher levels in the twelfth
grade, the disparities between white students and students of color persist.
Figure 1.7 shows a similar pattern of disparities in the reading assessment
of black and Hispanic students and their white counterparts. We have
reported the NAEP scores for mathematics and reading because skills in
these areas are fundamental to success in school at any level. The results
of the NAEP assessments in science and writing are consistent with this
pattern of disparity in achievement as well (NCES, 1997d; NCES, 1998).

FIGURE 1.6

Percentage of White, Black, and Hispanic Fourth- and Twelfth-Grade Students
at Different NAEP Mathematics Achievement Levels, 1996

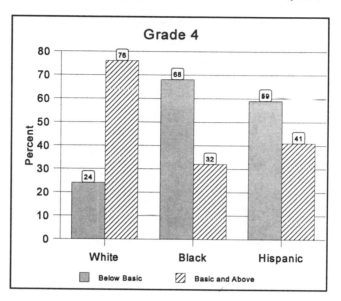

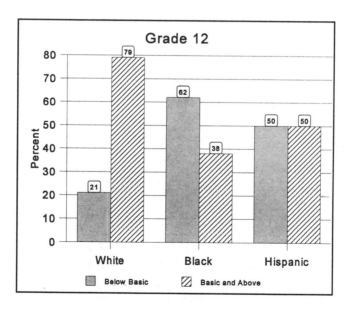

Source: NCES, 1997c

FIGURE 1.7
Percentage of White, Black, and Hispanic Fourth- and Twelfth-Grade Students at Different NAEP Reading Achievement Levels, 1998

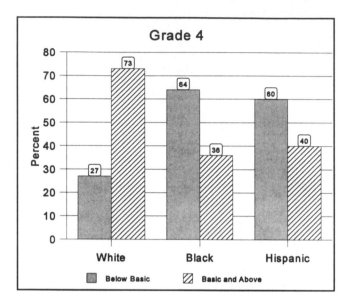

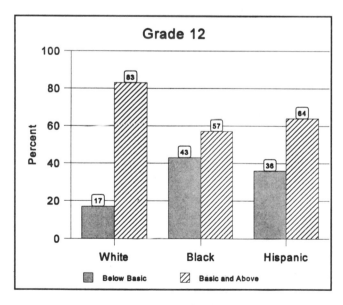

Source: NCES, 1999c

The failure of the schools to teach students from poor families of all racial/ethnic backgrounds effectively is also reflected in gaps between the performance of students of different socioeconomic backgrounds on the NAEP. Figure 1.8 compares the different achievement levels on the 1996 NAEP mathematics assessment for students who were eligible for the free and reduced-price lunch program (a proximal indicator of socioeconomic status) and for students who were not eligible for the program. As this figure shows, proportionately more students who were eligible for the program scored "below basic" than students who were not eligible. Again, the patterns are similar in both grades; considerably higher percentages of less affluent students had "below basic" scores, while higher percentages of more affluent students attained the basic level or above.

Scores on standardized tests are not the sole indicator of the inequitable distribution of educational benefits among groups. Data published by the Educational Research Service (1995) and the National Education Goals Panel (1994) provide evidence of disparities in the high school completion rates of the white population and black and Hispanic groups, highlights of which are summarized in figure 1.9. The data for eighteen year olds show on-time graduation rates for the three groups. On-time graduation was defined by Educational Research Service (1995) as the percentage of eighteen year olds who either held a high school diploma or were in their fourth year of high school in a particular year. Assuming that all high school seniors graduated in 1992, 84 percent of white youth would graduate on time, compared to 72 percent and 64 percent for black and Hispanic youth, respectively.

Not graduating on time does not mean that students will not ultimately complete high school. Because it takes some students longer than others to attain this goal, it is helpful to examine high school completion rates for older cohorts, as in the other two sets of data in figure 1.9. These data show a similar pattern of disparity in the nineteen-to-twenty and twenty-three-to-twenty-four year-old cohorts. In both cases, the completion rates for black youth were a full 10 percentage points lower than for white youth. More alarming still were the twenty-seven and twenty-six percentage point differences between the white and Hispanic populations. Data from the Current Population Survey that combine eighteen through twenty-four year olds show this gap in high school completion rates persisting in 1996: 91.5 percent of white people in that age group had completed high school, compared to 83.0 percent of black people and 61.9 percent of Hispanics (NCES, 1999b).

While these differences in educational attainment have always been problematic, they are becoming ever more so. In the industrial-based society of the past, workers with less than a high school diploma could secure

FIGURE 1.8
Percentage of Students Attaining Different NAEP Mathematics
Achievement Levels by Free/Reduced-Price Lunch Program Eligibility, 1996

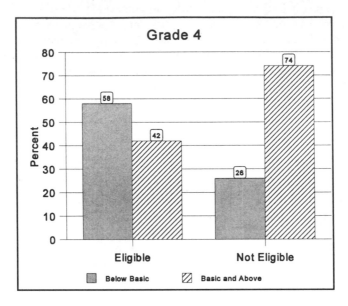

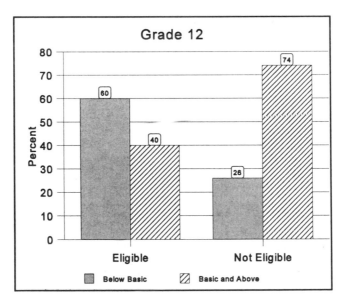

Source: NCES, 1997c

FIGURE 1.9
High School Completion Rates for Different Age Cohorts
for White, Black, and Hispanic Groups, 1992

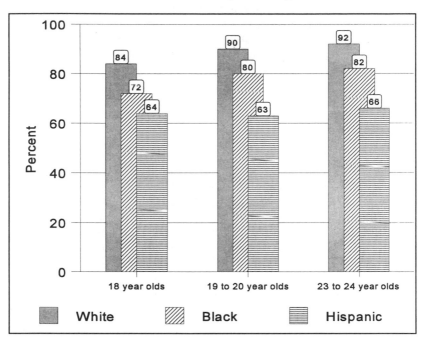

Sources: ERS, 1995; National Education Goals Panel, 1994

a job that would provide a living wage for a family. That world is rapidly disappearing. In the international information-based economy of the present and future, people without a high school education and some specialized training will be among the unemployed and underemployed as manufacturing jobs are replaced by jobs requiring knowledge of technology and access to information. Comparisons of income levels and unemployment rates provide evidence of disparities associated with educational attainment. Between 1973 and 1994, real incomes declined by 37 percent for families headed by high school dropouts and by 20 percent for families headed by high school graduates, while they increased for families headed by college graduates (Barton, 1997). It has also been reported that low-skilled workers have five times the unemployment rate of college-educated workers (Wilson, 1996). Ironically, while it is now essential to attain higher education in order to escape poverty, it is also becoming more difficult for those in poverty to make it into and through the higher education system. In 1979, eighteen to twenty-four year olds from the top income quartile were four times more likely to graduate from college than those from the bottom quartile; by 1994, they were ten times more likely to do so (Barton, 1997). These educational disparities and the income inequality associated with them are growing rapidly, despite our overall economic well-being (Freeman, 1999; Reich, 1999). They represent wasted human potential, as more people are relegated to inescapable poverty and chronic underemployment. Further, the two-tiered society that we have become flies in the face of our ideals of democracy and social justice. We can hardly maintain the "moral authority that [has] defined us as a nation" (Reich, 1999, ix) if we do not address these undisputed disparities in educational and economic attainment.

The demographic trends presented above paint a picture of a changing student population. While the details of the experiences and perspectives of the majority of students of the future may be different from those of the largely European population of years ago, diversity has characterized the United States since its beginning. This diversity carries with it an infusion of resources that have served this country well in the past. At the same time, the differences within the changing population of today and the ways in which they depart from the dominant white, middle-class, native-English-speaking population pose new challenges to the educational system. The demographics and student outcomes data speak for themselves; it is up to the nation and, of particular interest here, the educational system—including teacher education—to respond productively to the changes that the data reflect.

CURRENT AND FUTURE TEACHERS

The demographic profiles of the K–12 teaching force and student body contrast dramatically in terms of race, social class, and language background. The racial/ethnic disparity is clearly evident in figure 1.10, which presents information for the 1995–96 school year, the most current data available on the racial/ethnic distribution of the teaching force. While students of color comprised over 35 percent of total elementary and secondary public school enrollments that year, people of color constituted only about 9 percent of the teaching force (NCES, 1997b). There is also a social class gap between many teachers and their students. As discussed earlier, 21 percent of all children (those eighteen years of age and younger) lived in poverty in 1995 (Kilborn, 1996). By contrast, the overwhelming majority of teachers in this country are from lower-middle-class and middle-class backgrounds (Fuller, 1992; Zimpher, 1989). The language backgrounds of the teaching force and the student population are also disparate. While more than one in seven students speak a language other than English at

FIGURE 1.10
Distribution of the Student Population and the
Teaching Force in Public Schools by Race/Ethnicity, 1995–96

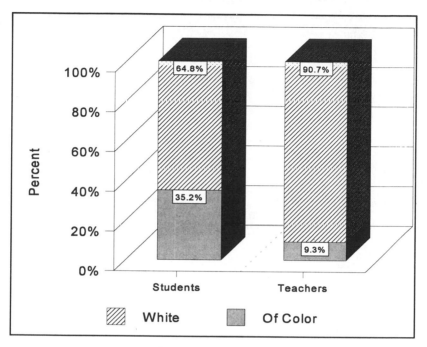

Source: NCES, 1997b

home (Federal Interagency Forum on Child and Family Statistics, 1999), the typical teacher is English monolingual (Zimpher, 1989).

A look at the education pipeline shows that the racial/ethnic makeup of the future teaching force is not likely to change much in the years ahead (see figure 1.11). Of all undergraduates preparing to be teachers in schools, colleges, and departments of education in fall 1994, 87.5 percent were white, and only 12.5 percent were of color, including 7 percent black, 3.6 percent Hispanic, 1.3 percent Asian/Pacific Islander, and .6 percent American Indian/Alaska Native.[5]

REPERCUSSIONS OF THE RACIAL/ETHNIC, ECONOMIC, AND LANGUAGE GAP BETWEEN STUDENTS AND TEACHERS

Why is it a problem that so many white, middle-class, English monolingual teachers teach students who are increasingly different from them

FIGURE 1.11
Undergraduate Enrollment by Race/Ethnicity in Schools,
Colleges, and Departments of Education, Fall 1994

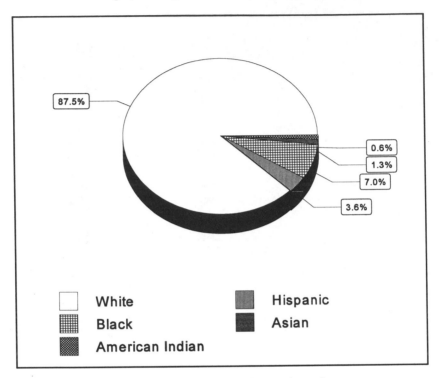

Source: AACTE, 1997. Calculations by authors.

racially, linguistically, and socioeconomically? The simplest response to this thorny question is that the sharp differences in the biographies of the teachers and their students make it difficult for the instructors to build cultural bridges between home and school for the students. When teachers know little about their students' experiences and perspectives, it is difficult for them to select materials that are relevant to the students' experiences, to use pertinent examples or analogies drawn from the students' daily lives to introduce or clarify new concepts, to manage the classroom in ways that take into account cultural differences in interaction styles, and to use evaluation strategies that maximize students' opportunities to display what they actually know in ways that are familiar to them. To remedy this serious problem, teacher education must help prospective teachers become culturally responsive teachers—that is, to develop strategies for learning about their students' individual and cultural background knowledge and experiences and for using this insight in their teaching. We discuss these responsive teaching strategies in chapter 3.

There is a more fundamental problem with the growing cultural mismatch between teachers and students. Research shows that many teachers from mainstream backgrounds view student diversity as an obstacle to overcome rather than as a resource to build upon and that they hold low expectations for poor students of color (Gomez, 1996; Irvine, 1990a, 1990b). Many blame students' academic difficulties on parents' lack of interest in and support for education, on dysfunctional family and community life, and on students' lack of motivation and skills, while overlooking the role that inequalities in society and schools play in the construction of academic failure (Paine, 1989). From their perspectives as relatively privileged members of society who generally have had little contact with people very different from themselves, they tend neither to see the need for social transformation nor to view schools as sites for social transformation. Many are convinced that teaching is a politically neutral activity and that teachers should not take political stands. They, therefore, tend not to view themselves as moral actors who have an obligation to provide a quality education for all students (Goodlad, 1990b). Teacher education must also tackle this second, more complex problem if teachers are to be effective in our increasingly multicultural society. In chapters 2 and 4, we discuss strategies for helping teachers-to-be examine and modify such attitudes and beliefs.

It is also important to ask why the relative absence of teachers of racial/ethnic and language minority backgrounds is problematic. The most frequently cited reason is that minority teachers serve as vital role models for all students, but especially for minority students (AACTE, 1989; Bass de Martinez, 1988; Cole, 1986; Graham, 1987; Mercer and Mercer, 1986). They give minority children hope that they too can grow up to occupy responsible positions in our society (Franklin, 1987; Stewart, Meier, La Follette, and England, 1989), a message that is especially important for those who come from impoverished homes and have few models in their communities of successful professionals who are racially, ethnically, and linguistically like themselves. Second, minority candidates bring to teaching firsthand knowledge about minority cultures and languages and personal experience with what it is like to be a member of a racial, ethnic, and/or language minority group in this country. Such a shared background makes it easier for teachers to build the necessary bridges between home and school for students from subordinated groups (Hidalgo and Huling-Austin, 1993; Huling-Austin and Cuellar, 1991; Irvine, 1990a; King, 1993; Ladson-Billings and Henry, 1990), and to challenge these young people to examine critically the consequences of disengaging from academic learning (Delpit, 1988; Foster, 1993; Ladson-Billings and Henry, 1990).

While the life experiences of people of color can give them an advantage in teaching students of color, this resource will have little payoff unless teacher education programs prepare them to draw on it in their teaching. It is foolish to think that a mere increase in the number of teachers of color will improve the school experiences of students of color, as much of the current literature on this topic seems to imply. Teacher education, therefore, not only must recruit more candidates of color but also must prepare them to be culturally responsive teachers (Villegas, 1997).

White Americans have consistently accounted for at least 86 percent of the teaching force in elementary and secondary public schools since 1971, the first year for which race information was reported for teachers in the *Digest of Education Statistics*. Between 1971 and 1980, the representation of black Americans in teaching held steady at 8 percent or slightly higher. In 1981, however, the proportion of black Americans began to drop until it reached a low of 6.9 percent in 1986. Concern in the education community over the loss of black teachers (see AACTE, 1987; Bass de Martinez, 1988; Cooper, 1986; Earley, 1987; Franklin, 1987; Graham, 1987; Irvine, 1988; Matcznski and Joseph, 1989; Post and Woessner, 1987; Spellman, 1988; Waters, 1989) resulted in a number of initiatives that boosted the fraction of black Americans in the teaching force back up to 8.0 percent by 1991. Since then, their share has declined again. As figure 1.12 shows, black teachers comprised only 7.3 percent of the total in 1996 (NCES, 1997c, 1999b). Some fear that the fraction of black educators will drop even further in the future.

The representation of Hispanics, Asians/Pacific Islanders, and American Indians/Alaska Natives in the teaching profession has also fluctuated since 1971, when collectively these groups accounted for 3.6 percent of all public school teachers. As figure 1.12 shows, in 1994 they comprised 6.1 percent of the teaching population. By 1996, however, their representation had dipped to 2.0 percent. This decline has led to calls for more aggressive recruitment of people from these racial/ethnic minority groups into teaching, especially from among the Latino population.

The underrepresentation of African Americans and other racial/ethnic minorities in the teaching force has been attributed to a variety of factors, most notably the inadequate education that many students of color receive in elementary and secondary schools, which limits the numbers who are eligible to go on to higher education in general and teacher education programs in particular. Equally problematic, the poor academic preparation of large numbers of those who complete high

FIGURE 1.12

Racial/Ethnic Distribution of the Teaching Force in Elementary and Secondary Public Schools for Selected Years

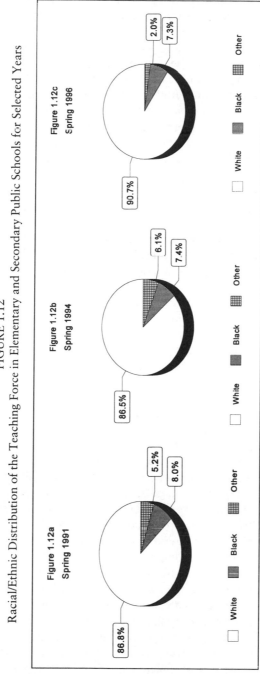

Source: NCES, 1997b, 1999a

school and go on to college (ETS, 1994) places many minority students at risk of dropping out of postsecondary education (King, 1993; Villegas, 1997).

The inability of teacher education to attract students of color also contributes to their underrepresentation in the teaching force (Coley and Goertz, 1991; Education Commission of the States [ECS], 1990; Irvine, 1988; King, 1993; Kirby and Hudson, 1993). Some of the reasons cited for the lack of popularity of teaching among people of color include increased opportunities for them in higher paying fields since the early 1980s (Kirby and Hudson, 1993), the difficult conditions of teaching (AACTE, 1987; Middleton et al., 1988; Zimpher and Yessayan, 1987), and increased use of loans as part of financial aid packages for postsecondary education, which deters minority students from choosing a career in a relatively poorly paid profession such as teaching (Dilworth, 1990).

Teacher education programs are also partly at fault for the relative absence of people of color in the teaching profession. While other academic fields compete actively for academically prepared students of color and offer potential candidates appealing incentives, teacher education programs generally pay scant attention to increasing their minority enrollments (Hood and Parker, 1991), nor do they allocate resources to retaining those minority students who enroll (Coley and Goertz, 1991; Darling-Hammond, 1990). In chapter 5, we discuss ways to recruit more people of color into higher education in general and into teacher education in particular.

Teacher certification tests, which were introduced during the early 1980s as part of the accountability movement and have since become widely used, are another major barrier to increasing minority representation in the teaching force. While the long-term impact of teacher testing on minorities is not known, available data show that candidates of color have considerably lower pass rates than white candidates (Haney, Madaus, and Krietzer, 1987; Smith, 1992). Clearly, these tests have resulted in the exclusion of large numbers of people of color from teaching (Dilworth, 1990; Goertz and Pritcher, 1985; Smith, 1992).

It is highly unlikely that the teaching force will match the student population in terms of race/ethnicity in the foreseeable future. By highlighting disparities here, we do not mean to imply that teachers must be of the same backgrounds as their students to be effective. Nor are we advocating assigning teachers to students based on these social characteristics. We do want to emphasize, however, that most teachers and prospective teachers have no windows into the lives of increasingly greater numbers of their students. As we stated earlier, teacher education institutions can address this problem on two major fronts. They can prepare all prospective teachers, including candidates of color, to be responsive educators. At the same time, they can attract more candidates of color into teacher education and provide them with the academic and social support they need to graduate and become certified teachers. In the remainder of this book, we detail our proposal for transforming teacher education, giving emphasis to both of these goals.

CHAPTER 2

Developing Fundamental Orientations for Teaching a Changing Student Population

To respond to the changing student population in elementary and secondary schools, teacher education programs will need to reconsider the content of the established preservice curriculum. As we have explained, we take a broad view of the curriculum, seeing it as comprising all the courses prospective teachers take in colleges of education and arts and sciences, as well as the field experiences they carry out in communities and schools. In this chapter and the next, we present the curriculum framework that gives conceptual coherence to our proposal for preparing teachers to be responsive to students from diverse cultural backgrounds.

Developing such an organizing framework has been challenging. During the past fifteen years or so, educators have come to use the term *knowledge base* to refer to the knowledge and skills that support teaching and learning (Murray, 1995; Reynolds, 1989). In discussions of the knowledge base, the question typically asked is, What must teachers know and be able to do to teach effectively? But preparation for teaching entails more than knowledge and skills. Without certain fundamental attitudes, such as a belief that all students are capable of learning to high levels, it is doubtful that a teacher can be effective in a multicultural society. Because we believe that culturally responsive teaching has a strong attitudinal component, we find the customary notion of a knowledge base too narrow.

However, as useful as it is to think about the curriculum for preservice teachers in terms of specific attitudes, knowledge, and skills, this conceptualization also has limitations. First, it would be unwieldy to discuss each attitude, each type of knowledge, and each skill needed by culturally responsive teachers. Such an approach would quickly deteriorate into a list that would inevitably be construed as a rigid prescription for program development, a trap we have sought to avoid. Second, while we may need to talk about attitudes, knowledge, and skills for analytic purposes, this separation is artificial. They are interconnected, intertwined like the strands of thread in a piece of cloth. Thus, we prefer to think about the curriculum for preservice teachers as a series of strands that constantly intersect and that depend on one another to form a cohesive whole—strands that blend dispositions, knowledge, and skills.

Six strands, or organizing constructs, give coherence to our curriculum proposal for preparing culturally responsive teachers: (1) gaining sociocultural consciousness; (2) developing an affirming attitude toward students from culturally diverse backgrounds; (3) developing the commitment and skills to act as agents of change; (4) understanding the constructivist foundations of culturally responsive teaching; (5) learning about students and their communities; and (6) cultivating culturally responsive teaching practices.[1]

Two assumptions undergird our curriculum proposal—that a central role of schools is to make society more equitable and just and that learning involves the construction of knowledge. Those who embrace these assumptions are likely to find our curriculum framework appealing, even if they think it preferable to arrange or label the strands somewhat differently. Those who do not share the underlying assumptions of our curriculum proposal are apt to disagree with at least some aspects of it. Despite such disagreements, they are likely to find our comprehensive review of the literature on culturally responsive teaching useful and the idea of adopting a framework to give coherence to the learning experiences of prospective teachers provocative.

While we believe that our six strands lay out the essential dispositions, knowledge, and skills for teaching the changing student population, we recognize that this is not the only way to conceptualize the preservice curriculum. Ultimately, the benefit that can be derived from a curriculum framework depends upon the extent to which all involved in preparing teachers at a given institution come to share the vision of culturally responsive teaching inherent in that framework. Such a vision cannot be imposed from the outside. It grows out of the hard work of negotiating differences to reach common ground, a process we discuss in chapter 5. We believe our curriculum proposal provides a good starting point for the needed conversations.

In the balance of this chapter, we present the initial three strands that comprise what we believe are the fundamental orientations for teaching a changing student population. This aspect of our curriculum proposal aims to engage prospective teachers in an examination of assumptions they have about schools and their relationship to society, about students who are poor and of color, and about the work of teachers. For each strand, we propose a general path for prospective teachers to travel en route to becoming responsive educators. While we discuss each orientation separately, their interconnected nature will become evident to the reader. In chapter 3, we discuss the last three curriculum strands, which deal more centrally with the practice of culturally responsive teaching.

STRAND ONE:
GAINING SOCIOCULTURAL CONSCIOUSNESS

The first strand in our curriculum proposal challenges aspiring teachers to expand their sociocultural consciousness. By sociocultural consciousness, we mean awareness that one's worldview is not universal but is profoundly shaped by one's life experiences, as mediated by a variety of factors, chief among them race/ethnicity, social class, and gender (Banks, 1993a, 1994, 1996; Bennett, 1995; Cochran-Smith, 1993; Grant, 1991; Howard, 1999; Sleeter, 1992). A white, upper-middle-class man who was born and raised in a wealthy suburban New Jersey community experiences the world very differently from a poor, Mexican-American woman born and raised in East Los Angeles, and both have worldviews that differ from that of a middle-class man who was born in Hong Kong and moved to the United States when he was sixteen. Understanding that a person's perspective, while accurately reflecting his or her personal experiences, is not necessarily shared by others is a prerequisite for effective communication in a multicultural society (Banks, 1991b, 1994; Bennett, 1995; Darling-Hammond, 1996; Howard, 1999; Martin, 1995b; Rosenberg, 1993; Sleeter, 1992; Zeichner, 1993). Given the growing disparity between the racial/ethnic, social class, and language backgrounds of teachers and that of their students, aspiring teachers need to expand the horizons of their perceptions of the world if they are to learn to see life from the perspectives of their future students—that is, they need to become socioculturally conscious.

An initial step in becoming socioculturally conscious is to learn that differences in social location are not neutral. In all social systems, some positions are accorded greater status than others. With this status differentiation comes differential access to power. The white, upper-middle-class man from New Jersey, for example, has advantages that the poor Mexican-American woman from East Los Angeles does not have. Because differences in access to power profoundly influence one's experience in the world, prospective teachers need to learn about the system of social stratification in this country. While a thorough treatment of this complex topic is beyond the scope of this book, we will venture a few comments.

It is generally agreed that social stratification has multiple dimensions in the United States. They include race/ethnicity, social class, native language or language variety, gender, and sexual orientation. The dimensions that have received most attention in the literature, however, are race/ethnicity, social class, and gender. A brief consideration of these three dimensions is instructive for understanding how economic resources, and the political power derived from those resources, are differentially distributed in society.

Although definitions of social class abound, wealth and income are typically used as its salient indicators. One measure of wealth is net worth. In 1993, the median net worth of households in the highest income quintile was $118,996 compared to only $4,249 for households in the lowest income quintile (U.S. Census Bureau, 1999a). Stated differently, the average net worth of the highest-earning 20 percent of families in this country was nearly thirty times that of the lowest earning 20 percent of families. Income, the money earned in wages and salaries throughout a year, is also unequally distributed. In 1994, the top fifth of U.S. families earned about 47 percent of all income; the bottom fifth, on the other hand, earned only 4 percent of the total (U.S. Census Bureau, 1999b). Since 1970, inequality in income and wealth has widened considerably in this country, causing leading economists to warn that the United States is rapidly becoming a two-tiered society in which the more affluent class lives in radically different ways than does the less affluent class (Reich, 1999). It is disturbing that U.S. society, one committed to the ideal of political "classlessness," is currently the leader in income and wealth inequality among all industrialized nations in the world (Freeman, 1999).

Race/ethnicity is another correlate of differential power in the United States. Racial/ethnic disparities in economic standing are obvious manifestations of this power differential, with people of color, but especially African Americans and Hispanics, faring less well economically than white Americans. Relative wealth illustrates existing disparities. In 1993, the net worth of all white households was $45,740, compared to only $4,656 for Hispanic-origin households and $4,418 for black households (U. S. Census Bureau, 1999a).[2] That is, the median net worth of Hispanic and black households was only about 10 percent that of white households. A similar pattern of disparities between the white population and the Hispanic and black populations is evident in income. In 1996, for example, the median family income of the white population was $44,756, a figure that was more than $18,000 above that attained by both the black and Hispanic groups, who earned $26,522 and $26,179, respectively (U.S. Department of Commerce, 1998). Stated differently, the median income of African American and Hispanic families was less than 60 percent that of white families in the United States for that year. Racial/ethnic discrepancies of large magnitude also exist in health and life expectancy (Russell, 1996; U. S. Department of Health and Human Services, 1996) and medical care (U.S. Census Bureau, 1995), as well as other areas.

Gender is another base for inequality in this country, as gleaned from traditional economic indicators. As a group, women earn far less and are more apt to suffer from poverty than men; this is particularly true for women of color. According to the U.S. Department of Labor (1997), the median weekly earnings of females over sixteen years of age who worked full time in the second quarter of 1997 was only 75 percent that of males ($428 and $572, respectively). Comparisons among white, black, and Hispanic men and women reveal even greater disparities (data for other racial/ethnic groups were not available). In every group, men earned more than women. The level of earning was highest for white men and lowest for Hispanic women. The median weekly earnings for all groups were as follows: white men ($589), white women ($443), black men ($424), black women ($379), Hispanic men ($368), Hispanic women ($320). Thus, median weekly earnings for Hispanic women were 87 percent of Hispanic men's earnings but only 56 percent of what white men earned. African American women earned 89 percent of what African American men earned but only 66 percent of the earnings of white men. Accompanying women's lower incomes is their greater poverty. In 1997, 41 percent of female-headed families lived in poverty, compared to less than 19 percent of male-headed families (Kilborn, 1996). Thus, more than twice the proportion of families with single mothers were poor as compared to families with single fathers.

A person's position in the class hierarchy, as measured by wealth and income, is the strongest predictor of his or her academic success and future social standing (Apple, 1990; Bowles and Gintis, 1976; Natriello, McDill, and Pallas, 1990). Given the lower economic position of people of color, both men and women, the disparities in educational outcomes between white students and students of color discussed in chapter 1 are not surprising.

This discussion raises disturbing questions in a society that, like the United States, espouses egalitarian ideals. How are these class, racial/ethnic, and gender inequalities maintained, reproduced, and legitimated? How is the tension between existing inequalities and egalitarian principles resolved in people's minds? Like Bowles and Gintis (1976), Sturm and Guinier (1996), and others, we contend that this system of dominance is produced and perpetuated through systemic discrimination and then justified through a societal ideology of merit, social mobility, and individual responsibility. And in this reproduction and legitimation process, schools play a leading role. They purport to offer unlimited possibilities for social advancement while simultaneously maintaining structures that severely limit the probability of advancement for those at the bottom of the social scale (Labaree, 1997).

From childhood, we have been socialized to believe that schools are the great equalizers in American society. We are told that schools "level the playing field," providing opportunity for all, regardless of social background, by serving as the impartial grounds on which individuals freely prove their merit. One function of schools, then, is to sort students according to merit—which is equated with "talent" and "effort." Those deemed meritorious are promised access to the higher-status positions, while those found lacking in merit are told they must be content with the lower-status positions since that is all they have earned. Two key assumptions undergird this function of schools: first, that individual merit can be identified and measured on the basis of objective criteria, and, second, that schools are fair in their practices. This ideological formulation, which is deeply ingrained in the everyday consciousness of most people in this country, validates social inequality by portraying it as a necessary device for motivating talented individuals to achieve high-status positions. It also justifies the existing social order by giving it normative dignity—that is, treating it as the natural order within a meritocracy where some "deserve" more benefits due to their greater talent and effort. In this process, the system of domination is perpetuated.

However, schools, as we have indicated already and will discuss in more detail later in this chapter, are far from being the impartial settings they are professed to be. Built into the fabric of schools are curricular, pedagogical, and evaluative practices that intentionally or unintentionally privilege the affluent, white, and male segments of society. Since schools mirror the culture of the powerful, the academic success of those who share in this power and the academic difficulties of those who lack access to it are not surprising. However, the process through which we have been socialized into thinking that biased practices—such as inequality in school funding and instructional tracking—are impartial and natural has a powerful impact on our thinking. And our belief in the meritocracy is further strengthened by the fact that some individuals from oppressed groups do manage to succeed academically despite the limited probability of their doing so. As a result, most people tend to explain academic success and failure on the basis of individual characteristics of the learner rather than institutionalized discrimination. Such explanations are offered by prospective teachers no less than by others (Davis, 1995; McDiarmid and Price, 1990; Paine, 1989).

To gain sociocultural consciousness, aspiring teachers must come to understand the intricate connection between schools and society. That is, they must come to see that, as typically organized, schools help to reproduce existing social inequalities while giving the illusion that such inequalities are natural and fair. Teacher educators who have attempted to engage their students in the study of this phenomenon report tremendous resistance from them (see Ahlquist, 1991; Cochran-Smith, 1991, 1995a, 1995b; Davis, 1995; King, 1993; Ladson-Billings, 1991; Sleeter, 1992, 1995a, 1995b; Tatum, 1992). Why is this so? We contend that a major reason for this resistance is fear of seriously scrutinizing the meritocratic ideology. In admitting that schools privilege some students—whether based on race, social class, gender, language group, or any other factor—prospective teachers begin to pull a thread that inevitably leads to the unraveling of their commonsense understanding of social stratification in the United States, a society that most have come to see as a meritocracy. Underlying their tenacious commitment to the meritocratic view of society is an intense belief that each individual is responsible for his or her own social standing, that upward mobility is based on merit rather than privilege, and that the education system is fair and neutral. Disrupting this tightly knit belief system will present tremendous challenges, as many teacher educators have already learned. Beliefs, particularly when they are deep-seated in a person's worldview, are extremely resistant to change (Floden, 1991; McDiarmid, 1991; Richardson, 1994; Tatto, 1996).

It is not simply that people hold fast to their beliefs, however. The belief in the meritocracy is rendered especially intractable by the relative success that most prospective teachers have experienced in the education system prior to entering teacher education (Davis, 1995). Because the education system has worked for them, they are not apt to question school practices, nor are they likely to doubt the criteria of merit applied in schools. Questioning the neutrality of the school system, which is the foundation for the meritocratic vision of society, forces them to question the reasons for their own academic success and the legitimacy of the social rewards that success promises to bring them. Thus, their personal experiences and interests make many aspiring teachers resistant to considering ideas that contradict the common-sense assumptions they have about the world.

Another factor that prevents many prospective teachers of mainstream backgrounds from recognizing the inequalities built into the education system and the larger society is the pervasive segregation in the United States. People in different racial/ethnic and socioeconomic groups live in "parallel universe[s] which rarely, if ever, intersect" (Reich, 1999, x). This spatial segregation provides most white teacher candidates with little opportunity for contact with people from oppressed groups, thus depriving them of a window into the day-to-day realities, concerns, interests, dreams, and struggles of these groups. Such isolation allows them the comfort of accepting the status quo and prevents them from recognizing the need to critically examine the meritocracy.

Despite the discomfort involved, prospective teachers must be helped to recognize ways in which their taken-for-granted notions regarding the legitimacy of the social order are flawed. If they do not come to see that the so-called meritocracy works largely for those who are already advantaged in society by virtue of their social class of origin and color of skin, for example, they will fail in their attempts to understand and respond to students who are socioculturally different from themselves, particularly when the students are from oppressed groups (Banks, 1991b; Gomez, 1994; Noel, 1995; Villegas, 1991; Zeichner, 1993). To reach such students, prospective teachers need to move beyond the unreflective and uncritical "habit of mind" that King (1991) calls "dysconsciousness."

It is useful to think about sociocultural consciousness along a continuum, with dysconsciousness at one end and consciousness at the other (see figure 2.1), keeping in mind that most of us—no matter how aware we might be—fall somewhere between the two extremes. In this conception, those at the dysconsciousness end of the continuum see their own worldviews as universal and are unaware that their particular take on the world reflects a given social space in a stratified system in which people are sorted according to class, race/ethnicity, and gender, among other factors. That is, dysconscious individuals fail to see themselves as racial, cultural, and gendered beings. They are insensitive to the fact that power is differentially distributed in society, with those who are affluent, white, and male having an advantage over those who are poor, of racial/ethnic minority groups, and female. They lack an understanding of institutional discrimination, including how routine practices in schools benefit young people from dominant groups while disadvantaging those from oppressed groups; and they have an unshakable faith that American society operates according to meritocratic principles and that existing inequalities in social outcomes are thereby justified.

By contrast, those at the consciousness end of the continuum are fully aware that a multiplicity of perspectives on the world exists and that each person's perspective reflects his or her location in the social order. They are conscious of themselves as individuals of a particular class, race/ethnicity, and gender; they understand that power is differentially distributed in society and that social institutions, including the educational system, are generally organized to advantage the more powerful groups; and they are critical of existing inequalities. A crucial task of teacher educators in preparing prospective teachers to be responsive to a changing student population is to help them locate themselves along this dysconsciousness-to-consciousness continuum and then to support their movement toward greater consciousness.

FIGURE 2.1
Curriculum Strand One:
Gaining Sociocultural Consciousness

Sociocultural dysconsciousness ————> ———> ———> Sociocultural consciousness

Worldview:

Unreflective way of thinking that takes one's worldview as universal; lack of awareness that one's experiences in life, as mediated by factors such as social class, race/ethnicity, and gender, influence how one comes to see the world.

Worldview:

Heightened awareness that there are multiple perspectives on the world and that a person's worldview reflects his/her location in the social order relative to such factors as class, race/ethnicity, and gender; clear insight into one's perspective and how it has been shaped by one's biography.

Power differentials:

Unawareness of power differentials in society and how existing differences in power are structured into the standard practices of the various institutions—including the education system; uncritical belief in the neutrality of school practices; unquestioned adherence to a meritocratic view of American society, which supports justification of existing inequalities.

Power differentials:

Profound understanding that power is differentially distributed in society and that social institutions, including the educational system, are typically organized to advantage the more powerful; critical of existing inequalities.

Teacher educators can use a variety of approaches to engage their students in this personal and difficult process of self-examination. Aspiring teachers can clarify their own perspectives through autobiographical and journal writing, studying their families and communities, and completing surveys about their experiences. As a mirror for their own experiences and as a way to broaden their understanding of various worldviews, they can learn about the experiences of others different from themselves. For example, they can read autobiographies, study history from the perspectives of different groups, and view documentaries about current and past experiences of other groups. Because this process is bound to provoke discomfort and resistance, especially for those who begin with little sociocultural consciousness, teacher educators need to be prepared to address difficult feelings that might surface, for example, by creating a safe classroom environment with clear rules for dealing with topics that generate conflict. In chapter 4, we elaborate on these and other strategies that teacher educators can use in this process.

While all aspiring teachers need to heighten their degree of sociocultural consciousness, candidates of color are apt to enter teacher education better prepared for this challenge than most of their white counterparts. Prospective teachers of color know from personal experience what it is like to be a member of a racial/ethnic minority group in the United States. Many come from economically poor backgrounds; if they are not poor themselves, they are likely to have close relatives and friends who are. They also know from firsthand experience that schools and society are not neutral and that to do well in school and in life, they cannot afford to ignore the perspectives and norms of the dominant group. In fact, to have reached this far academically, prospective teachers of color must already have a high degree of facility at crossing sociocultural boundaries. If properly tapped by teacher educators, these experiences and insights will serve as resources for the further expansion of their own sociocultural consciousness (Villegas, 1997).

Contact with aspiring teachers of color is also a crucial resource for white teacher candidates, many of whom have led culturally encapsulated lives and have therefore been limited in their opportunities to develop sociocultural consciousness. Classroom discussions and interactions with people of color can provide the stimulus that many white prospective teachers need to challenge their assumptions about schools and society. The presence of people of color in their classes and the sharing of their stories give white teachers-to-be access to other perspectives on the world that many of them lack. Learning directly from peers about experiences and perceptions radically different from their own can serve as a powerful impetus for reflection. This reflection can, in turn, lead white prospective teachers to reconsider the legitimacy of the standards for conceptualizing the world and ultimately for constructing pedagogy. These are some of the benefits that teacher education programs derive from the presence of students of color.

STRAND TWO:
DEVELOPING AN AFFIRMING ATTITUDE TOWARD
STUDENTS FROM CULTURALLY DIVERSE BACKGROUNDS

An affirming attitude toward students who differ from the dominant culture is the second fundamental orientation for successfully teaching a changing student population. Because much has been written on this topic, our discussion of this curriculum strand is lengthy. Before beginning, however, we want to make explicit the definition of culture we have adopted for this book. We use culture pragmatically to mean the way life is organized within an identifiable community or group. This includes the ways that community or group members use language, interact with one another, take turns at talk, relate to time and space, and approach learning. While we acknowledge that the organization of community life is continuously evolving in response to changing societal conditions and that the ways of thinking, talking, and interacting of individual members of any group vary widely, we also recognize that group patterns exist. These patterns, in fact, reflect the standards or norms used by community members to make sense of the world.

Once again, this second orientation can be conceptualized as a continuum, with a deficit perspective at one end and an affirming perspective at the other (see figure 2.2). Each perspective can be thought of as a lens through which teachers view the dominant or mainstream culture (i.e., the culture of the white middle class), the cultures of nondominant groups, and students who depart from the dominant cultural norms. As in the discussion of the continuum of sociocultural consciousness above, our description of teachers on either end of this continuum is an abstraction. The attitudes of real educators, including ourselves, fall somewhere between these extremes.

Teachers looking through the deficit lens believe that the dominant culture is inherently superior to the cultures of marginalized groups in society. Within this framework, such perceived superiority makes the cultural norms of the dominant group the legitimate standard for the United States and its social institutions. Cultures that differ from the dominant norm are believed to be inferior. Cultural differences, therefore, are viewed as problems. Students who do not conform to the dominant culture, which is the unquestioned standard of schools, are seen as "deficient" from the start and in need of "fixing." Such perceptions

FIGURE 2.2
Curriclum Strand Two:
Developing an Affirming Attitude toward Students from Culturally Diverse Backgrounds

Deficit perspective ———> ———> ———> ———> ———> ———> Affirming perspective

Attitude toward the dominant culture:

The culture (e.g., ways of thinking, talking, behaving) of the white middle class is inherently superior and, therefore, the legitimate standard for U.S. society and its institutions.

Attitude toward cultural diversity:

Ways of thinking, talking, and behaving that differ from the dominant cultural norms are inherently inferior. Cultural differences are problems.

Attitude toward culturally different students:

Students who don't conform to the dominant culture are "deficient" and in need of "fixing." Emphasis is placed on what students are lacking.

Attitude toward the dominant culture:

The culture of the white middle class is valid, as are the cultures of other groups. The greater status of this dominant culture derives from the power of the white middle class, not from an inherent superiority.

Attitude toward cultural diversity:

Ways of thinking, talking, and behaving that differ from the dominant cultural norm are valid (not inherently inferior or deficient). Cultural differences are to be respected and affirmed.

Attitude toward culturally different students:

All students—not just those who conform to the dominant cultural norms—have experiences, knowledge, and skills that can be used as resources to help them learn even more.

inevitably lead teachers to emphasize what students who are poor and of color cannot do rather than what they already do well. In effect, deficit-oriented teachers see the education process as one of *replacing* nonmainstream ways of thinking, talking, and behaving with mainstream ways. As this suggests, the deficit perspective is consistent with a socioculturally dysconscious orientation.

By contrast, teachers who view their students through the affirming lens acknowledge the existence and validity of a plurality of ways of thinking, talking, behaving, and learning. While recognizing that white, middle-class ways are most valued in society, they understand that this status derives from the power of the white, middle-class group rather than from any superior quality inherent in their sociocultural attributes. Such teachers, therefore, make it a priority for their students to develop facility with the mainstream ways so that they can effectively function in society as it is now structured. However, they treat the necessity for such facility as serving an instrumental purpose for their students rather than reflecting the greater value of those ways. They see all students, including children who are poor and of color, as learners who already know a great deal and who have experiences, concepts, and language that can be built upon and expanded to help them learn even more. They thus see their role as *adding to* rather than replacing what students bring to learning. They are convinced that all students, not just those from the dominant group, are capable learners who bring a wealth of knowledge and experiences to school. As this implies, teachers with an affirming perspective are also socioculturally conscious.

Teachers' attitudes toward students significantly shape the expectations they hold for student learning, their treatment of students, and what students ultimately learn (Irvine, 1990a, 1990b; Pang and Sablan, 1998; Rist, 1970; Rosenthal and Jacobson, 1969). Teachers with deficit attitudes are more apt to make negative judgments about students' potential. Lacking faith in the students' ability to achieve, these teachers are more likely to form low academic expectations of the children and ultimately to treat them in ways that stifle their learning (Irvine, 1990b; Payne, 1994). This process begins by assigning labels to students, such as "disadvantaged," "semi-lingual," and "at-risk," terms that usually carry negative connotations (Richardson et al., 1989). Once labeled, the children are often placed in instructional groups or tracks designated for "low achievers" and designed to provide them with "remediation" to correct the perceived deficiencies. Remediation too frequently is part of the problem, not a solution. Students are exposed to an overly simplified curriculum that emphasizes basic skills while ignoring the development of higher-level thinking skills (Anyon, 1981; Irvine, 1990b; McDiarmid and Price, 1990). The pace of instruction is slowed to the point that learning becomes boring (Hilliard, 1989). Instructional tasks decontextualize learning and rely heavily on drill, worksheets, and rote memorization (Anyon, 1981; McDiarmid and Price, 1990). The focus is placed on students' behavior at the expense of academic content (Anyon, 1981; Ekstrom and Villegas, 1991). And, too often, there is little encouragement for learning and little praise for good work (Irvine, 1990b). These and other similar "remedial" practices devalue the individual and cultural strengths that students from nondominant groups bring to school; they also produce low academic outcomes and promote a sense of alienation and disempowerment among these children.

An affirming perspective, on the other hand, has been shown to support student achievement (Bartolomé, 1994; Ladson-Billings, 1994; Lucas, 1997; Lucas, Henze, and Donato; 1990; Moll et al., 1992; Nieto, 1996). Teachers who respect cultural differences are more apt to believe that students from nondominant groups are capable learners, even when these children enter school with ways of thinking, talking, and behaving that differ from the dominant cultural norms (Delpit, 1995). They convey this confidence in numerous ways, such as exposing students to an intellectually rigorous curriculum, teaching students strategies that they can use to monitor their own learning, setting high performance standards for the students and consistently holding them accountable to those standards, encouraging students to excel, and building on the individual and cultural resources that the children bring to school (Delpit, 1995; Foster, 1989; Heath, 1983a). Strategies such as these that convey respect for students and affirm their differences become the basis for meaningful relationships between teachers and students and produce favorable academic results (Foster, 1989; Irvine, 1990b; Lucas, Henze, and Donato, 1990; Moll, 1988).

Given the evidence, teachers-to-be need to develop an affirming orientation toward student diversity. As a start, teacher educators can help aspiring teachers understand the consequences of teacher attitudes on student learning. But presenting and discussing the research on this topic, convincing as the evidence is, will not suffice. The more challenging tasks will be to motivate teacher candidates to inspect their own beliefs about students from nondominant groups and confront negative attitudes they might have toward these students. One way of approaching this delicate task is to guide prospective teachers through an exploration of their assumptions and beliefs regarding the well-documented pattern of academic difficulties observed among students who are poor and of racial/ethnic minority groups.

We have outlined a continuum of often unconscious attitudes toward nondominant cultures, ranging from a deficit to an affirming perspective. The work of researchers and theorists who have explored this domain in an intentionally explicit way tends to fall into three broad categories. First are theories organized around the notion of cultural deficits in students, their families, and their culture. The second cluster of theories may be characterized as "cultural difference" explanations, focusing on a mismatch between the cultural practices of home and school. Third are the theories of structured inequality, which emphasize biased educational, social, political, and economic policies and practices that disfavor students who are poor and of color. Each of these explanations represents a different point along the continuum from deficit perspective to affirming perspective, as we explain below. Although a comprehensive review of this extensive literature is beyond the scope of this book, we will highlight the thinking advanced by researchers and theorists who espouse these three views. This analysis will provide insight into both the path teacher candidates need to travel toward the development of an affirming orientation and the barriers they are likely to encounter along the way.

Deficit Theories

The conceptual underpinnings for the deficit orientation toward student diversity are the IQ and cultural deficit theories. While most of the literature supporting these theories is several decades old, the views they reflect still have considerable influence. According to the IQ deficit theory, genetic deficiencies of students of racial/ethnic minority and lower socioeconomic backgrounds explain why they do poorly in school (Herrnstein, 1973; Jensen, 1969). In developing their arguments, both Herrnstein and Jensen point to evidence of a pattern of differential IQ, with people of color and poorer people generally attaining lower scores on IQ tests than their white and middle-class counterparts. They claim that intelligence is largely inherited, citing as evidence studies of twins reared apart and of adoptive children. Arguing that IQ is a better predictor of scholastic performance than any other measurable attribute of the child, they conclude that the academic lag of many poor children and children of color results from genetic deficiencies. This explanation was influential in the 1960s and early 1970s then fell into disrepute shortly thereafter, only to re-emerge in 1994, when it once again received considerable attention with the publication of *The Bell Curve* (Herrnstein and Murray, 1994). In that book, the authors argued anew that there are inborn and largely fixed differences in intelligence among racial groups. Investments in education, they concluded, are not likely to close the achievement gap between students of color and white students in any appreciable way.

The second major deficit explanation for the documented academic lag of racial/ethnic minority and poor students posits that the source of the problem is cultural rather than genetic. Proponents of this cultural deficit position contend that the students' poor school performance stems from one or more of the following sources: (1) deficiencies in the home environment (e.g., "disorganized family life," "inadequate sensory stimulation," "inadequate child-rearing practices," "poor language modeling"), which are said to deprive poor and racial/ethnic minority children of the kinds of experiences needed to do well academically (see Bereiter and Engelmann, 1966; Brooks, 1966; Deutsch, 1963; Hunt, 1964; Riessman, 1962); (2) lack of parental interest and involvement in their children's education, which deprives students of opportunities for reinforcement of school learning at home and also signals to them that what goes on in schools has little value (Coleman et al., 1966); (3) and lack of motivation to learn on the part of students (often interpreted as a sign of laziness), which limits their willingness to apply themselves seriously to academic tasks (Bereiter and Engelmann, 1966; Riessman, 1962).

While differing somewhat in their explanations of failure, the IQ and cultural deficit theories have one common feature—both place the onus of failure on students and their families. Because this way of thinking is consistent with the belief widely held by prospective teachers that the system is fair and that school success results from hard work and innate ability, which we discussed in strand one, many tend to find deficit theories intuitively appealing. Few will publicly admit to subscribing to the overly deterministic IQ deficit theory. However, many openly embrace cultural deficit explanations, and in so doing they find scientific legitimacy for their negative beliefs about students from nonmainstream backgrounds.

To move from a deficit orientation toward an affirming orientation, teacher candidates must first become dissatisfied with their deficit conceptions. As teacher educators, we can help create such dissatisfaction by pointing out to our students the many technical and practical inadequacies inherent in deficit theories of differential school performance. The IQ deficit theory, for example, has been criticized on several grounds. It has been argued that IQ tests do not measure important features of intelligence and are culturally biased (Anastasi, 1988; Gardner, 1988; Hilliard, 1990) and that factors related to the administration of these tests (e.g., student anxiety, test environment, and examiner effect) make it impossible to assess students' intelligence reliably, especially for pupils of racial/ethnic minority or poor backgrounds (Steele, 1997). The very notion that intelligence is a global ability that draws largely on linguistic and analytic competence has been challenged (Gardner, 1983; Sternberg, 1996), as have the views that intelligence is inherited (Feuerstein, 1979) and that it is fixed at birth (Ceci, 1993; Gould, 1994).

The cultural deficit theory is also problem-ridden. Critics have argued that while differences in the cultural experiences of children from dominant and nondominant groups are undeniable, the cultural ways of the latter groups do not result in cognitive defects. As we discuss below, research shows that, contrary to what cultural deprivationists believe, children from poor and racial/ethnic minority communities possess rich and complex ways of thinking, talking, behaving, and learning (Au and Jordan, 1981; Cazden, John, and Hymes, 1972; Heath, 1983a, 1983b; Labov, 1973; Philips, 1972; Piestrup, 1973). Similarly, while parents who are poor and of color tend to participate less actively in their children's schooling than white, middle-class parents, this should not be interpreted as a sign of lack of support for, interest in, or value for education. A host of other factors interferes with their participation, such as the necessity to work long hours to support their families, previous negative experiences with the school system, unfamiliarity with the system, and lack of fluency in English (Chavkin, 1993; Delgado-Gaitan, 1990, 1992; Epstein, 1991; Hoover-Dempsey and Sandler, 1995, 1997; Nelson-Le Gall, 1994; Vaden-Kiernan, 1996). Rarely is attention given to devising strategies to welcome such parents into the schools and to tap their resources to support their children's learning. Furthermore, while it may be true that many students of color and of poor backgrounds lack interest in school learning, such behavior should not automatically be seen as a sign of laziness or lack of motivation. There are good reasons for this lack of interest. Poor, racial/ethnic, and language minority students bear the brunt of biased school practices. For example, they are overrepresented in low-track remedial classes, which are notoriously unchallenging and stigmatizing (Harklau, 1994a, 1994b; Oakes, 1985; Ekstrom and Villegas, 1991); many attend poorly maintained and overcrowded schools with few resources, materials, and qualified teachers (Darling-Hammond, 1995; ETS, 1991; Kozol, 1991); and they are aware that successfully completing high school and higher education is no guarantee of a better life, given the inequalities in the larger society (Fordham and Ogbu, 1987; Ogbu, 1995a, 1995b).

Teacher educators can further promote discomfort with the deficit orientation by helping teacher candidates understand that deficit theories lack constructive suggestions for solving the school problems of students from poor and racial/ethnic minority backgrounds. If the problems reside in the students and their families, there is little that teachers and schools can do to solve them, other than to provide a remedial education—which, as we have explained, does not solve the problem of underachievement. Embracing a deficit perspective, then, poses a moral dilemma for prospective teachers who envision themselves as making a difference in the lives of the young people who will be their students.

Grappling with this dilemma, with support from teacher educators, can move them toward a more affirming view of young people of diverse backgrounds.

Cultural Difference Theory

When prospective teachers begin to see the inadequacies and limitations of deficit thinking, they are more likely to entertain alternative explanations for the academic difficulties of students who are culturally different from the white middle class. The cultural difference theory is an alternative that many teacher candidates find appealing. In its broadest expression, this theory attributes the academic problems of these students to cultural disjunctures between home and school. While attention has been paid to differences in language varieties (Adger, 1997; Collins, 1988; Labov, 1973; Piestrup, 1973; Wolfram and Christian, 1989; Wolfram, Adger, and Christian, 1999) and cognitive styles (Ramirez and Castañeda, 1974), the primary focus of this line of investigation has been on subtle differences in language use and interaction patterns at home and in school and on the failures in communication resulting from these differences. Once again, this work is several decades old, but it continues to offer powerful insights for teacher education programs that aim to prepare culturally responsive teachers.

A well-known study conducted by Philips (1972, 1983) in the Warm Springs Indian Reservation of central Oregon and in the schools attended by the children of that community illustrates the dynamics of cross-cultural miscommunication between home and school. The perceived reluctance of children from the reservation to participate in classroom instruction was the focus of this study. According to Philips, this apparent reluctance of American Indian children has perplexed non-Indian educators, many of whom have interpreted it as a sign of linguistic or intellectual deficiency or of shyness on the part of the children. Her analysis, however, suggests a different explanation.

As the teachers had reported, Philips found that the children spoke little in school. Upon closer examination, however, she discovered that the children were most reluctant to talk during whole class or group lessons directed by the teacher—a type of instruction that requires students to speak out individually in front of their peers. When the children were asked to work independently, they occasionally volunteered to speak to the teacher. But, when working in small groups in which the children (rather than the teacher) controlled the interaction, the American Indian children spoke freely with their peers. These differences in the children's patterns of participation in teacher-directed lessons, individualized activities, and collaborative group work led Philips to hypothesize that the silence of the Warm Springs children observed in the classroom was a function of the way the teachers organized instruction rather than a deficiency on the part of the youngsters.

To gain insight into the participation patterns of the children in school, Philips studied how learning occurred in the Warm Springs community. She found that children in the community were accustomed to a high degree of self-determination with little direction from adults. A system of sibling caretaking was evident as well. Under this system, children learned to turn to other children rather than to adults when they needed assistance. When learning from adults, the children did so primarily by observing them rather than receiving verbal instruction from them. They followed this period of observation with private practice and self-initiated testing. With this orientation toward learning, it was not surprising to find the children at a loss during teacher-directed instruction, with its emphasis on learning through verbal instruction, public display of knowledge by individuals, and tight adult control over the interactions. Nor was it surprising that children reared in the manner described by Philips were more apt to participate in activities that gave them considerable control over the interaction, such as group projects. Philips concluded that because the teacher-directed lesson prevailed in these classrooms, rather than the more culturally compatible group project, the environment did not promote optimal learning for the Warm Springs children and, in fact, inadvertently relegated them to a silent role. As a consequence, the children fell further and further behind in their school work with each passing year.

Many other examples of clashes in cross-cultural communication between home and school are reported in the literature (see Au, 1980; Barnhardt, 1982; Delpit, 1995; Erickson, 1975; Greenbaum and Greenbaum, 1983; Heath, 1983a, 1983b; Jacob and Jordan, 1987; McCullum, 1989; Michaels, 1981; Mohatt and Erickson, 1981; Wong-Fillmore, 1990). This research demonstrates that classrooms are not neutral settings. Learning—whether in or out of school—occurs in a cultural context. Built into this context are subtle and invisible expectations regarding the manner in which individuals are to go about learning. The tacit demands of the conventional classroom are more compatible with the home upbringing of some children than of others. Many white, middle-class children, in particular, find the school experience an extension of the home experience. But, for many students from poor and racial/ethnic minority backgrounds, the way life is organized in the typical classroom clashes with the way life is organized in their homes and community, as Philips and others have shown. Of what use is prior experience to these children if their established ways of using language, interacting, and making sense of the world are deemed unacceptable or are prohibited in the classroom?

In our work as teacher educators, we have found that prospective teachers are receptive to the cultural difference theory and accompanying research and find the new ideas compelling. From reading this literature, they begin to understand that the way children are socialized to use language, interact with peers and adults, and go about learning may differ across communities. They also begin to learn that schools generally assume a particular type of socialization, one that corresponds most closely to the experiences of white, middle-class students but clashes with the home and community experiences of many students who are poor and of color. These insights lead many teacher candidates to conclude that standard classroom practices need adjustments in multicultural settings in order to prevent potential miscommunication between teachers and students. In so doing, they begin to shift some of the onus for academic failure and responsibility for academic success from students and their families to schools.

Despite these important changes in their thinking, however, many teachers-to-be persist in believing that ways of using language, interacting, and learning that "differ" from the white, middle-class ways are "deficient" and must therefore be corrected. That is, they continue to use a deficit frame of reference to interpret cultural differences.

To leave behind the deficit perspective and truly embrace an affirming orientation toward diverse students, aspiring teachers need to examine why the cultures of people who are poor and of color hold less status in society than the culture of the white, middle-class group. Because the cultural difference theory is silent on this topic, it is seriously limited (Villegas, 1988). Prospective teachers need to recognize that it is simplistic to claim that cultural differences between home and school are the root of the widespread academic problems of poor and racial/ethnic minority children, while leaving unexamined why some differences are accorded greater status in schools and society than others.

While differences exist and do, in fact, create communication difficulties in the classroom for both teachers and students, those differences are best understood by aspiring teachers when placed in the context of a broader struggle for social and economic advantages in a stratified society. In this struggle, the dominant group has the upper hand, given its greater resources—including more economic power, more political clout, more knowledge of how the system works, and more control of social institutions. It is no mere accident that students from poor and racial/ethnic minority backgrounds experience gaps between home and school, while their middle-class, white peers experience a more seamless connection between the two. Openness on the part of prospective teachers to exploring this proposition will signal that they are ready to seriously examine the theory of structured inequalities.

Structured Inequalities

To stop blaming the academic difficulties experienced by children from nondominant groups on their cultural backgrounds, future teachers need to understand how schools systematically discriminate against these children. We have already discussed how the white, middle-class bias that tacitly permeates the cultural texture of schools leads teachers to regularly underestimate the academic potential of students who are poor and of color, to lower their expectations of these children, and to teach them in ways that alienate, demoralize, and miseducate them. Below we examine two other salient ways in which the educational system constructs failure for these students: by teaching them in segregated and poorly funded schools and by implementing a noninclusive and disempowering curriculum. We do not intend this discussion to be encompassing of all types of inequalities that are built into the daily practices of schools; rather, we offer it as an illustration of the kind of analysis that will help prospective teachers to understand the debilitating impact of schools—as customarily organized—on students from marginalized groups. Without this understanding, it is doubtful that prospective teachers will ever come to see the culture of children from nondominant groups as worthy of affirmation.

Segregated and Unequally Funded School Systems   Although it is generally assumed that students in U.S. schools have similar educational experiences, at least through eighth grade, this is far from the reality. One major difference is that formal education occurs in contextually distinct settings such as public or private schools and urban, suburban, or rural schools. These settings vary considerably by economic and racial/ethnic compositions and by the type of educational experiences the students are provided. A comparison of urban and suburban schools will illustrate some of these differences.

It is common knowledge that students who are poor and of color are overrepresented in urban schools and that suburban schools are attended largely by students who are white and more affluent. Most teacher candidates accept this as fact, but few ever question how such economic and racial/ethnic polarization came to be. As educators of future teachers, we need to guide our students through such questioning. A brief review of circumstances that led to the prevailing spacial segregation gives insight into societal inequalities and some of the ways schools replicate them. One of the most insightful analyses of this phenomenon, as it occurred in the eastern United States, is offered by Kantor and Brenzel (1992). According to them, two processes converged to transform the racial/ethnic and economic mix of metropolitan areas subsequent to World War II. One of these processes was the migration of large numbers of African Americans and Hispanics to cities, fueled largely by the growing demand for manual labor in factories, particularly in the northeastern region of the United States. Statistics presented by Kantor and Brenzel bear this out. In 1940, for instance, almost 80 percent of the African American population lived in the South, and 63 percent lived in rural areas; thirty years later, only 33 percent lived in the South, and 75 percent lived in urban settings. In the 1970s, the movement of Hispanics into northern cities increased dramatically, as African American migration slowed.

While this migration of people of color into the cities was taking place, the migration by white people out of the cities and into the suburbs, which had begun prior to World War II, accelerated dramatically. Supporting this second process were public policies providing incentives for people to buy homes in the suburbs. These incentives, from which many white families benefited, were not readily available to people of color, however. In fact, a number of policies and practices were in place to keep racial/ethnic minorities from moving into the suburbs. As Kantor and Brenzel explain, these included restrictive covenants that made it illegal for white people to sell their houses to people of color; zoning practices restricting the types of dwellings that could be built in the suburbs, thereby foreclosing these areas to people of color, who generally had limited economic means; policies issued by the Federal Housing Administration that discouraged loans in racially mixed areas; and open hostility of whites toward minorities. Even with the passage of antidiscrimination laws during the 1960s and 1970s, which opened the suburbs to people of color with rising incomes, this group generally was ghettoized into areas that had been vacated by white residents.

The economic disparity that has accompanied this racial/ethnic polarization between cities and suburbs is also considerable. According to Kantor and Brenzel, the postwar economic expansion led to a rise in median family income in both cities and suburbs; nevertheless, the income gap between families in the two settings, which was already noticeable in 1950, grew steadily through the 1980s. By 1983, for example, the median income in inner-city households was about 62 percent of that in the suburbs. By 1989, this gap had widened even further. The median income of people living in inner cities was only 53 percent of the median income of those living in suburban areas (U.S. Census Bureau, 1993).

Nowhere was this shift in the economic and racial/ethnic composition of the city more clearly seen than in the public schools. As the pace of the white, middle-class exodus from cities picked up around 1950, the proportion of students of color rose in public schools in nearly all major cities in the country (Orfield, 1983). But suburbanization has not simply resulted in the isolation of children who are poor and of color in city schools. Because public education is funded mostly through local property taxes (ETS, 1991) and because the average tax base has come to be substantially lower in urban areas due to higher concentrations of poverty, urban school districts have vastly inferior resources for educating their students (Kozol, 1991; Natriello and Zumwalt, 1993). Despite ongoing legal battles over funding disparities in numerous states, these inequalities persist.

Compared to schools in most suburban districts, impoverished urban schools have out-of-date, dilapidated, and often dangerous physical facilities; poorly equipped science laboratories, libraries, and computer labs; less qualified and experienced teachers; and unacceptably large class sizes (Darling-Hammond, 1994b, 1995; ETS, 1991; Firestone and Pennell, 1993; Greenwald, Hedges, and Laine, 1996; Kozol, 1991; Sutton, 1991). This fundamental resource inequality between urban and suburban schools contributes in no small way to the achievement gap between urban students and their suburban counterparts.

For optimal learning, students need access to physically safe and well-equipped schools. Unfortunately, many urban schools are neither. Kozol (1991) provides unforgettable descriptions of schools where sewage fills the classrooms, hallways, and kitchens; where ceilings are falling in and windows are broken out; where gymnasiums are unsafe for use; where coal dust fills the air in winter; where woodworking tools are from the 1950s and football uniforms from the 1970s. He describes schools with few or no VCRs, computers, and electric typewriters, little or no science equipment, and insufficient numbers of textbooks and library books. As a high school teacher in a public television special based on Kozol's work pointed out, we expect children (and teachers) to go to school every day in buildings most of us would not even enter if they were places of business (Hayden and Cauthen, 1996).

Another factor that has been found to have a clear impact on student learning is the quality of teachers. Qualified and experienced teachers can provide appropriate and challenging instruction and classroom environments that promote high levels of learning for diverse students (Darling-Hammond, 1994b, 1995; Greenwald, Hedges, and Laine, 1996; Oakes, 1990). Again, urban students have less access to such teachers than their suburban counterparts, due largely to funding inequalities. In addition to the unsafe and demoralizing facilities they offer their teachers, poorer inner-city districts generally pay teachers less than wealthy suburban school districts. Cities, therefore, cannot be as selective in hiring teachers as more affluent suburbs because they have fewer qualified applicants from which to choose. Teachers in cities are more likely to be less experienced, to be uncertified, and to be teaching outside their areas of expertise than teachers in other settings (Darling-Hammond, 1994b, 1995).

Overcrowded classes also interfere with student success in poor urban schools. Common sense tells us that smaller student-teacher ratios enhance the quality and quantity of student-teacher interactions, the pedagogical flexibility available to teachers, and the attitudes of teachers toward their work. While there is some disagreement about the impact of class size, considerable research has supported the common-sense perception, showing that student achievement is positively affected by smaller class size (Greenwald, Hedges, and Laine, 1996; Wenglinsky, 1997). Finn and Achilles (1990) have shown that students of color benefit from smaller classes even more than do white students. However, because smaller classes cost more than larger classes in teachers' salaries and classroom space, poorer schools, where students of color are most numerous, can least afford them.

As this analysis suggests, the suburbanization of the United States has created two racially segregated and economically unequal systems of education—one urban, mostly for children who are poor and of color; the other suburban, largely for white, middle-class children. We believe, as do Kantor and Brenzel (1992), that it was not a coincidence that these separate and unequal systems came into being "just as the Supreme Court was mandating the dismantling of the old dual system of schooling" (284) in the *Brown v. Topeka Board of Education* decision. A second divided system arose in its place.

If future teachers are to truly comprehend urban education, which is largely the education of children who are poor and of color, they need to learn about the circumstances that led to the current plight of city schools. Such insight will prepare them to understand that the pattern of low academic performance among children from nondominant groups does not derive from deficient genes or inferior cultural upbringing, as is popularly believed. Rather, inequalities in educational outcomes are part of a broader struggle in society, with those in power generally seeking to retain their advantage and/or improve their relative positions. The history of the suburbanization of this country during the post–World War II period makes this clear. As the discussion above suggests, many white families attained the "American dream" of owning a house in the suburbs by taking advantage of mortgage incentives available largely to white people. Their skin color gave them not only access to loans but also the right to live in the suburbs. The shift in wealth from cities to suburbs and the practice of funding schools through property taxes also worked to their advantage by securing better funded schools for their children; this resulted in an educational experience of much higher quality for suburban children than that available to city children in poorly funded urban schools. By restricting access of people of color to the suburbs through institutional means—such as housing and banking policies and practices—the system advantaged white people of greater economic means, while disadvantaging those who were poorer and of color. Thus, the plight of urban schools today is a socially constructed reality shaped largely by discriminatory policies and practices.

To say that white families profited from institutionalized racism does not mean that they did not have to work hard to amass sufficient money for a down payment on their suburban houses and to continue to make monthly mortgage payments. Clearly, without much hard work, they could not have made their way into the suburbs. But to ignore the role that systemic discrimination has played in the suburbanization of America and to overlook the many advantages that white, middle-class people have derived from these biases serves to perpetuate institutionalized discrimination and legitimate resulting inequalities.

Teacher candidates who are white and have lived their lives in the suburbs—that is, the majority of today's aspiring teachers—are apt to resist this sociohistorical analysis. Those whose personal experiences have reinforced the belief that schools distribute opportunities to learn fairly and that society is largely unbiased will find the notion of institutionalized discrimination difficult to understand and even more difficult to accept. Because the analysis brings the impact of institutionalized discrimination into their own lives by suggesting that their families (and therefore they themselves) have directly participated in and benefited from discriminatory practices, they are apt to find it problematic. No doubt, classroom discussions of these issues will be tense.

Prospective teachers of color of middle-class backgrounds who have grown up in the suburbs are also likely to experience discomfort with this analysis. Their suburban background is bound to limit their understanding of the experience of the numerous people of color who are trapped in the cycle of poverty in inner cities. Nevertheless, many of these aspiring teachers have family members who continue to live in cities and are poor, which gives them a window into this world. They are also likely to recall personal experiences of racism in their own communities. Aspiring teachers of color from poor backgrounds will also be rattled by this sociocultural analysis, but for different reasons. While such discussions can be welcome acknowledgments of the realities of their lives, they may also serve as distressing reminders of the extent to which they and their families have suffered as a result of social injustices. Thus, these discussions are bound to stir feelings of pain and anger among the students who have suffered the most from institutionalized racism and classism.

Despite the difficulty involved, those of us who teach prospective teachers must push on with these tense conversations. In doing so, we will help our students to gain insight into institutional discrimination, locate themselves in history, understand that social inequalities do not exist independent of human actions, and unpack their assumptions about cities and the poor people and people of color who live in them. Such dialogue will provide the stimulus prospective teachers need to develop a heightened sense of sociocultural consciousness and an affirming orientation toward student diversity.

The Noninclusive and Disempowering School Curriculum   The curriculum is another aspect of schools that contributes to the reproduction and perpetuation of social inequalities. We are using the term *curriculum* broadly to mean the learning experiences to which students are exposed as part of their schooling. This includes the content taught in schools, the textbooks and materials used to teach this content, and the ways in which learning experiences are organized in schools and classrooms—all of which are closely interconnected.

According to Banks (1991a), school knowledge "should reflect the interests, experiences, and goals of all of the nation's citizens and should empower all people to participate effectively in a democratic society" (126). We share this vision. Unfortunately, the knowledge that is institutionalized in schools does not live up to Banks' standards. Instead, it largely represents the interests of one segment of the population—the dominant group—and it fails to prepare students—particularly students from oppressed groups—for productive participation in society (Apple, 1990; Banks, 1991a; Crichlow, Goodwin, Shakes, and Swartz, 1990; Nieto, 1996).

The bias in favor of the dominant group is most clearly seen in the content of the social studies curriculum. The customary development of historical topics, such as the declaration of independence from England by those residing in the American colonies, illustrates this point. As adopted in 1776, the Declaration of Independence states that "all men are created equal." What it does not specify, however, is that this powerful statement applied only to white men who owned property. Men of color as well as white men who were too poor to own property were not included in this category of equally created individuals, nor were women, regardless of racial or economic background. This hierarchy of power evident in the original intentions of the Declaration of Independence reflects the structure of dominance of colonial times. That is, those with power—affluent white men—defined *equality* in ways that suited their particular interests. Yet, when the Declaration of Independence is taught in schools today, rarely are students engaged in a discussion of the classist, racist, and sexist thinking inherent in the seem-

ingly neutral and frequently celebrated statement that "all men are created equal." Omissions such as this serve to legitimate the experiences
of the dominant group and teach children from oppressed groups that
the interests of the powerful are more important than their own interests. In the process, schools alienate students from subordinated groups.

In addition to presenting content primarily from the perspective of
those in power, the curriculum also perpetuates unequal social relations
by minimizing the discussion of controversial topics (Apple, 1990;
Banks, 1991a; Crichlow et al., 1990; Sleeter and Grant, 1991). For
example, the roles of African slaves in the history of the United States
rarely receives the attention it deserves. When slavery is studied, the
events leading to the "emancipation" of slaves are often examined more
closely than the long period of slavery itself and the impact of this
degrading practice on its victims. This silencing strategy applies to present times as well. Only in the past ten years or so have some students
learned about the internment of Japanese-American U.S. citizens during
World War II. Discussions of racism continue to be rare, with emphasis
given to "progress" toward interracial harmony rather than past or continuing racial inequities.

Underlying this curricular emphasis on harmony and consensus is a
profound fear that intellectual conflict will threaten the smooth functioning of the social order. This conflict-containing strategy, however,
works to the detriment of students from oppressed groups. For one
thing, it keeps important aspects in these children's everyday lives from
becoming legitimate topics of conversation in school. This can only serve
to distance them from schools. Equally problematic, by being taught
that conflict is negative and that "controversial" issues are off limits for
discussion, they are indirectly also learning that few if any institutionalized avenues exist for them to express their own interests. While they are
explicitly told that the United States is a democratic country in which
every voice counts, the implicit message they get throughout the curriculum undermines that explicit message. The silence about issues of
oppression and inequities that are part of their everyday lives speaks
louder to them than the clichéd pronouncements about participatory
democracy in civics classes.

Textbooks used in schools also reinforce the dominance of the European perspective and perpetuate stereotypes of other groups. Sleeter and
Grant (1991) examined textbooks used in grades K–8 and found that
white Americans—white males, in particular—still dominate in both
text and images and that little is included about contemporary race relations or about other issues of concern to people of color. While representation of people from oppressed groups has increased in the last two
decades, the stories of women and people of color inserted into text-

books are typically those that are most acceptable to the dominant group (Banks, 1991a). As Banks points out, for example, the life of Booker T. Washington is more likely to be featured in textbooks than that of Nat Turner.

Not only are the experiences of past and present members of oppressed groups underrepresented in the curriculum; the knowledge and experiences of individual students from these groups are consistently ignored in schools as well (Bartolomé, 1994; Freire and Macedo, 1987; Nieto, 1999). Most teachers are not prepared to draw on the background knowledge and experiences of poor and racial/ethnic minority students because they know little about these students' lives. More to the point, however, because many educators view students who are poor and of color through deficit lenses, they do not perceive the students' lives to be fruitful or appropriate resources for learning. Unfortunately, by avoiding discussions of the children's everyday experiences, teachers tend to alienate these young people and distance them from the learning process.

Given the length of our discussion of this second curriculum strand, a summary is in order. In this strand we have argued that to successfully teach students who are poor and of color, prospective teachers need to adopt an affirming view toward diversity. We have suggested that teacher educators can help future teachers develop affirming attitudes by guiding them through an exploration of the major explanations given for the academic lag of these students—the IQ and cultural deficit theories, the cultural difference theory, and the theory of structured inequalities. We further have argued that these explanations represent perspectives that fall at different points along the continuum from a deficit to an affirming view.

The IQ and cultural deficit theories reinforce the view that students who are poor and of color enter schools with deficiencies that must be corrected (that is, the extreme deficit orientation). The cultural difference theory supports a view that is closer to the affirming end of the continuum by acknowledging that all children—not just white, middle-class children—have complex ways of thinking, talking, behaving, and learning. By attributing the academic difficulties of students from non-dominant groups to cultural clashes between home and school, schools are acknowledged as at least partly responsible for the problem. This theory, however, fails to explain why society and schools value the culture of the dominant group more highly than the cultures of other groups. Such failure allows prospective teachers to continue to see departures from the dominant culture as deficiencies. The theory of structured inequalities addresses this question directly. It posits that the centrality of the dominant culture derives from its social, economic, and political power rather than any inherent superiority over other cultures and that schools actually perpetuate inequitable power relations in society by privileging the culture of the dominant group. It is an understanding and acceptance of this explanation that makes it possible for prospective teachers to move beyond a deficit view and to embrace an affirming perspective of students from nondominant groups.

STRAND THREE:
DEVELOPING THE COMMITMENT AND SKILLS
TO ACT AS AGENTS OF CHANGE

The third strand in our curriculum proposal asks prospective teachers to develop the commitment and skills to act as agents of change. Like Fullan (1993, 1999), we see change agentry as a moral imperative. Teachers are moral actors whose job is to facilitate the growth and development of other human beings. Students depend on teachers to have their best interests at heart and to make sound educational decisions. Teachers have the moral obligation to do all they can to fulfill these expectations and to do so for all children, not just for some (Goodlad, 1990b; Tom, 1984, 1997). By actively working for greater equity in education, teachers can increase access to learning and to educational success and can challenge the prevailing perception that differences among students are problems rather than resources.

Like strands one and two, strand three can be portrayed as a continuum (see figure 2.3). On one end of this continuum is a conception of teachers as technicians, and on the other end is a conception of teachers as agents of change. One role of teacher educators is to help prospective teachers locate themselves along this continuum and move them toward a perception of themselves as agents of change. Below, we discuss these contrasting views of the roles of teachers. Our discussion draws heavily on strands one and two, illustrating the interconnectedness of the first three curriculum strands. As with the previous continua, the two ends of this continuum are abstractions; the views of teachers, prospective teachers, and teacher educators fall somewhere in between the two extremes.

Those who view teachers as technicians tend to see schools as neutral and meritocratic institutions that function separately from the larger social order. Grounded in this uncritical view of schools, they think of teaching as a politically neutral activity. From this perspective, teaching is seen as primarily involving the development and refinement of technical skills—specific instructional methods, classroom management techniques, and assessment strategies (Bartolomé, 1994; Giroux, 1989).

FIGURE 2.3
Curriclum Strand Three:
Developing the Commitment and Skills to Act as Agents of Change

Teachers as technicians ⟶ ⟶ ⟶ ⟶ ⟶ Teachers as agents of change

View of schools:

Schools are neutral settings that function separately from the struggle for power in society and are not affected by this struggle. They provide all students with an equal opportunity to prove their merit.

View of schools:

Schools are intricately connected to society. Typically, they reproduce existing social inequalities by privileging the culture and interests of the dominant group. However, they have the potential to serve as sites for social transformation.

View of teaching and teachers:

Teaching is principally a technical activity that involves the application of clearly defined instructional procedures or methods. Standard school practices are accepted uncritically. There is no need for teachers to develop a personal vision. The role of teachers is to impart to students the knowledge and skills that are packaged in the school curriculum. Teachers should strive to be "objective" in their words and deeds.

View of teaching and teachers:

Teaching involves much more than applying instructional methods. It is essentially a political and ethical activity. Teachers are participants in a larger struggle to promote equity in society. They must develop a personal vision of why they are teachers and what is important in education and in the larger society. As agents of change, they assume responsibility for identifying and interrupting inequitable school practices. Their actions are never neutral; they either support or challenge the existing social order.

There is no need for teachers to reflect on their own personal vision of teaching and education. The role of teachers is to use accepted and proven means to impart the knowledge and skills prescribed by the school curriculum, which is designed by experts and selected by administrators and policy makers, none of whom work in the classroom (Cochran-Smith, 1991; Giroux, 1989; Giroux and McLaren, 1986). Teachers are held accountable for their effectiveness in imparting the curriculum by their students' scores on standardized tests. In this process, teachers are largely passive participants, expected neither to create curriculum nor to critique it, but simply to implement it (Beyer, 1996; Zeichner, 1996b). Teachers who see themselves as technicians strive to be objective in word and deed; they do not contest educational practices. They consider their political and social values irrelevant to their jobs as teachers, and they take pains to separate those values and associated activities from their work.

In contrast, those who view teachers as agents of change see schools and society as interconnected. They believe that, while education has the potential to challenge and transform inequities in society, without intervention, schools tend to reproduce those inequities by giving greater status to the ways of thinking, talking, and behaving of the dominant cultural group. Those with this perspective recognize that teaching is a complex activity that is inherently political and ethical. They are aware that institutional structures and practices do not exist in a vacuum, but that people build and sustain them, whether consciously or unconsciously. They therefore believe that teachers must have a clear vision of their own roles as teachers and of the goals of education (Fullan, 1993). They view teachers as participants in a larger struggle for social justice whose actions either support or challenge current inequalities (Cochran-Smith, 1991, 1997). They are "morally sensitive and inquiry oriented teachers, not classroom technicians" (Tom, 1997, 3).

A host of factors work against teachers becoming agents of change, as Fullan (1993) points out: "The way that teachers are trained, the way that schools are organized, the way that the educational hierarchy operates, and the way that education is treated by political decision-makers results in a system that is more likely to retain the *status quo* than to change it" (3). Teacher education is at the top of Fullan's list of impediments to educational change. Indeed, teacher education programs have generally not given much attention to socializing future teachers to see themselves as change agents or to helping them develop skills for behaving as change agents once they become teachers (Snell and Swanson, 2000; Wasley, 1991). Most teachers who are inclined to work for change must educate themselves about the process and their role in it once they are teaching. Below, we highlight a number of other factors that prevent prospective teachers from becoming agents of change. These are summarized in figure 2.4. Then we discuss broad strategies that teacher educators can use to prepare future teachers to be agents of change.

Institutional barriers to change agentry by teachers present themselves at every turn. The hierarchical nature of the educational system places those who are outside the classroom in roles of authority, providing few formal means for teachers to become involved in decision making anywhere other than their own classrooms. The bureaucratic nature of the work of educators burdens teachers with paperwork and disciplinary tasks and constrains them through external controls on curriculum, assessment, and, increasingly, pedagogy (Wasley, 1991). While teachers tend to have some degree of autonomy inside their classrooms, they have little autonomy regarding their professional activities in other contexts (Firestone and Pennell, 1993). Teachers have little time in their work day for anything other than teaching and carrying out their bureaucratic duties (Collinson and Cook, 2000). Contact with colleagues is often limited to brief interactions during lunch; opportunities for collaboration are rare. For beginning teachers, the challenges of learning how to teach are so great that they have little time or energy to think about trying to change things. For prospective and beginning teachers, the disheartening mismatch between their idealistic desire to change the world (Oakes and Lipton, 1999) and the very real institutional barriers to change they are likely to encounter in field experiences, practica, and their initial teaching experiences can be a serious impediment to their becoming change agents. These features of educational

FIGURE 2.4
Factors That Prevent Teachers from Being Agents of Change

- Institutional factors:
  - > Hierarchical nature of the educational system.
  - > Bureaucratic nature of the educational system.
  - > Insufficient time.
  - > Insufficient opportunities for collaboration with colleagues.
  - > Challenges of learning to teach during the first years of teaching.

- Resistance by those in privileged positions to equity-oriented changes.

- Lack of personal understanding of oppression and empathy for those who are oppressed.

- Despair that change is possible.

institutions loom large as teacher educators try to prepare future teachers for their professional lives.

Another barrier for teachers who want to reduce inequities in the educational system is the fact that many reforms to increase educational equity do not serve the immediate interests of those in positions of power (Fullan, 1999; Oakes et al., 1998). Resistance to such change efforts can be powerful and insidious—a response that has been especially well documented with regard to efforts to reduce tracking (see Wells and Serna, 1996). Schmidt (1996) describes the disappointing efforts of one kindergarten teacher who tried to introduce multicultural literacy learning to colleagues in her predominantly white suburban school. Although she was initially supported by other teachers and administrators, resistance became apparent as the year progressed. Teachers—even those who had volunteered to participate in the project—did not follow through on activities, and administrators, fearing that the project would become "a big issue in the school district" (26), ignored requests for translators and curriculum development time. At one point, the teacher was accused by a colleague of "forgetting about America" because she was including different cultural perspectives in her class (25). Such overt and covert antagonism toward reform aimed at increasing social justice can silence those who initiate it.

Further preventing teachers and prospective teachers from becoming agents of change is the fact that many of them—the great majority of whom are white and middle class—do not have sufficient awareness of inequalities in schools to be inspired to become agents of change. Many lack a personal understanding of oppression and of the need for change to increase social justice. As we discussed above, due to pervasive segregation, many have had little contact with people who are different from themselves and, in particular, with those more oppressed than themselves. They have had little firsthand experience with or understanding of inequities and the ways inequities are structured into the educational and social systems. Because there are few personal relationships in this country across racial/ethnic and socioeconomic boundaries, many teacher candidates have no way to associate oppression with real people. They have had few opportunities to develop empathy for those different from themselves (Fullan, 1999); oppressed people are largely stereotypes and myths to them. Given this background, it is no wonder that many prospective teachers see no pressing need to change the system.

The final and perhaps most debilitating barrier to teachers becoming agents of change is despair. Change agents need hope. Hargreaves and Fullan (1998) argue that "hope is the ultimate virtue on which a decent and successful school system depends" (57). The kindergarten teacher described by Schmidt (1996) illustrates the importance of hope. Despite the resistance she encountered in her first efforts to promote multicultural literacy learning in her school, she "remained hopeful" that her colleagues and the administration "would eventually come to terms with cultural diversity," and she planned to continue her efforts (27). For many, however, such hopefulness is difficult to sustain. The postmodern critique of power relations and the recognition of the pervasiveness of structures of domination and hegemony have had an important impact by bringing covert oppression and antidemocratic practices into the light of day. Much of our analysis in strands one and two is, in fact, grounded in this body of thought. But the force of this critique can create a sense of despair, a sense that all actions are oppressive and that human agency is an illusion (Apple, 1996; Carlson, 1997; Mehan, 1994). Another source of despair is the frequency with which educational innovations come and go. After a few experiences embracing a new idea only to have it disappear by mandate or lack of support from above, teachers become understandably cynical about the chances of any new idea taking hold. Without hope that their actions will make a difference, how can prospective teachers be expected to find the will to engage in action to increase social justice?

If we as teacher educators are serious about preparing future teachers to be agents of change, we can take steps to "deliberately socialize" them for that role (Cochran-Smith, 1991, 285). Our challenge is to encourage both critique and hope in equal measure (Nieto, 1999). Awareness of the pervasiveness and longevity of the inequities in schools and of the structures and practices that perpetuate them can be disheartening for prospective teachers. But it is essential that they recognize these realities. If they see schools through the rose-colored glasses of the meritocratic myth, they will unwittingly perpetuate inequities. At the same time, if we promote awareness of these inequities without engendering an accompanying belief that schools can change, we will discourage the very people needed to teach the changing student population from becoming teachers at all. As we discussed above, teachers need to believe that schools can be sites for social transformation, even as they recognize that schools have typically served to maintain social inequities. They need to have faith in the ongoing project to fashion a democracy, acknowledging that there will be failures as well as successes along the way. They need "a fine sense of historical agency" (Apple, 1996, xviii) that allows them to see that schools have become more equitable over time and that change is a slow process. Thus, as teacher educators, we must go beyond promoting awareness of the ways that schools perpetuate these social inequities; we must also help aspiring teachers see that it is possible to reconstruct education to give all students opportunities to learn in academically rigorous ways.

Teachers who are change agents are aware of the need for educational and social change and have a desire to participate in bringing about such change. This desire goes along with a high degree of sociocultural consciousness and affirming attitudes toward students of diverse backgrounds, which we discussed at length in strands one and two. It also grows out of a sense of the moral purpose of education (Fullan, 1993, 1999; Goodlad, 1990b; Tom, 1984, 1997); a personal vision of their own roles as teachers and of what is important in education (Fullan, 1993); empathy for students of diverse backgrounds; a passion for and commitment to students, teaching, and social justice (Firestone and Pennell, 1993; Firestone, Rosenblum, and Webb, 1990; Hargreaves and Fullan, 1998; Swanson, 2000); hope and optimism that change is possible (Apple, 1996; Freire, 1968; Hargreaves and Fullan, 1998); and a sense of self-efficacy and agency (Bandura, 1977; Smylie, 1990). Teachers who are change agents are knowledgeable of the change process (Fullan, 1993). They engage in ongoing reflection on and critical analysis of their own practice and factors that impinge upon and influence their practice. They value and pursue collaboration with colleagues. Actions that teacher educators can take to prepare teachers to be change agents are summarized in figure 2.5.

One way teacher educators can contribute to the change agentry of future teachers is to emphasize the moral dimension of education (Ful-

FIGURE 2.5
Actions of Teacher Educators to Prepare Teachers to Be Agents of Change

- Emphasize the moral dimension of education.
- Guide prospective teachers in developing their own personal vision of education and teaching.
- Promote the development of empathy for students of diverse backgrounds.
- Nurture passion and idealism as well as a realistic understanding of obstacles to change.
- Provide evidence that schools can become more equitable.
- Teach about the change process.
- Promote activism outside as well as inside the classroom.
- Emphasize the importance of and develop skills for collective action and collaboration.

lan, 1993, 1999; Goodlad, 1990b; Tom, 1984, 1997). As Tom (1997) cautions, moral prescriptions are not advisable. Instead, future teachers can be made aware of and guided to reflect on the moral dimensions of teaching as they fashion their own moral identity as educators. At the same time, we believe that teacher education must explicitly address the need for change that is driven by a commitment to social justice (Beyer, 1996; Cochran-Smith, 1991; Gay, 1993; Zeichner, 1996b). Teachers can work for changes of many sorts that will not increase access and equity. In fact, many calls for school reform to promote "higher standards," more "accountability" through testing, and more "choice" through privatization would do just the opposite (Apple, 1996; Villegas, 1998). An emphasis on developing sociocultural consciousness and affirming attitudes toward students of diverse backgrounds can provide a social-justice perspective for examination of the moral purpose of education.

To make the moral purpose of teaching central and to highlight the place of social justice in that purpose, we as teacher educators can engage future teachers in critical analysis of and inquiry into the political nature of education, social and institutional practices, and the nature and consequences of social inequities, as well as reflection on their own reactions to those consequences and their own roles within social and institutional contexts. We have discussed this type of analysis and reflection above in strands one and two. Many prospective teachers have given little thought to the varying degrees to which different social groups have a voice in economic, political, and social domains and access to the benefits available within these domains. They have not considered what the goals of education in a democracy should be. They have not examined ways in which the educational system gives different students radically differential degrees of access to knowledge. They have not critically examined their own experiences, nor have they reflected on their own perceptions and values with regard to these issues. Many prospective teachers are simply unaware of these inequities; when they discover the hard facts, they are shocked and dismayed. As discomforting as it is, awareness of how inequalities in schools and society are structured accompanied by a growing awareness of their own social positions, values, and perceptions can be a powerful catalyst for inspiring teachers to be change agents. We describe pedagogical practices that can nurture critical analysis and reflection in chapter 4.

In addition to emphasizing the moral dimension of education, we can prepare teachers to be agents of change by encouraging them to develop a personal vision and professional identity that incorporate a commitment to social justice. Once they recognize social injustice and structured inequalities in schools and are conscious of their own values with regard to social justice, prospective teachers can no longer assume an objective stance. They are forced to make a decision either to ignore social injustice (and therefore perpetuate it) or to actively work against it. If they have an ethical commitment to reducing injustice, teachers will be more likely to make the latter decision. Such a commitment requires that they go beyond an intellectual understanding of the issues; it is a personal vision of education based on a passion for children, for teaching, and for justice that will carry them on to action (Apple, 1996; Hargreaves and Fullan, 1998).

Another way for teacher educators to cultivate commitment to bringing about change is to foster the development of empathy in future teachers for all students, including those who are different from themselves (Comer, 1993; Fullan, 1999; Lucas, 1997). To become change agents, prospective teachers will need the skills and inclinations to make personal connections with children from communities previously unknown to them. As teacher educators, we can emphasize the need for teachers to get to know their students and their students' communities, help prospective teachers develop strategies for doing so, and engage them in learning about diverse communities as part of their teacher education program. Through this process, they will develop personal links with people different from themselves as well as the skills to learn about their future students as individuals and about their students' cultures. We discuss this approach in depth in strand five. We can also nurture the development of empathy by tapping the experiences of prospective teachers who have encountered poverty, racism, xenophobia, sexism, homophobia, and other oppressions. Hearing about the experiences of their own classmates can build awareness and understanding among those who have lived more privileged lives. The creation of classroom communities of learners, which we discuss in chapter 4, can make such sharing possible. A third way to heighten the sense of personal connection between mainstream prospective teachers and oppressed people is to engage the former in reflection on ways they have experienced prejudice themselves. For example, women may develop empathy for people who have experienced other forms of oppression once they have reflected on the extent to which sexism has influenced their lives. We discuss the role of reflection in developing culturally responsive teachers in chapter 4.

As we mentioned above, the disparity between the idealism of many prospective teachers and the institutional barriers to change they encounter in field experiences can discourage them from becoming change agents. Many, perhaps most, people enter the teaching profession because they sincerely want to make a difference in the lives of individual students and in communities. Such passion and idealism must be nurtured by teacher educators. At the same time, however, prospective teachers need a realistic understanding of the impediments to change that are built into the educational system—the isolated and fragmented nature of teachers' work, the lack of time for professional development and collaboration, the value placed on accountability as measured by test scores and the pressure to teach to tests, and the emphasis on the efficacy of teaching technique rather than human connections, to name a few. Beginning teachers will burn out quickly if they are unrealistic about the difficulties they will face in trying to bring about change (Cherniss, 1995). They will become disillusioned if they expect to reverse inequitable practices single-handedly. Our goal, then, should be to strike a balance between idealism and realism. We can encourage prospective teachers not only to envision a morally grounded education that promotes social justice inside and outside the classroom, but also to take into account the social and institutional contexts within which they will work and the ways in which those contexts will constrain their own actions (Zeichner, 1996b).

We can further counter pessimism and instill a sense of hope in the possibility of change by providing evidence that schools can indeed be transformed to become more democratic and equitable. Prospective teachers can read published accounts of successful efforts to reconstruct schools in the service of social justice and can participate in field experiences where teachers are actively working to change inequitable school practices. We elaborate on these activities in chapter 4. By seeing evidence of successful change, future teachers can develop a sense of what aspects of the educational system need to be changed and, equally important, what aspects should not be changed (Apple, 1996). By seeing this work in progress, they can envision it for themselves. By getting to know teachers who are doing this work, they can begin to see themselves as part of a community of educators actively working for social justice.

We can also prepare future teachers to be change agents by explicitly teaching them about the change process, including the obstacles they will face and the skills they will need to overcome those obstacles. Change agents need moral purpose, a personal vision, empathy, passion, and idealism. But these worthy qualities must be accompanied by skills if change is to occur. "Moral purpose without change agentry is so much wishful valuing; change agentry without moral purpose is change for the sake of change" (Fullan, 1993, 6). We cannot expect future teachers to figure out for themselves the strategies and tools for bringing about educational and social reform. We can give them opportunities to learn about and practice different aspects of the change process through various activities in coursework and field experiences. We discuss some of these activities in chapter 4.

Another way to help aspiring teachers positively address institutional constraints to change is to emphasize the importance of participating in change efforts at multiple levels—in the classroom, in the school, within the educational system, and in the larger community (Feiman-Nemser, 1990). This approach can help them focus their energies on those contexts in which their efforts can be successful, avoiding dead-end situations that will create a sense of defeat. They can also avoid the "moral martyrdom" that can result from focusing change efforts only at the individual and classroom levels (Fullan, 1993, 11). If they ignore the contextual factors that impinge upon teaching, teachers not only can become discouraged but are also less likely to make real headway toward change inside the classroom. We need to make prospective teachers aware of possibilities for collaborative action outside schools. As we discussed above, changes in schools are not sufficient to bring about social justice. It is easy for teachers—even those who are committed to working for change—to despair because so many forces external to schools serve to maintain inequities. By becoming involved in collaborative communities working for change in domains other than education, teachers can forestall some of that despair, bolstering optimism and sustaining commitment.

Giving attention to different dimensions of the educational and social system also encourages prospective teachers to see the profession of teaching and their efforts to increase social justice as part of a collaborative project. Individuals, no matter how committed, cannot hope to overcome the very real social and institutional constraints they face in trying to bring about change (Cochran-Smith, 1991, 1995a; Fullan, 1993; Liston and Zeichner, 1991; Nieto, 1999; Tom, 1997; Weiner, 1993; Zeichner, 1990b, 1996b). At the same time, individual action and personal change are the starting places for institutional change (Fullan, 1993). Therefore, we need to encourage both collective and individual analysis, reflection, and action. We have already discussed the importance of facilitating the development of personal vision, empathy, and passion among prospective teachers. We also need to emphasize the importance of collective action and collaboration. Collective action across institutional boundaries and collaboration within a mutually supportive community can amplify the impact of one individual's actions and help to sustain optimism. As we discuss in chapter 4, teacher educators can engage students in collaborative projects, in sharing their work and their ideas, and in substantive classroom discussions. We can provide them with opportunities outside class to meet, discuss, and work together.

As teacher educators, we can also cultivate collaboration between prospective teachers and practicing teachers. Cochran-Smith (1991) has made a strong argument for the necessity of fostering collaborative relationships between future teachers and educators who are actively engaged in the pursuit of social justice. She asserts that such relationships can help link theory and practice for student teachers, promote their ongoing learning in the company of experienced teachers engaged in reform, and help them see that schools and universities need to work together to change schools. We discuss the nature of these collaborations in chapter 4. We also believe that such collaborative relationships can inspire optimism. When beginning teachers recognize that their vision of education that fosters equity and justice is shared by experienced teachers, they begin to develop an identity as part of a supportive professional community with a commitment to a common cause. When they see that experienced teachers have not lost hope and have had successes, they learn that continued hope and commitment are warranted. These experienced teachers can serve as powerful personal and professional role models.

Given the disparities in educational achievement for students of diverse racial/ethnic, socioeconomic, and linguistic backgrounds that we described in chapter 1, we believe that teachers have a moral obligation to be agents of change. It follows that those of us who are teacher educators have a moral obligation to support the development among prospective teachers of a commitment to act as agents of change. Teachers face numerous obstacles in their efforts to transform schools, some of which we have highlighted above. We can take a number of steps to equip them with the resolve and tools to deal with those obstacles. Taken together, the actions we have discussed can foster in prospective teachers hope for a more just social system and a more equitable educational system, optimism that change is possible, and a sense that they are capable of contributing to the process. Through such efforts as those described here, we can prepare teachers who no longer accept the pervasive view of teaching as a technical activity and acquiesce to the pressure for teachers to take an "objective" stance toward social issues. Instead, we will contribute to the development of teachers who see teaching as a political and ethical activity, schools as potential sites for social transformation, and themselves as the agents of that transformation.

CHAPTER 3

Fostering Culturally Responsive Teaching

In chapter 2, we introduced the initial three strands of the teacher education curriculum we are proposing. We argued that to teach a changing student population successfully, prospective teachers need to reformulate their conceptions of society and the role schools play in it, their understanding of diversity and of learners from diverse backgrounds, and their view of the roles of teachers. Specifically, we suggested that as teacher educators, we need to help future teachers develop along three continua: from lesser to greater sociocultural consciousness, from deficit-oriented to affirming attitudes toward diverse students, and from seeing teachers as technicians to seeing them as agents of change.

In chapter 3 we present the last three curriculum strands, which focus more sharply on aspects of teaching and learning. Strand four addresses the conceptions of knowledge, teaching, and learning that support our vision of culturally responsive teaching. In strand five, we argue that to successfully teach students from nonmainstream backgrounds, teachers need to learn about them and their communities. We discuss what teachers need to know about the students they teach and about the communities in which those students live, and we suggest strategies they can use for learning about them. In strand six we explain how teachers can use their insight into the lives of students to make their teaching culturally responsive.

STRAND FOUR:
EMBRACING THE CONSTRUCTIVIST FOUNDATIONS
OF CULTURALLY RESPONSIVE TEACHING

Prospective teachers enter teacher education programs not only with strong beliefs about society, diversity, schools, and the roles of teachers, but also with firmly imprinted images about the nature of knowledge and the processes of teaching and learning (Ahlquist, 1991; Cabello and Burnstein, 1995; Feiman-Nemser and Melnick, 1992; Feiman-Nemser and Remillard, 1996; Floden, 1991; Goodwin, 1994; Harrington and

Hathaway, 1995; Lortie, 1975; McDiarmid, 1990a, 1991; Powell, 1996; Richardson, 1995; Tom, 1997). Teachers-to-be derive these images from their personal histories as students in elementary and secondary schools (Lortie, 1975) and in college (McDiarmid, 1992). Generally, these educational experiences support the view that knowledge is a commodity to be transmitted by teachers and acquired by students. Thus, most prospective teachers begin their formal professional preparation with what we are calling "transmission views" of knowledge, learning, and teaching. Below we review the assumptions that shape these views and examine their limitations. We then discuss an alternative to transmission thinking—constructivist views of knowledge, teaching, and learning. We argue that constructivist views support educational practices that foster learning for understanding, acknowledge the critical role that student diversity plays in learning, and prepare children to be active participants in a democracy. Figure 3.1 provides a framework for our discussion.

Transmission Views

While transmission views of education have dominated school practices throughout history, it was not until the development of behaviorist theories of learning in the twentieth century that longstanding school customs received their modern scientific sanction (Oakes and Lipton, 1999). The view of knowledge implicit in the transmission framework reflects the Western empirical tradition. Specifically, knowledge is assumed to be a reality that exists separate from the knower and that has always been "out there" waiting to be "discovered." The discovery process calls for the application of scientific rules and procedures that are considered purely "objective." Such objectivity is said to eliminate personal and collective bias. It is further believed that if properly followed, those rules and procedures invariably lead all knowers—regardless of their backgrounds—to the same conclusions. Knowledge, then, is conceived of as discrete, fixed, and disinterested.

In this view, school knowledge is a collection of facts, concepts, principles, and theories that were discovered by experts in the different academic disciplines and packaged into the formal curriculum (Banks, 1991a, 1993a, 1994; Floden, 1991; McDiarmid, 1991; Nieto, 1999). Because the process by which this knowledge was discovered is deemed impartial, the content of the curriculum is presumed to be neutral and objective (Banks, 1994; Grant, 1997; Nieto, 1999; Wilson, 1991). Most questions asked in school are thought to have a single "right" answer that has been predetermined by experts. To facilitate the learning process, the content of each school subject is broken down into small bits of information that are then organized in a linear fashion from basic facts and skills to more complex processes and ideas. This bottom-up approach characteristic of the traditional school curriculum is in keeping with behaviorist principles of learning that call for students to master the basics before they attempt to deal with complicated content (Oakes and Lipton, 1999; Resnick, 1989). As this suggests, the school curriculum not only tells the teacher what to teach but also dictates the order in which he or she must teach the predetermined content. In brief, school knowledge is conceived of as a stable commodity for students to consume and teachers to dispatch (Feiman-Nemser and Remillard, 1996; Sfard, 1998; Tom, 1997).

Within the transmission model of education, the role of students is largely that of "receiving" the discrete bits and pieces of knowledge comprising the established curriculum. Knowledge is deemed to originate outside the learners and to reside in teachers (who have already mastered the content of the curriculum) and textbooks (which were written by people who are knowledgeable about the subject matter). In fact, teachers and textbooks are the two principal sources of information available to students in schools (Banks, 1993a; Floden, 1991). Students are said to have "learned" when they memorize what the teacher has told them and what is recorded in textbooks and can then reproduce this information upon teacher request, either verbally or in writing. As this suggests, knowledge and learning are decontextualized from the world outside school. Thus, learning is viewed as the consumption, storage, and recall of decontextualized bits of information by individual students. The prevalent image of the learner is that of an empty receptacle or container passively waiting to be filled with knowledge. The more knowledge a student retains, as demonstrated in tests that focus mostly on factual information, the more successful a learner he or she is perceived to be.

Teaching, it follows, involves transmitting the content of the curriculum to students. Teachers function primarily as unidirectional "conduits" through which knowledge passes from subject matter experts to pupils (Grant, 1997; Oakes and Lipton, 1999; Tom, 1997). The main responsibility of teachers is to "cover" content, which is believed best accomplished by adhering closely to the prescribed curriculum. The transmission model is therefore consistent with the conception of teachers as technicians, which we discussed in strand three. Because it is assumed that all students learn the same way and that their background experiences play no appreciable role in learning, a uniform method of instruction is generally considered appropriate. This method calls for teachers to present small chunks of information to all the students using a lecturelike format, give the pupils repeated drill and practice to help

FIGURE 3.1
Curriculum Strand Four:
Embracing Constructivist Views of Knowledge, Learning, and Teaching

Transmission Views ———>———>———>———>———>———>———> *Constructivist Views*

Knowledge:

A reality that exists independent of the knower and is waiting to be discovered. "Scientific" methods of discovery, which are considered neutral and objective, lead all knowers to the same conclusions. Objectivity of methods is said to eliminate personal and collective bias. Knowledge is seen as discrete, fixed, and disinterested.

School Knowledge:

Body of accepted facts, concepts, principles, and theories discovered by experts in the different disciplines and packaged into the school curriculum according to subject areas. The content of the curriculum is organized sequentially from basic facts and skills to more complex processes and ideas. The curriculum is believed to be fixed, agreed upon, and neutral. Teachers and textbooks are the principal sources of information for students.

Knowledge:

Always filtered through knowers' frames of reference, which are influenced by their experiences in the world. Given the subjectivity involved in the act of knowing, its product—knowledge—is necessarily a human construction. Knowledge is depicted as value-laden, partial, interpretive, and tentative.

School Knowledge:

The meanings students give to the content of the school curriculum (e.g., collections of facts, concepts, principles, theories, and skills) based on their preexisting knowledge and experiences. Because the curriculum is believed to be value-laden and partial, schools have the responsibility to help students understand the perspective(s) reflected in and excluded from it.

School Learning:

A relatively passive act of receiving the content of the school curriculum; memorizing what teachers say and what textbooks report. Students are seen as empty receptacles into which knowledge is poured. The more knowledge a student retains, the more successful a learner he or she is perceived to be.

Teaching:

Transmitting or delivering the content of the school curriculum to students. Emphasis is on "covering" the content of the school curriculum and testing students' recall. The uniform method of instruction involves presentation by teacher and practice by students until mastery is shown on tests. Differences among students are ignored or treated as deficiencies. Use of rewards and punishments to motivate students to learn.

School Learning:

An active process by which students give meaning to new input based on their preexisting knowledge and experience. While each student must construct his or her own understanding of new ideas and experiences in his or her own mind, the new conceptions originate in social interactions within a given learning community. Students are seen as builders or constructors of knowledge.

Teaching:

Supporting students in their attempts to make sense of new input by helping them build bridges between their prior knowledge and experiences and that input. Emphasis is on monitoring students' developing understanding of ideas. Teachers motivate students to learn by engaging them in purposeful activities, such as solving problems. Differences among students are acknowledged and treated as resources for learning. The complex nature of learning demands that teachers continuously adjust their plans of action.

them gain mastery of the content, and ask mostly factual questions to ascertain whether the students have indeed "learned" what they were "taught." It is believed that if the teacher presents information clearly and gives students sufficient practice with it, they will learn the material (Glasersfeld, 1995; Oakes and Lipton, 1999). To motivate students to learn, teachers reward correct answers with different sorts of approvals; grades, however, are perceived to have an especially strong reinforcement value. This systematic use of drill and reinforcement characteristic of transmission teaching reflects the influence of behaviorist thinking.

As others before us have argued, the transmission model of education has serious limitations. While effective in training children to remember factual information, the emphasis on memorization fails to prepare learners to think for themselves. Even when students are given problems to solve, the stress is often placed on remembering the rules and procedures that will enable them to arrive at predetermined solutions rather than on developing an understanding of the problems themselves (Oakes and Lipton, 1999). Numerous researchers have found, however, that learners who do not understand the reasoning behind what they are expected to memorize generally cannot access the information and apply it in novel situations (Brown and Palincsar, 1989; Floden, 1991; Glasersfeld, 1995). Clearly, this type of instruction falls far short of the goal of educational excellence to which our society and schools aspire.

The stress on memorization of prescribed knowledge is troublesome in a second fundamental way. Excessive use of memorization at the expense of thinking skills supports the development of an attitude of obedience and passivity on the part of students (Banks, 1993a; Glasersfeld, 1995; Suzuki, 1984). In fact, Freire (1985) contends that the purpose of transmission teaching, which he calls the "banking system of education," is to "domesticate" students' minds by rewarding those who relinquish thinking critically. This emphasis on conformity and inattention to critical thinking is dangerous in a democratic society where all citizens must have the ability to analyze and interpret complex information, understand social problems, and envision potential solutions to those problems.

While all children schooled through the transmission approach lose out in the process, those from poor and racial/ethnic minority groups pay an especially high price. As we discussed in chapter 2, schools do not dispense value-free and objective knowledge. Instead, institutionalized knowledge reflects the interests, concerns, and norms of the dominant groups in society. For example, the social studies curriculum continues to show European men as the heroes who brought "civilization" to North America through conquest that is treated as inevitable, therefore natural, and ultimately benign. When such a curriculum is presented as neutral, schools legitimate the experiences of the dominant group and marginalize the experiences of subordinated groups. In this process, schools disempower students from subordinated groups by implicitly teaching them to accept rather than challenge their marginal social position.

The assumption regarding student homogeneity built into transmission teaching—namely, that all students should acquire the same knowledge, at the same pace, when taught the same way—penalizes students from subordinated groups in another serious way. As we explained already, the "standard" student for whom schools have traditionally been designed more closely resembles the white, middle-class child than the child who is poor and of color. Consequently, poor and racial/ethnic minority students, whose cultural capital is largely ignored by schools, frequently encounter difficulties mastering the content of the traditional school curriculum. Yet, because teaching is presumed to be impartial within this framework, those who hold transmission views of education often conclude that the children themselves are fully responsible for their academic problems. Making matters worse, the pedagogical solution to the difficulties experienced by the so-called "slow learners" is to assign those students to "low ability" groups or classes where the unlearned material can be broken down into the smallest possible fragments of information and hammered into them at a slow pace. Students taught in such a decontextualized and purposeless manner cannot possibly assimilate the new information (Lave and Wegner, 1991; Resnick, 1989). While every student needs to learn basic skills, instruction that focuses exclusively on the basics is doomed to fail because students are bound to lose interest in the work when they cannot see the purpose of the activity (Irvine, 1990b; Moll, 1988).

No doubt, the decontextualized nature of traditional school knowledge, remote as it often is from students' everyday lives, affects all learners negatively. Yet children from mainstream cultural groups typically overcome this problem, while those from poor and minority backgrounds frequently do not. McDiarmid (1991) offers an insightful explanation for these different responses. According to him, children who grow up around adults for whom schools have served as an avenue for upward social and economic mobility—as is the case for many mainstream students—tend to put up with a curriculum they find meaningless because they trust that doing well in school will benefit them in the long run, just as it benefited others they know. By contrast, young people who have few, if any, adult role models for whom schools have served as a means to social and economic success—as is often true for children from poor and racial/ethnic minority backgrounds—have no tangible reason to trust schools. Without an incentive to learn the bits and pieces of information they find meaningless, these children often disengage from school learning.

Despite the many problems inherent in the transmission approach to education, it continues to hold a privileged position in schools today, much as it has in the past. It is so deeply imprinted in the minds of anyone who has attended schools, including prospective teachers and educators of teachers, that envisioning a credible alternative is extremely difficult. Fortunately, a different theory of knowing, one that breaks away from conventional views, offers such a possibility. This theory contends that knowledge is a human construction, not a set of absolute truths that reside outside the knower. According to Donmoyer (1996), the conception of knowledge as a human construction draws support from a number of disciplines, including philosophy, the history of science, the sociology of knowledge, critical theory, feminist pedagogy, postmodern social criticism, anthropology, and cognitive science. In the field of cognitive science, the term *constructivism* is often used to describe this line of work. Because the alternative views described below build largely on cognitive science research, we are calling them "constructivist." We believe that constructivism provides a solid foundation for a pedagogy that promotes the goal of academic excellence with respect for cultural differences.

Constructivist Views

Since the 1960s, the conception of knowledge as a set of universal truths has come under increasing criticism. While the existence of a world "out there" is generally not disputed, critics of the conventional view of knowledge argue that what can be known about this world is always filtered through the knower's frame of reference—beliefs, assumptions, and theories that are deeply and often unconsciously held. This frame of reference is shaped by the learner's experience of the world (Banks, 1993a; Berger and Luckmann, 1967; Code, 1991; Habermas, 1971; Kuhn, 1970; Mannheim, 1936). A salient aspect of this experience is the knower's position within the social order as indicated by his or her race/ethnicity, social class, and gender, along with other factors (Banks, 1994, 1995, 1996; Code, 1991). Because subjectivity is involved in the act of knowing, its product—knowledge—is necessarily a human construction. The claim to pure objectivity inherent in conventional thinking is seen from this perspective as little more than an attempt to make the interests of some, typically those with power in society, appear universal. In short, when knowledge is conceived of as constructed, it is admittedly value-laden, partial, interpretive, and tentative (Banks, 1995; Grant, 1997; Powell, 1996; Tom, 1997).

The conception of knowledge as a human construction has been slowly making its way into educational thinking over the past fifteen years or so. While schools have a formal curriculum that includes facts, concepts, principles, and theories, there is growing recognition that this collection of information and ideas is far from being disinterested and neutral. Not only do ideas comprising the curriculum reflect the assumptions of the disciplines themselves, but they also mirror the values of those who have the power to separate out what is worth teaching in schools from all that is known (Villegas, 1998). The realization that knowledge is not neutral has led some educators to pressure schools to make the curriculum more inclusive of the social and cultural diversity found in the United States. It has also led to calls for schools to teach students to examine the content of the curriculum critically (Apple, 1990, 1993, 1996; Banks, 1991a, 1993a, 1995; Grant, 1997; Ladson-Billings, 1994; Nieto, 1999). Banks (1993a), for example, argues that the school curriculum is valid only when students understand the perspective(s) reflected in it. According to him, such critical examination provides pupils with

> opportunities to investigate and determine how cultural assumptions, frames of reference, perspectives, and the biases within a discipline influence the ways the knowledge is constructed. Students should also be given opportunities to create knowledge themselves and identify ways in which the knowledge they construct is influenced and limited by their personal assumptions, positions, and experiences. (1993a, 3)

Within the constructivist framework, it is virtually impossible to separate knowledge from the act of knowing. While students' knowledge construction is admittedly constrained by the conventions of the various disciplines and the political process by which the content of the school curriculum is selected, learners do not merely receive prescribed knowledge. The content of the curriculum becomes "knowledge" for students only when they infuse it with meaning. Thus, learning is defined precisely as that process by which students generate meaning in response to new ideas and experiences they encounter in school. In this interpretive process, learners use their prior knowledge and beliefs— which they store in memory as mental structures (described variously by cognitive scientists as knowledge frameworks, schemata, mental models, and personal theories)—to make sense of the new input (Floden, 1991; Glasersfeld, 1995; Piaget, 1977; Resnick, 1989). As this suggests, children's preexisting knowledge, derived from personal and cultural experiences, is what gives them access to learning. To overlook the resources children bring to school is to deny them access to the knowledge construction process. The conventional "empty vessel" metaphor of the learner yields to the image of a "builder" who is constantly striving to construct meaning. Similarly, the traditional belief that knowledge resides, intact, outside the learner gives way to an understanding that knowledge is inseparable from the learner.

A number of cognitive scientists have emphasized the individual mental operations involved in the construction of knowledge (see Floden, 1991; Glasersfeld, 1995; Piaget, 1977). According to these theorists, when the knowledge frameworks that students bring to learning are consistent with the new input encountered in school, the children can assimilate the new ideas into their existing ways of thinking. For example, students who think that the earth is round have little difficulty understanding how a person can travel east from New York City and ultimately arrive in San Francisco. As the students assimilate the new ideas into workable knowledge frameworks, they can later access those ideas at will and apply them in different situations. But learning can easily go awry when the new ideas to which students are exposed contradict their preexisting knowledge and beliefs. When this happens, learners must change or reconfigure their mental schemes in order to accommodate the new input. Learners, however, tend to cling to those schemes that are intuitively appealing to them or that have proven useful in their everyday lives, even when confronted with contradictory evidence (Brown and Palincsar, 1989; Glasersfeld, 1995). So, for example, a child who believes that all physicians are male might wonder when introduced to a female physician why this woman is pretending to be something she is not. This resistance to changing mental schemes leads students to distort their perceptions of contradictory experiences in order to make them fit into what they already believe and know. The danger of distortion inherent in the learning process presents a tremendous challenge to teachers, particularly when they lack an understanding of their students' knowledge frameworks and sense-making strategies.

While learning has a strong intrapersonal dimension (i.e., as an individual mental activity), it also involves an interpersonal component (see Bruner, 1966, 1996; Cole, 1996; Vygotsky, 1978). Vygotsky's foundational work gives insight into the social development of the knowledge construction process. According to him, children appropriate new ideas and modes of thinking through practice in social interactions with more competent individuals. To support learning, he argued, those interactions must occur within the learner's zone of proximal development. This zone mediates between those activities the learner can accomplish alone and those that he or she could not do under any circumstances. In the zone of proximal development, through interactions with a more competent other, the learner can carry out activities that would otherwise be impossible. From this perspective, learning is situated in a given sociocultural context and is inseparable from the social relationships embedded in that context. One of the critical roles of teachers, then, is to organize social interactions in the classroom in ways that maximize children's access to more knowledgeable others—both adults and peers—who can support or "scaffold" their learning (Brown and Campione, 1994; Brown and Palincsar, 1989; Oakes and Lipton, 1999).

Such a dynamic conception of learning makes teaching a complex and demanding undertaking. The overriding goal of the constructivist teacher is to help students build bridges between what they already know and believe about the topic at hand and the new ideas and experiences to which they are exposed. This involves assisting students to activate appropriate knowledge frameworks that will enable them to interpret the new input and assimilate the new understandings into their mental schemes. It also involves supporting students' efforts to change prior schemes when these clash with accepted ideas within the various disciplines (e.g., many children believe that the earth is flat).

From the constructivist viewpoint, knowledge is not something that can be passed on directly from teachers' minds to students' minds. As we have discussed above, each student must ultimately build his or her own understandings of the ideas encountered in school. Since students bring different knowledge and belief frameworks to learning, they will not necessarily construct the same understandings of any given topic. This presents a major challenge to teachers. If they are to guide their students' knowledge construction efforts, teachers must have a clear understanding of how the children are thinking about the topic at hand (Doll, 1993; Floden, 1991; Howey, 1996; Oakes and Lipton, 1999; Phillips, 1995). Teachers, therefore, must continuously monitor the students' developing understanding of new ideas. This might include asking students to define their terms or to explain how they solved a problem and observing students engaged in learning activities.

While transmission-oriented teachers motivate students to learn largely through the use of rewards and punishments, constructivist educators see little merit in this approach. From a constructivist perspective, motivation to learn stems from a drive within students to investigate problems that are of interest to them (Dewey, 1938, 1991; Glasersfeld, 1995). Such a conception of student motivation places a responsibility on the teacher to create ample opportunities for pupils to apply what they already know to real problems that are related to their lives and are interesting to the students. In fact, it is through active participation in purposeful activities, such as solving problems, that students ultimately come to develop a broad and deep understanding of the concepts embedded in those activities (Barell, 1995).

For constructivists, then, teaching entails engaging students as active learners to expand or reconfigure their preexisting knowledge frameworks. Teachers do this by building on students' experiences and interests. They also motivate students by engaging them in activities that are purposeful and meaningful. Given the diversity in students' backgrounds and the complex nature of the knowledge construction process, constructivist teachers continuously adjust their plans of action in order to meet students' needs while simultaneously building on their strengths. Clearly, teaching cannot be reduced to a rigid prescription that if faithfully followed automatically results in student learning. On the contrary, teaching demands thoughtful decision making in situations that are ever changing and characterized by uncertainty (Oakes and Lipton, 1999; Richardson, 1999).

We have grounded our curriculum proposal on constructivist views because we think they are respectful of diversity, supportive of the principles of democracy and social justice, and have the potential to move education beyond rote memorization to understanding for all students. To begin with, the new ways of thinking acknowledge the critical role that student diversity plays in the teaching and learning process, and they assume that differences—whether individual or cultural—are strengths to be built upon, not problems to be managed. All students, regardless of background, are depicted as capable thinkers who continuously strive to make sense of new information and who bring rich experiences and ideas to this sense-making process. This represents a significant departure from the conventional mind-set in which students who do not conform to the ways of speaking, thinking, and acting that schools have traditionally been organized to expect are automatically seen as deficient and in need of fixing. Implicit in this shift in perspective is also a recognition that educators have a responsibility to adjust their practices in order to build on the diverse backgrounds of the students.

A constructivist education is also more likely to prepare children to fulfill their roles in a democratic society than an education that is rooted in conventional thinking. Conventional schools, while preaching a lot about the value of democracy, are typically structured in ways that contradict the democratic principles they formally espouse. As we discussed above, the emphasis on rote memorization teaches students to conform without question, the consistent exclusion from the curriculum of certain perspectives alienates the children whose voices are silenced, and the tendency to rank learners based on how much knowledge they are thought to "possess" demoralizes those who are relegated to the lower positions in the pecking order. These are but a few manifestations of the hierarchical and authoritarian nature of traditional education. This type of socialization is more conducive to getting children to fit into the existing social order than to participate in the democratic process to make society more just. A truly constructivist education, however, would cultivate students' ability to think critically, solve problems, work collaboratively, make collective decisions, and understand the multiplicity of perspectives in the world. This type of socialization is much more likely to empower children to participate actively in a democracy than the socialization children receive through the transmission approach.

Constructivist ways of thinking are also more supportive of academic rigor for all students than are transmission views. While transmission approaches foster memorization of facts and decontextualized bits of information, constructivist strategies support the development of a broad and profound understanding of ideas and their subsequent application in a variety of settings. In classrooms that are guided by constructivist principles, students' thinking is as important as the products of that thinking, and their problem solving is as important as the solutions that result from it. The goal is to help students learn to think like experts, not merely to memorize the answers previously generated by experts.

As the above analysis suggests, teacher education programs that aim to prepare future educators to teach for understanding, to respect diversity, and to promote active involvement in the democratic process would do well to help their students adopt a constructivist perspective. This involves assisting prospective teachers in locating their views along the transmission-to-constructivist continuum shown in figure 3.1 (at the beginning of this chapter) and supporting their movement toward the constructivist end of the continuum.

A point of clarification is in order, however. While we strongly support constructivist views, we do not mean to suggest that there is no place in schools for memorization, basic skills instruction, direct teaching, and other elements that are salient in the transmission model of education. For example, after children have conceptually understood the function of multiplication, having them memorize the multiplication tables would give them greater facility with computations. Undoubtedly, all students must learn basic skills. But for reasons we have explained already, it is better to embed the development of those skills in purposeful and meaningful activities than to teach them in a decontextualized and mechanical fashion, as is typically done in conventional classrooms. Direct instruction can also be a helpful tool for learning. In certain situations it might be useful for students to be told explicitly by their teachers about the specific problems they are having in constructing knowledge, especially when those same problems crop up repeatedly. Students should not be left entirely on their own to construct knowledge; they need input from their teachers. However, when memorization of information, the development of basic skills, and the use of direct instruction become the engines driving the educational process—as is the case in transmission teaching—their pedagogical value is greatly diminished, much to the students' disadvantage.

Changing the conventional conceptions of knowledge, teaching, and learning that the overwhelming majority of prospective teachers bring to teacher education is a formidable task. Adult learners, no less than children, are reluctant to give up deep-rooted beliefs. It is doubtful that simply telling prospective teachers about the merits of constructivist views will produce the desired conceptual change. To succeed in getting prospective teachers to embrace constructivist views, those of us who educate them will need to apply constructivist principles in our own teaching. First, we can help prospective teachers become aware of their taken-for-granted assumptions about knowledge, teaching, and learning. Among the strategies that have been found useful in fostering such awareness are the following:

- asking future teachers to reflect on their personal experiences as learners with a focus on recalling how subject matter was portrayed to them, what roles they played as students, what roles their teachers played, and what types of learning activities they were exposed to (Ahlquist, 1991; Tom, 1997);
- involving them in telling stories about teaching and in identifying different metaphors for teaching (Tom, 1997);
- asking them to write letters that explain what teaching means (Feiman-Nemser and Melnick, 1992); and
- eliciting their views on different situations depicted in teaching cases (Parker and Tiezzi, 1992)

The benefit of activities such as these is maximized when accompanied by discussions in which prospective teachers are able to critically examine their beliefs in a nonthreatening atmosphere (Feiman-Nemser and Melnick, 1992; Harrington and Hathaway, 1995; Richardson, 1995). Without first understanding those beliefs, prospective teachers will not be able to break out of transmission teaching.

We can then raise questions about the conventional views of knowledge, teaching, and learning to prompt discomfort with those views among prospective teachers who believe them. If sufficient discomfort is created, prospective teachers will have a reason to seek out and ultimately embrace alternative views. At this point, we can introduce the constructivist framework as an alternative to transmission views. This can be done by having teacher candidates review teaching cases that provide clear descriptions of constructivist classrooms (Parker and Tiezzi, 1992; Tom, 1997) or by asking them to conduct observations in multicultural classrooms that reflect constructivist principles (Feiman-Nemser and Rumillard, 1995). These activities are more likely to succeed when prospective teachers also have opportunities to consider why the constructivist approach might represent an improvement over conventional practices.

Unless prospective teachers have direct experience as learners with the knowledge construction process, they are not likely to adopt constructivist views of education or to use constructivist strategies in their own teaching (Floden, 1991; Feiman-Nemser and Melnick, 1992). Therefore, the courses prospective teachers take, both in colleges of education and of arts and sciences, need to model constructivist practices, as we discuss in chapter 4. Teacher candidates who are not given opportunities to critically examine the assumptions embedded in the version of American history they are exposed to in college courses, for example, will most likely not involve their future students in a critical inspection of the perspectives reflected in and excluded from the social studies curriculum they will teach (Banks, 1991b). Similarly, prospective teachers who as learners are not provided frequent opportunities to interpret ideas, solve problems, explain solutions, defend explanations, and refute arguments will probably not engage their future students in these types of exchange either (Barell, 1995; Feiman-Nemser and Melnick, 1992). Ultimately, teachers will teach as they were taught.

STRAND FIVE:
LEARNING ABOUT STUDENTS AND THEIR COMMUNITIES

Within the constructivist perspective, the overriding role of the teacher is to help students build bridges between their prior knowledge and experiences and the new ideas to be learned. This involves drawing on students' strengths, challenging their misconceptions, embedding new ideas in problem-solving activities that are relevant and meaningful to the children, explaining new concepts with illustrations or examples taken from their everyday lives, and providing opportunities for them to display what they know about the topic at hand in ways that are familiar to them, among other strategies. To build these types of bridges to learning teachers need to know their students well. Obviously, teachers who are not familiar with their pupils are not well positioned to represent subject matter in ways that are meaningful to them (Cochran-Smith, 1997; Lee and Fradd, 1998; McDiarmid, 1991; Noordhoff and Kleinfield, 1993; Villegas, 1991). By making school knowledge relevant to students, teachers both engage the children's attention and promote their desire to learn (Banks, 1993a; Mehan et al., 1995).

Teachers also need to know their students in order to establish the types of relationships that will help them feel connected to school. Specifically, teachers who can develop trusting and caring relationships with their students are better able to engage them in learning (Delpit, 1988; Foster, 1989; Lucas, 1997; McDermott, 1977). While it is theoretically possible for young people to be successful learners without such relationships, connections to teachers who know and respect them provide extra motivation for those who might otherwise disengage from school. Young people who are most alienated from mainstream school practices arguably stand to benefit more from such relationships than students from the dominant group. Because schools as institutions tend to devalue the ways of speaking, interacting, and thinking of these students, they send a message to the children that they are not valued by society. Thus, relationships with the people in schools are all the more critical in giving them a reason not to disengage from learning (Stanton-Salazar, 1997). The interest of teachers who take the time to know about students from oppressed groups can provide some connectedness to school that they might otherwise not feel.

What Teachers Need to Know About Students

To help students from diverse backgrounds build bridges between home and school, teachers need to know about the lives of the *specific children* they teach. While prospective teachers cannot develop this knowledge in advance in programs of preservice teacher education, they should be helped to understand what they need to know about their future students and to develop strategies for familiarizing themselves with those students. Such a context-specific approach to learning about students underscores the fact that individual differences exist within any single group and that culture is constantly evolving as it adapts to changing social, economic, political, and environmental conditions. Before discussing strategies for learning about students, we will review the key types of information teachers need about their particular students. As shown in figure 3.2, this includes information about students' lives outside school, their perceptions of school and school knowledge, their relationships to subject matter, and their communities.

Students' Lives Outside School   While young people spend a considerable amount of their time in school, they spend even more time outside school with their families and friends. It is tempting for educators to

FIGURE 3.2
What Teachers Need to Know about Their Students
to Help Them Build Bridges to Learning

Students' lives outside school

- Family life: family makeup, immigration history, language use, mobility, educational history, child-rearing philosophy and practices, major activities, labor history, skills and knowledge used regularly.
- Social life: use of leisure time, favorite activities, language use, what students excel at, interests, hobbies, concerns.

Students' perceptions of school knowledge and belief in the potential of schooling to improve their lives in the future

- Past experiences in school with subject matter and impressions of school knowledge derived from these experiences (e.g., interesting/boring; relevant/irrelevant; meaningful/meaningless).
- Trust that schools will improve their adult lives.

Students' relationships to subject matter

- Experience of subject matter knowledge outside school.
- Preexisting knowledge and beliefs about specific instructional topics.
- Areas of potential conflict between students' cultural values and the cultural demands built into the various school subjects.

Community life

- Demographic profile: economic makeup, racial/ethnic composition, linguistic makeup, patterns of language use, patterns of segregation.
- Formal and informal holders of power and influence.
- Available resources: businesses, institutions, agencies, people.
- Perceptions of school and school knowledge and participation in schools.

---

compartmentalize what happens outside and inside school and to act as if the only events and relationships in their students' lives that are relevant to school learning are those that take place during the school day and inside the school walls. However, as we have discussed above, learners apply all of their experiences and knowledge to learning. Thus, educators need to know about students' lives outside school.

Teachers who know about their students' family lives are better prepared to understand the children's in-school behavior and to incorporate the "funds of knowledge" those families possess in classroom activities

(Lucas, 1997; Moll et al., 1992; Moll and Gonzalez, 1997). Similarly, teachers who know about their students' social lives outside school can systematically tie the students' interests and concerns into their teaching (Darling-Hammond, 1996; Ladson-Billings, 1994; Noordhoff and Klein-field, 1993). Figure 3.3 lists sample questions that teachers could use to guide their efforts to learn about students' family lives and social lives outside school.

FIGURE 3.3
Learning about Students' Lives Outside School

Learning about Students' Family Lives—Sample Questions

- Who constitutes the student's family?
- Has the family immigrated to this country? If so, from where and how long ago?
- What language(s) is/are spoken in the home? How proficient are adults in English?
- Has the student's family moved frequently in the past few years?
- What is the educational history of family members?
- What is the child-rearing philosophy that prevails in the household? Who in the family has major responsibility for child-rearing? To what extent are older children involved in the upbringing of younger siblings? How much autonomy and self-determination do children have in their own upbringing?
- What are the student's responsibilities in the family?
- What are the major family activities?
- What are the aspirations for children in the family?
- What is the labor history of family members?
- What skills, abilities, and types of knowledge are regularly used in the family?

Learning about Students' Social Lives—Sample Questions

- How do students spend their leisure time?
- What are students' favorite activities? Are these activities organized along competitive or cooperative lines?
- What language(s) do students use with friends?
- What do students excel at?
- Do students belong to community groups such as basketball teams or church choirs?
- What are students' interests and hobbies?
- What are the main concerns in students' lives?
- Who do students look up to in the community?

Students' Perceptions of School Knowledge and Belief in the Potential of Schooling to Improve Their Lives in the Future   Teachers also need insight into how their students' past learning experiences have shaped their current views of school and school knowledge (Anderson, 1991; Feiman-Nemser and Melnick, 1992; McDiarmid, 1991; Powell, 1996). For example, children who have been taught subject matter as discrete bits of information that bear little or no relationship to the world beyond the school walls are likely to see school knowledge as boring, alien to their lives, and devoid of personal meaning. Similarly, children who have a history of not being told where the information they are expected to learn in school comes from or why they need to learn that information will most likely lack enthusiasm for learning. Students who have been subjected to hours of mindless grammar drills or meaningless arithmetic exercises, for instance, cannot be expected to figure out on their own the importance of such activities for their lives. As we discussed already, these perceptions of school knowledge are particularly problematic for children from historically oppressed groups. While they might be told that doing well in school will ultimately bring tangible social and economic rewards, these young people are not apt to believe it since they generally know few, if any, adults for whom schools have served as a path to a better life. Seeing no value in school knowledge for themselves, these students might become resistant to learning.

Responsive teachers make it a point of finding out whether this profile is applicable to any of their students. Because such children are in danger of disengaging from learning and ultimately dropping out of school, they are apt to need focused attention. Clearly, these children will benefit from the type of teaching that seeks to build multiple bridges between home and school and that aims to develop their understanding of ideas. In addition, however, responsive teachers make certain that these students know why they need to learn the various topics studied in school and how this knowledge relates to their current and future lives.

Students' Relationships to Subject Matter   Teachers who know about their students' experiences outside school with reading, writing, mathematics, science, music, art, and other school subjects can draw on those experiences to represent school knowledge to them meaningfully and to embed learning activities in contexts that are familiar to the students. In so doing, teachers make school knowledge more relevant and accessible to their pupils (Anderson, 1991; Feiman-Nemser and Melnick, 1992; Kennedy, 1991; McDiarmid, 1991; Moll and Gonzalez, 1997). Figure 3.4 shows sample questions that educators could use to focus their explorations of the roles that different subject matter plays in their students' lives.

FIGURE 3.4
Learning about Students' Relationships to Subject Matter

Literacy—Sample Questions

- Does anyone in the family write or receive letters? If so, in what language(s) are these letters written?
- Are there magazines, newspapers, or books in their homes? If so, who reads them? In what language are they written?
- Are religious texts, such as catechisms, used by the students?
- Does anyone use lists for organizing and remembering things?
- What role does literacy play in the community?
- How is storytelling used by community members?

Mathematics and Science—Sample Questions

- Does anyone build or repair things, thus using principles of mathematics and physics? What specific principles are involved in these recurrent activities, and how did those who perform such activities learn them?
- Do students regularly deal with money? If so, in what situations?
- Does anyone make clothing or do other types of sewing that require measuring with precision?

The Arts—Sample Questions

- Do students or members of their families play musical instruments? What instruments do they play?
- What type of music do the children like?
- What type of music is heard with frequency in the community?
- What artists live in the community? What artistic forms do they use?
- Are there museums in the neighborhood?

As we have already discussed, instruction is likely to fail if teachers do not take into account how students use their preexisting knowledge to make sense of new ideas. This implies that teachers need to know their students' initial understandings of the various instructional topics they aim to teach in order to help guide their construction of knowledge. For example, teachers who want their students to learn about the civil rights movement of the 1950s and 1960s in this country would seek answers to questions such as the following:

- What are the students' understanding of concepts such as justice, equality, fairness, segregation, discrimination, racism?

- What do the students know about people such as Martin Luther King Jr., Rosa Parks, Malcolm X, and James Farmer?

- Do they know about other individuals who have fought against discrimination based on race or any other factors?

- Do they believe that racism still exists in society?

- Have they experienced racism or prejudice themselves?

- Do they perceive any connections between the events that took place during the civil rights movement and their current lives?

- Do students see any value in learning about the civil rights movement?

Such insight into their students' prior knowledge, experiences, and beliefs about the civil rights movement enables teachers to build on the concepts that are familiar to the children and confront any misunderstandings they might have. It also allows them to point out to children connections they may not be seeing between events of the past and their current lives. Awareness of such connections can motivate students to participate actively in their learning rather than to sit passively in the classroom receiving disembodied information.

Teachers also need to be familiar with their students' cultural backgrounds—including prevalent values, preferred approaches to learning, and customary styles of interaction—and to understand how compatible these are with the cultural demands built into the school subjects they teach. For example, Anderson (1991) argues that certain metaphors used in science (e.g., control over nature and objectivity) are less accessible to children raised in oral rather than highly literate communities. Similarly, Lee and Fradd (1998) point out that students from an oral language tradition are likely to experience difficulty using particular language functions—such as predicting, inferencing, and hypothesizing—that are central to science. They also contend that children who have been socialized to value living in harmony as a group more highly than individualism are apt to encounter difficulty arguing their perspectives and criticizing the ideas of others, skills that apply to science as well as other school subjects. There is also considerable evidence that how children learn and use subject matter knowledge in nonmainstream communities often conflicts with how subject matter is traditionally taught and used in schools (see Au and Kawakami, 1994; Cazden, John, and Hymes, 1972; Jacob and Jordan, 1987; Villegas, 1991). The study of children from the Warm Springs Indian Reservation conducted by Phillips (1983), which we discussed in strand two, is a clear example of this. Teachers who can anticipate sources of potential cultural conflict for their students will be better able to help them cross cultural boundaries and thus gain access to mainstream knowledge. Just as important, this understanding will allow teachers to acknowledge the existence and validity of different cultural ways.

Community Life   Learning about life in the communities in which students live as well as how community members perceive schools and what is taught there gives teachers considerable insight into the ways in which community residents, including the children they teach, make sense of their experiences. A list of sample questions that can help guide teachers' explorations of their students' communities appears in figure 3.5; these reflect the more general elements of community life included in figure 3.2, above.

In this section, we have highlighted those aspects of children's lives that we consider important for designing instruction that is relevant and meaningful to them. We do not mean to suggest, however, that teachers must have all of this information about each child in their classes in order to be successful. Our point is that responsive teachers strive to know as much as possible about the children they teach in order to facilitate their learning. But teachers may not be able to make productive use of what they learn about individual students unless they have some frameworks for interpreting this information—frameworks that come largely from a grounding in academic disciplines.

From their coursework in history, for example, teachers-to-be need to learn that there is no one "true" historical record but that past events are recounted differently depending upon the perspective of those doing the recounting. They also need to learn about particular historical periods and events, including the enslavement, conquest, and colonization of people of color by the dominant European groups. They need to come to understand that, despite progress toward making society more equitable over time, oppression continues to take a toll on the lives of people of color through subtle and not-so-subtle policies and practices that limit their access to jobs, homes, services, and education. They also need to learn about the ongoing struggle of people of color for liberation. Without this historical perspective, it would be very difficult if not impossible for future teachers to make sense of the persistent pattern of low educational attainment among students of color and their general distrust of schools and frequent resistance to learning in such settings.

Knowledge of the literature of different sociocultural groups can serve as a powerful complement to historical accounts. The rich texture of people's lives—their hopes, aspirations, dreams, disappointments, pain, and joy—may be more vividly portrayed through fiction than

FIGURE 3.5
Learning about Students' Communities

Community Life—Sample Questions

- What is the socioeconomic makeup of the community? What is its racial/ethnic composition?
- What languages are used in the community and for what purposes? If students speak languages other than English, what are the attitudes toward their native languages within the communities where they live?
- Are there clear patterns of segregation in the community? If so, what are these?
- Who has the formal and informal power in the community? Are those in power representative of community residents?
- What businesses are located in the community? Who owns these businesses?
- What are the key institutions (e.g., churches, community centers) in the community?
- What service agencies/community groups exist, and what are their functions?
- What human resources are available within the community (e.g., people who can talk about their careers and/or businesses, people who can teach about the history of the community, storytellers, artists, community organizers)?
- What are the most significant events of the year for community members?
- How does news travel within the community?
- What salient issues do community members find socially relevant?
- What kinds of knowledge and skills are valued in the community? Do community members value what is taught in schools?
- How do community members feel about school? What do adults in the community say to children about school? Do they have faith that schools will serve their children well? What suggestions do they have for improving schools?
- Who from the community is represented on the school board and on committees or task forces that deal with school-related issues? Are students' parents/guardians and other community members active in schools in other capacities?
- What school staff members live in the community?

---

through history. Thus, fiction can make a stronger impact on prospective teachers, relating past events and their ongoing influence on life in ways that many historical accounts do not. Through exposure to the extensive body of literature that portrays past and present experiences of diverse groups in this country, teachers-to-be can deepen their empathy for members of those groups.

Courses in anthropology can help prospective teachers develop an understanding of the nature of culture. We have suggested already that a pragmatic view of culture—one that defines it as the way life is organized in a community, including prevalent ways of using language, interacting, and approaching learning—is valuable to teachers. It allows them to identify subtle aspects of the students' home and community experiences that are relevant to instruction but are usually overlooked. These courses can also reinforce the fact that, while discernable patterns for cultural groups exist, at the same time culture is dynamic and constantly evolving, it varies among individual members within a cultural group, and it varies across communities within a larger cultural group.

Courses in sociolinguistics can help prospective teachers understand the nature of language variation and the relationships among social context, language use, and language form. From such courses, they can also learn that all varieties of language are complex and rule-governed and that some varieties of English are considered "standard" because of the power of those who speak these varieties, not because the so-called nonstandard varieties or "dialects" are any less sophisticated linguistically. Without such knowledge, teachers are apt to interpret the varieties of English used by children from different racial/ethnic and socioeconomic groups as evidence of lack of intelligence or ability.

Prospective teachers would also benefit from coursework that focuses on language development. Because of the increasing number of students who are speakers of languages other than English, all teachers need at least a basic understanding of second language acquisition, ways to promote second language development, and ways to promote the development of academic skills and knowledge for students learning English as a second language (Castañeda et al., 1996; Hamayan, 1990; Hernandez, 1995; Levy, 1995; Milk, Mercado, and Sapiens, 1992; Necochea and Cline, 1995). Without such understanding, teachers can easily become confused about the various language-related influences on children's learning and can misinterpret problems that children may be having. For example, the learning of children who speak native languages other than English is influenced by their degree of oral fluency in English, their level of literacy development in English, and their level of education and literacy development in their native language. Teachers who can distinguish among these influences are more apt to make educational decisions that support these children's development.

In-depth knowledge of the particular students they teach and insight into the history, literature, and language of the students' sociocultural groups will have optimal payoff for teachers only if they also have a comprehensive grasp of subject matter. Teachers-to-be need to develop a deep understanding of the concepts in different academic disciplines and how those concepts relate to one another; the structures, the principles of inquiry, and the nature of discourse in those disciplines; and the roles that those disciplines play in society (Ball, 1991; Darling-Hammond, Wise, and Klein, 1995; Kennedy, 1991; McDiarmid, 1991; Wilson, 1991). Without this academic grounding, prospective teachers will not be able to facilitate their students' understanding of subject matter knowledge.

Strategies for Learning about Students

Programs that aim to prepare teachers who are culturally responsive equip them with strategies they can later use to learn about their future students. For example, prospective teachers can be given practice conducting home visits during which they interview students' parents or guardians to build a fuller understanding of their family life (Cochran-Smith, 1995a; Gonzalez, 1995; Gonzalez and Amanti, 1997; Ladson-Billings, 1994; Moll, 1992; Moll et al., 1992; Moll and Gonzalez, 1997; Villegas, 1991). Moll and colleagues, who have used household research extensively in their work with teachers, contend that educators must be theoretically and methodologically well prepared to conduct these information-seeking home visits. Theoretically, they need to see all households as containing funds of knowledge—that is, skills, expertise, and ideas—that can be incorporated into classroom activities to help children learn even more than they already know. According to these researchers, the role of the teacher during these visits is to learn from family members, not to instruct them. Methodologically, teachers need to develop the skills of entering households with a set of open-ended questions that can give focus to the information-gathering meetings while maintaining a relaxed conversational style that enables family members to feel at ease throughout the exchange. During these conversations, teachers must be willing to share information about their own lives as they elicit information from the families.

Talking with people who live in the students' communities—in addition to the children's parents or guardians—can also broaden teachers' understanding of life in those settings. Thus, it is useful for prospective teachers to begin to envision different types of community members with whom they might consult in the future. For example, many paraprofessionals employed in urban schools reside in the same neighborhoods in which the students live (Haselkorn and Fideler, 1996; Hidalgo and Huling-Austin, 1993). Their personal insight into the lives of the children could be a valuable resource to teachers who are not familiar with those communities. Other sources of cultural expertise for teachers might include those individuals who command respect in the community. Teachers' ongoing communication with parents and other community members is essential to their developing a proper understanding of the students' culture. Without such understanding, well-intentioned teachers might punish behavior that is acceptable in the community or erroneously accept questionable behavior that they believe is culturally appropriate but that is actually considered unacceptable in the students' home and community.

To develop skills for learning about their future students, prospective teachers can also participate in community events, visit community centers and other agencies to learn about available services, volunteer time to help out in these settings, read local newspapers regularly, and frequent local businesses. Direct experience is the best way for teachers to learn about the life of their students' communities. Through interactions with people in the communities, as we discussed above, educators can identify key community events and sites to visit. Some future teachers may find it helpful to see themselves as "ethnographers" and to plan their first visits to unfamiliar communities as information-gathering trips. Setting up meetings with community agency representatives can also give a focus to community visits.

Teachers can also learn much about the students and their experiences outside school from the children themselves (Cochran-Smith, 1995a; Darling-Hammond, 1996; Grant, 1991; Ladson-Billings, 1994; McDiarmid, 1991; Nieto, 1999; Powell, 1996). It is therefore important to teach future teachers ways to learn directly from students. During classroom-based field experiences, for example, prospective teachers can be encouraged to create opportunities for learners to talk about their goals and aspirations for the future and the role they see schools playing in bringing these plans to fruition, what they value and find interesting about the different school subjects, what they like and dislike about schools, and what they think about the school curriculum. Teachers-to-be can ask children to talk about their interests, hobbies, concerns, strengths, uses of leisure time, and favorite activities. Questionnaires eliciting such information can easily be used with older students. They can also have students write about different aspects of their lives outside school or involve the children in carrying out research projects in their own communities. For example, students can be asked to identify ways in which mathematics is used in their neighborhoods and report the findings back to the class.

Teacher educators can also help future teachers develop a variety of strategies to discover what students believe and think about different instructional topics and how they use these frameworks to make sense of new ideas (Anderson, 1991; Darling-Hammond, 1996; Floden, 1991; Oakes and Lipton, 1999). Such strategies include

- engaging students in substantive conversations that elicit their understandings of concepts relevant to specific instructional topics;
- having students keep learning logs and reading them regularly;
- conferencing with individual students;
- taking note of the knowledge and skills students display when they participate in class activities;
- attending to students' questions;
- observing students' in-class presentations;
- posing a problem for students to solve and observing how each goes about solving it; and
- probing students' understanding by asking them to explain the reasoning they used to arrive at their answers.

These information-gathering strategies are of upmost importance if teachers are to guide their students' construction of knowledge. While teachers-to-be can gain some valuable experience in using such strategies during their preservice preparation, they will need mentoring and ongoing learning opportunities in their early years of teaching to use them skillfully.

Because all prospective teachers, including candidates of color, will eventually teach children from cultural groups different from their own, all will need to develop strategies that they can use to learn about their future students, as discussed above. Strategies alone, however, are insufficient. Teachers must approach learning about their students with a heightened sociocultural consciousness, an affirming attitude toward diversity, a belief in themselves as agents of change, and an understanding of the constructivist nature of learning.

STRAND SIX:
CULTIVATING THE PRACTICE OF
CULTURALLY RESPONSIVE TEACHING

If all students entered school with identical background knowledge and experiences and all learned the same way, then teaching would be a relatively simple task involving the use of a uniform instructional method regardless of the setting. The diversity of experiences that characterizes the student population today, however, precludes the use of a teaching script. In a multicultural society, responsible educators continuously tailor instruction to individual children in particular cultural contexts. This demands both that teachers know their students well and that they have the skills to transform what they know about the students into appropriate classroom practices. As this suggests, culturally responsive teaching is a profoundly adaptive and creative activity.

This final strand in our curriculum proposal brings together the essential knowledge, skills, and orientations for teaching a changing student population discussed in the previous five strands into a vision of culturally responsive teaching. We want to emphasize that our view of culturally responsive teaching does not represent an add-on strategy to be used only with students from nonmainstream cultural backgrounds. Nor is it a band-aid approach for teaching poor and racial/ethnic minority students. Schooling should be responsive for all children. Traditionally, however, schools have built on the social and cultural backgrounds of mainstream students while largely ignoring the social and cultural experiences of children from nonmainstream groups. The critical challenge for educators today is to find ways of restructuring schooling to draw on the strengths of all children, not just some. Below we discuss five broad practices that support this goal. These are (1) involving all students in the construction of knowledge, (2) building on students' personal and cultural strengths, (3) helping students examine the curriculum from multiple perspectives, (4) using varied assessment practices that promote learning, and (5) making the culture of the classroom inclusive of all students. These practices are not intended as specific prescriptions for teachers to follow. Instead, they are meant as general guidelines; teachers need to work out the details within the context of their particular classroom settings, drawing on knowledge about their own students.

Involving All Students in the Construction of Knowledge

A central task of culturally responsive teachers is to create a classroom environment in which all students are encouraged to make sense of new ideas—that is, to construct knowledge that helps them better understand the world—rather than merely memorizing predigested information. Teachers who strive to support students' knowledge construction actively involve children in learning tasks that promote the development of higher-order thought processes, including the skills of hypothesizing, predicting, comparing, evaluating, integrating, and synthesizing.

One way teachers can give students an active role in learning is by involving them in inquiry projects that have personal meaning to them. Rosebery, Warren, and Conant (1992) provide a good example of this practice, as used in a junior high school science class for Haitian students in Massachusetts. Most of the students in this class believed that the water from the school's third-floor fountains was better tasting than the water from the first-floor fountains. As they put it, the younger children—whose classrooms were located on the first floor—"slobber" when they drink water, thereby making it taste bad. To test their belief about the superiority of the third-floor water, the students designed and conducted a blind taste test of water taken from several fountains. They were surprised to find that a full two-thirds of them preferred the first-floor water. They then decided to expand the test to include students from other junior high school classes, a decision that created an opportunity for the children to discuss methodological sampling issues and strategies for minimizing response bias. They were again surprised to learn that while 88 percent of the students sampled had reported a preference for the third-floor water, more than half of them (55 percent) chose water from the first floor in the taste test. To try to make sense of their findings, the students analyzed the school's water and discovered that the first-floor water was twenty degrees colder than that from any other floor. They theorized that the water becomes warmer as it moves up the pipes to the third floor and concluded that temperature was a likely factor influencing respondents' water preference.

By involving the children in "doing" science, this inquiry project actively engaged them in learning. Like scientists in laboratories, these students posed questions, devised ways of testing their hypotheses, collected and analyzed data, reconciled contradictory data, and generated explanations. By embedding learning in a meaningful activity on a topic of interest to the students, the teacher provided them a strong motive to learn. The fact that the students were learners of English as a second language did not interfere with their carrying out a sophisticated scientific project. In fact, the project contributed to their language development.

Having students working collaboratively in small groups of mixed ability is yet another way of promoting active learning for all (Calderón, 1991; Cochran-Smith, 1999; Ladson-Billings, 1994; Nieto, 1999; Oakes and Lipton, 1994; Zeichner, 1993). When children work in groups to solve a problem or carry out a project, they share the cognitive demands built into the overall task. According to Brown and Palincsar (1989), the benefit of small-group tasks is maximized when each student adopts a different role. Some of the roles they identify include the doer who designs action plans or offers solutions to the problem posed, the critic who questions the ideas generated by the group, the instructor who reviews for all group members the ideas discussed, the record keeper who keeps track of the group's work, and the conciliator who settles conflicts. Brown and Palincsar contend that for peer interaction to be effective, however, two basic conditions must be met—all children in the group must have at least a partial grasp of the concepts involved in the task, and no single student must be so dominant that others defer all the work to him or her. Glasersfeld (1995) recommends that teachers place students into groups of three or four and assign the role of reporting back to the entire class to the one they consider to have the least command over the topic. As he explains, in order to have their collective thinking represented accurately, group members must explain their thoughts to one another, reflect upon what each is saying, and listen to each other's ideas. He contends that group work is a powerful learning tool because students tend to listen more openly and with greater interest to their peers than to teachers who present information to them. Group work can also promote cross-cultural communication and understanding, and it gives English language learners more opportunities to hear and use English than they would otherwise have (Lucas, 1997).

Open dialogues provide another avenue to actively engage students in the construction of knowledge. Effective dialogues involve everyone, including the teacher, in a genuine exploration of questions to which none of the parties claim to know the answers. This type of conversation contrasts markedly with the pseudo exchange that is the hallmark of transmission teaching. In such situations, teachers ask questions of the students to which they already have answers; their main purpose in asking known-answer or display questions is to assess whether the students can recall the information. One of the tasks of culturally responsive teachers is to promote a classroom atmosphere that is conducive to conversation, both between students and teacher and among students themselves. To engage in such conversations, students need to feel safe to ask questions, argue, and share views. This calls for an attitude of openness on the part of the teacher and a willingness to listen to the students (Glasersfeld, 1995; Nieto, 1999), as well as recognition that students who are not fully fluent in English may need extra time and support to participate (Lucas, 1997).

Culturally responsive teachers also support students' knowledge construction by having them gradually assume increasing responsibility for their own learning. Reciprocal teaching is a good example of this practice. As described by Brown and Palincsar (1989), reciprocal teaching involves a teacher and a group of students taking turns leading a discussion that centers on a portion of text they are jointly trying to understand. The discussion leader, who could be the teacher or a student, begins the exchange by asking questions and ends it by summarizing the main points raised in the discussion. Two other strategies are used during the discussion—clarifying any comprehension problems and predicting what will happen next. It is important to point out that students learn these strategies in the context of a collaborative attempt to interpret a portion of text, not as isolated skills. The role of the teacher in these situations is to model behavior, keep the discussion focused on content, and help student leaders see the discussion through to a satisfactory completion. Once again, teachers need to take into account the special linguistic demands of this process and make adjustments to ensure the successful participation of English language learners. Over time, the responsibility for the discussion—and the learning that comes with it—is transferred to the students. According to Resnick (1989), when students see themselves in control of their own learning instead of the teacher, they are more likely to construct knowledge rather than to merely memorize information.

When instruction is designed along the lines described above, students implicitly learn that concepts and ideas are phenomena to be generated and understood, not just facts to be memorized. This type of instruction—which engages students actively in purposeful, meaningful, collaborative, intellectually rigorous, and language-rich activities—also conveys to children that they are capable thinkers who can create new ideas. Students who are treated in this manner tend to push themselves to meet the teacher's expectations. Teachers who create such a classroom community have faith in the ability of all students to reach high levels of learning. That is, they possess an affirming view of students.

Building on Students' Personal and Cultural Strengths

Schools alienate learners when the substance of instruction neither relates to their lives nor invites them to use their preexisting knowledge and skills. To be responsive to future students, prospective teachers need to learn about the lives of those children, as we discussed in strand five. But knowledge of students' personal and cultural strengths will have little payoff for them unless they can translate those insights into pedagogical practices. Below we describe a variety of strategies that teachers can use to build on the knowledge of their students while stretching them beyond that which is familiar to them.

Helping Students Access Prior Knowledge and Beliefs   Because students use their prior knowledge and beliefs to give meaning to new ideas, teachers need to help them access the frameworks they already have relative to the topic of instruction. For example, a teacher might begin an instructional unit on the civil rights movement by describing for his students a class in which left-handed children are treated dramatically differently from their right-handed counterparts. The teacher might explain that left-handed students are seated separately from the others, assigned the least comfortable seats, provided fewer opportunities to answer questions, given less time to complete instructional tasks, and denied access to classroom computers, among other differences. The teacher could then ask the children to comment on the differential treatment of students in this imagined class. The children's comments would give the attentive teacher valuable insight into their understanding of the concepts of fairness and discrimination, both of which are central to an understanding of the civil rights movement. At the same time, such a discussion would help the children to activate a relevant framework, or mental scheme, that can assist them in organizing or integrating related pieces of information into a fuller interpretation of the civil rights movement. This assumes, of course, that the students already have a firm grasp of the concepts of fairness and discrimination.

While it is pedagogically useful to build on what students already know about a topic, the culturally responsive teacher also stretches students beyond that which is familiar to them. At times this could entail helping students develop mental schemes they do not have yet. To return to the example above, students who lack an understanding of the notion of discrimination are likely to have difficulty making sense of the civil rights movement. The responsive teacher would help those students develop such an understanding. This could be done, for instance, by involving them in an activity that arbitrarily assigns privilege to some members of the class while denying it to others, similar to the example given to the class initially (see Peters, 1987). Such an experience would provide the students a basis for constructing the meaning of fairness. The teacher could then invite the students to discuss their experience. The students' comments would give the instructor a window into the children's developing thinking relative to the target concept.

Stretching students beyond what they already know could also entail confronting misconceptions that might distort their understanding of a given topic. For instance, some students might believe that racial discrimination no longer exists in this country. This misconception is dangerous because it can support the view that people of color are to blame for their low socioeconomic standing relative to white people. Equally problematic, such a belief also promotes a lack of personal responsibility for challenging existing social inequalities. The culturally responsive teacher would help those students confront their misconception. She might ask them to review different newspapers over the past month to ascertain the extent to which issues of racial discrimination have made the news. If they find a number of examples of these issues (as we assume they would), then the teacher could engage the students in critically analyzing why, if racial discrimination is no longer an issue, it is being reported. For example, if students had examined newspapers in the New York City area during the spring of 1999, they would have found numerous articles about racial profiling and mistreatment of people of color by police officers in New York and New Jersey. Some students might still argue that the instances reported are exceptions to the rule. The teacher might then invite people who have personally suffered racial discrimination to come to class to share their experiences. By providing the children with evidence that contradicts their initial belief about the nonexistence of racial discrimination in this country, these activities might give the students a reason to modify their initial thinking.

Building on Students' Interests   When students are given opportunities to explore topics of interest to them, they are more apt to engage in learning than when instructional topics have little relevance to their lives (Glasersfeld, 1995; McDiarmid, 1991; Moll and Diaz, 1987). An example of how an ESL teacher successfully built on the interests of her secondary school students, taken from work by Moll and Diaz (1987), illustrates this practice. The action research project from which the example is drawn was carried out in a San Diego community with a large concentration of Latinos. The teacher—who knew that residents of the community, including her students, were highly interested in the topic of bilingualism—asked the students to survey the views of community members on this topic. As part of this writing module, the students were expected to develop a questionnaire, administer the questionnaire to several community members, and prepare a report of findings. The objective of ascertaining the community members' opinions gave purpose to all the writing connected with this module. Because the students were curious to find out the different views on bilingualism held in the community, they became fully engaged in the various writing activities. Students who had previously been considered incapable of writing in English were sufficiently motivated to produce essays in their second language. The key to the success of this module, according to Moll and Diaz, was the opportunity it gave the students to engage in purposeful writing on a topic of interest to them and of relevance to their community.

Teachers are often expected to teach topics that are of no apparent interest to students; students are disinterested largely because they do not see how those topics connect to their lives. Culturally responsive teachers find ways to generate interest in such topics. This practice was effectively demonstrated by a California elementary school teacher, an acquaintance of one of the authors. The teacher was beginning an instructional unit focusing on drought conditions in that state and the need for residents to conserve water. She reported that the drought topic had come up in class several times before, but the students had expressed little enthusiasm for it. To generate interest in the topic, the teacher began the unit by posing the following problem to the students: "You wake up tomorrow morning, and you turn on the faucet to wash your face, but no water comes out. You check on the faucet in the kitchen sink, and there's no water there either. You go next door to see if you can use your neighbor's bathroom to wash up, but you find out that they don't have any water either. Then you find out that none of your neighbors has water. Then you turn on the TV, and you find that there's no water in the whole city. How would this situation affect your lives? What would your day be like without water? What might it be like to go without water for a week?" This brief introduction to the unit, which helped the students envision a link between the content of instruction and their personal lives, provided the motivation the children needed to explore a topic about which they previously had shown little curiosity.

Culturally responsive teachers also promote candid discussions about topics that, while relevant to the lives of the students, are regularly excluded from classroom conversations. For example, the teachers who participated in a study conducted by Ladson-Billings and Henry (1990) openly discussed with their students issues related to drug use and teenage sex. As these researchers report, instead of offering moral pronouncements, the teachers helped the students to examine why such conditions existed in their communities. In so doing, the instructors validated the students' experiences. At the same time, they made those experiences problematic and an appropriate subject for critical inspection.

Building on Students' Linguistic Resources   Just as culturally responsive teachers build on students' interests, they also build on students' linguistic resources. Language, like culture, is part of who a person is. It is "intimately connected with loved ones, community, and personal identity" (Delpit, 1998, 19). To ignore or denigrate a student's language is to ignore or denigrate the student him/herself. Culturally responsive teachers use their knowledge of sociolinguistics and language development along with what they learn about their students' uses of language—as we discussed in strand five—to draw on language as a resource for learning rather than seeing backgrounds in languages other than English or in varieties other than standard school English as impediments to learning.

Culturally responsive teachers value bilingualism—that is, fluency and academic competence in English and in students' native languages. They encourage students to continue to develop their native language ability while becoming fluent in English. They also invite students to communicate in and use materials in their native languages if it will facilitate learning. They might, for example, pair students who speak the same native language so that they can help each other make sense of instruction in English. They take into account students' levels of proficiency in English and their native languages in designing classroom activities, such as cooperative groups and dialogue, as we have already mentioned. They engage students in classroom activities that will make the most of their native languages as well as facilitate their development of English skills. The students who conducted the survey on attitudes toward bilingualism described above, for example, were able to use both English and Spanish in carrying out the project. Culturally responsive teachers also advocate for adequate staffing and support for English language learners in their schools and districts and seek the advice of colleagues with expertise in bilingual education and second language learning.

Teachers who are culturally responsive also draw on the linguistic resources of students who speak varieties of English other than the standard school variety. They might, for instance, bring in examples of discourse that students are familiar with from their homes or communities. Below, we give an example of a student teacher who used a piece of rap music to teach poetry. Reading fiction and nonfiction written in dialects other than standard English can heighten awareness of linguistic varieties and illustrate the appropriateness and impact of using such varieties in published literature. Teachers might also have students formally analyze dialect differences and variation in language use across different domains (e.g., at school, at home with parents, with friends, at church). By recognizing the reality of language differences, showing that they value such differences, and making use of them in the classroom, culturally responsive teachers allow students to use their language abilities to facilitate learning rather than reducing their capacity to learn by taking such an important resource away from them (Lucas, 1997).

Using Examples and Analogies from Students' Lives   Using pertinent examples and analogies from learners' lives to introduce or clarify new concepts or principles is another way in which culturally responsive teachers help students build bridges to learning (Banks, 1996; Garcia, 1995; Irvine, 1992; McDiarmid, 1991; Resnick, 1989). For example, one of us recently observed a student teacher successfully introducing the concept of rhythm in poetry to African American and Latino students in an urban middle school by drawing on the students' familiarity with rhythm in rap music. She began the lesson by playing a selection of rap music that the children knew well, followed by a discussion of rhythm in that particular music selection. She then guided the students through a similar analysis of rhythm in a poem by Robert Frost, drawing parallels between the use of rhythm in rap and that in poetry. In exploring the analogy between the two poetic forms, this young teacher transformed the subject matter into an educational experience that was relevant to her students.

Analogies could play a powerful role in students' learning by serving as a bridge between the abstract and the concrete. Gay (1988) warns, however, that when the analogy used to introduce or clarify a given topic is unfamiliar to students, learning becomes even more difficult because the learners must decipher a double layer of abstraction—the concept and the analogy used to represent it. Culturally responsive teachers, therefore, are careful to select analogies that are familiar to their students. Resnick (1989) suggests that to maximize the use of analogies in teaching, instructors must discuss the analogy at length with the class in order to allow students to adequately grasp the similarities between the two systems or situations being compared.

Using Appropriate Instructional Materials   Culturally responsive teachers select or develop instructional materials that not only promote the learning goal but that are also relevant to the students' experiences (Danielson, 1996; Zeichner, 1993). Some of the questions teachers might consider in reviewing instructional materials for relevance to children include the following:

- Do textbooks and other written materials depict situations that are familiar to the students?
- Do word problems describe situations that the students can easily recognize?
- Is the language accessible to them?
- Are there appropriate materials in the students' native languages that could be used to enhance their learning?
- Are the examples used familiar to the students?
- Do the materials reflect the diversity of the class in terms of race/ethnicity, socioeconomic levels, language groups, and gender?
- Do they reflect the contributions of different groups, especially those represented in the class?

Similarly, culturally responsive educators review commercially developed materials carefully for bias, omissions, and inaccuracies. According to the Council on Interracial Books for Children (1997), the review process gives attention to the following concerns:

- Do the illustrations include oversimplified generalizations or stereotypes of any group?

- Does the text promote stereotypes of any groups?
- Does the text encourage a passive acceptance of oppressive conditions in society?
- Are people of color or females consistently depicted in subservient roles?
- Do the heroes of the story include representatives of different groups?
- Is the language of the text free from bias (e.g., describing someone as an "Indian-giver" or referring to specific groups with loaded adjectives such as "docile")?

Tapping Community Resources   Another strategy that culturally responsive teachers can use to help students build bridges between school learning and their lives outside school is to draw on the expertise of community members, including the children's parents. For example, a teacher of a large number of Hmong children in a San Francisco area school asked the father of one of the children to show the class how a traditional Hmong wooden top was made and used. He came to the classroom over a period of several weeks, first showing the children the raw materials and tools for making the top, then carving and painting the top, and finally teaching them how to use it. The class learned valuable lessons about measurement and woodcraft through this project. Another teacher in New York City, when teaching about immigration in the United States, invited the parents of several children in her class who had immigrated to this country to share their immigrant experience with the students. By asking the children's parents to share aspects of their funds of knowledge with the class, these two teachers not only strengthened the connections between home and school but also conveyed to the children that their families have knowledge and experiences that the school values.

Creating Different Paths to Learning by Using Varied Instructional Activities   Because active participation in classroom activities is a stimulus for learning, responsive teachers deliberately plan and implement instruction so as to involve all students. To accomplish this in today's diverse classrooms, they need to have a wide repertoire of strategies to represent each instructional topic (Irvine, 1990; McDiarmid, 1991; Noordhoff and Kleinfield, 1993; Villegas, 1991). These strategies include the mini-lecture, large group discussion, small group discussion, debates, cooperative group projects, peer centers, reciprocal teaching, and individual work on computers. Just as important, culturally responsive teachers are skilled at selecting from this repertoire those instructional modes that are appropriate to the students and the situation. To the extent possible, they create learning tasks that give students some choice in activities and flexible time for completion (Darling-Hammond, 1996). By building different paths to knowledge, culturally responsive teachers accommodate the wide range of individual and cultural approaches to learning found in our society.

To summarize, culturally responsive teachers tailor instruction to their students rather than impose a singular teaching style to which all students must adapt. By building on the children's personal and cultural strengths, they scaffold the children's learning. This scaffolding entails activating students' prior knowledge, building on their interests and concerns, building on their linguistic resources, using examples and analogies from their lives to facilitate the comprehension of new ideas, selecting instructional materials that are relevant to the learners, drawing on the expertise or funds of knowledge available within the students' communities, and using varied instructional activities to accommodate differences in learning. The aim of these responsive teaching practices is to add to what students already know, not to replace what they bring to learning. By acknowledging the students' strengths, culturally responsive teachers communicate respect for them and also validate their experiences. It is this respect and validation that serves as the basis for a meaningful relationship between teacher and students.

Helping Students Examine the Curriculum from Multiple Perspectives

We have already argued that knowledge is socially constructed and value laden. The knowledge comprising the school curriculum is no exception. It is useful to think of the curriculum as a story. Like all stories, that told in the curriculum reflects the perspectives of the authors. In the case of the curriculum, those who hold power in society have the privilege to write the text. It is not surprising then that the traditional school narrative largely reflects the experiences, values, concerns, and interests of the powerful groups, while muting the voices of the less powerful. A central role of the culturally responsive teacher is to help students interrogate the curriculum critically by having them address inaccuracies, omissions, and distortions in the text and by broadening it to include multiple perspectives. This type of curriculum interrogation and expansion is needed for two major reasons—to assist students from oppressed groups to overcome the sense of alienation many experience in school and to prepare all students to act against social inequality rather than merely assimilating into inequitable social arrangements (Banks, 1991a, 1993a, 1994, 1995, 1996; Cochran-Smith, 1995a, 1997,

1999; Crichlow et al., 1990; Ladson-Billings, 1992, 1994; Mehan et. al, 1995; Nieto, 1999).

Banks (1993a), who has written extensively about the need to transform the Eurocentric accounts that dominate the school curriculum, advocates that children be taught to examine concepts, situations, and events from multiple perspectives. He illustrates his vision of curriculum transformation with a social studies unit about the westward movement. The unit begins with the teacher asking the students to list the ideas and images that come to mind when they think of "The West." According to Banks, the intent of this activity is to build on the students' personal and cultural knowledge relative to the topic. The class is then asked to view *How the West Was Won*, a 1962 film that depicts a European family's struggle to settle in the West. Banks points out that American Indians are seen in the film only when attacking the family during their journey west. This image of aggression is reinforced further by occasional comments heard throughout the film in which the American Indians are referred to as "hostile." In his assessment, the overall impression promoted by the film is that the West was won by people who were pursuing freedom for all.

After engaging the students in a critical analysis of the film, the teacher summarizes for the class the thinking of the well-known American historian Frederick Jackson Turner, who in an influential paper written in 1893 describes the Western frontier as the site of a struggle between "savagery" and "civilization." At this point in the unit, the students are invited to view and analyze the film entitled *How the West Was Won and Honor Lost*. As described by Banks, this film focuses on broken treaties and the ultimate displacement of the American Indians by the westward-bound European Americans. To give students insight into how the images of American Indians portrayed in popular culture have both changed and persisted over time, the unit recommends that students watch *Dances with Wolves*, a movie that was popular several years back. The unit concludes with a discussion of the textbook version of the westward movement. In brief, by describing the westward movement from contrasting points of view, this unit aims to broaden and deepen students' understanding of the traditional school version of the story. In so doing, the unit also strives to help learners understand how knowledge is socially constructed.

Crichlow, Goodwin, Shakes, and Swartz (1990) illustrate another approach teachers can use to help students examine the curriculum critically. They describe a discussion in a seventh-grade class during which the teacher is working with her students to expand the traditional historical narrative. One portion of this conversation centers around a sentence from the social studies text, which states the following: "When

Washington was elected president, only men who owned property or were wealthy could vote." While "truthful," this statement glosses over important ideas that the teacher did not want the students to overlook. Through a series of questions, the instructor helps the students make the sentence "more accurate" by adding that it was only "white" men who were able to vote. The teacher also has the class explicitly name those who did not have voting privilege at the time—poor white men, enslaved black men, free black men, and women. According to Crichlow and colleagues, by helping the students distinguish between truth and accuracy, this teacher broadened the text to include voices that were clearly missing, thereby expanding the students' ways of thinking about the topic.

The two examples presented above show how culturally responsive teachers can help students identify and critically analyze the voices they hear in the materials they study as well as those that are silenced. They suggest possibilities for exploring conflicting interpretations of the same topic, raising questions of injustice and exclusion, and helping students formulate their own views on issues. These are precisely the types of skills students will need as adults to make society more democratic and just, a salient goal of our vision of culturally responsive teaching.

Taking a somewhat different approach to reconceptualizing the school curriculum, Lang (1995) shows how the science curriculum can be enriched by different cultural perspectives. He describes a component of a unit on weather that was designed to have students learn about weather-prediction practices from the perspectives of different cultural groups. He introduces this unit component by commenting on the ability of many elders in early African cultures to predict weather accurately before modern instruments were developed. As he explains, those predictions were based on careful observations of natural signs, such as the behavior of birds, cloud formations, and the color of the sky. Among the suggested activities in this aspect of the instructional unit are the following: asking the students to conduct library research to identify culturally related weather prediction strategies, having students interview older family members of different racial/ethnic groups to explore the accuracy of weather-prediction strategies identified in their library research (e.g., predictions related to body aches and pains, the sound and pitch of blowing winds, ants piling the dirt higher around the openings into their homes), and observing over a period of time the flight direction of birds and subsequent weather conditions to determine the relationship between the two. The multicultural integration approach to science illustrated in this unit component affirms the knowledge and traditions of different cultures.

To engage students in the types of curriculum reconceptualization described above, teachers need a solid and critical understanding of their subject matter, a clear grasp of how knowledge is socially constructed, a well-developed sense of sociocultural consciousness, affirming views of diversity, and a commitment to being agents of change. Without these essential dispositions and knowledge, teachers will most likely persist in presenting school knowledge to students as a given, while ignoring its contested nature.

Using Varied Assessment Practices That Promote Learning

A fourth practice of culturally responsive teaching is the use of varied approaches to student assessment. Standardized tests provide information about how a given student measures up to specified educational criteria relative to others who have taken the same test. The results of such tests can give important insight into progress made toward equalizing educational opportunities in society, or the lack thereof. For example, analysis of scores from the National Assessment Education Program (NAEP) over time show whether the gap between the achievement of white students and that of students of color has narrowed or widened. Such information is important for policymakers and educators. Traditionally, however, scores from standardized tests have been used largely to sort students into different instructional tracks (Darling-Hammond, 1995; National Coalition of Educational Equity Advocates, 1994). If the goal of schools is to educate *all students* to high levels of achievement—as we believe it should be—then tests and assessments must be used in the service of teaching and learning rather than for sorting pupils into different instructional groups or tracks. The overall purpose of assessment should be to help teachers identify the particular strengths and needs of their students so they can determine the most effective ways of building on what the children already know while helping them grow academically (Goodwin, 1997b; Goodwin and McDonald, 1997).

Assessments that serve as learning tools—that is, as tools that support the development of students' understanding—expand beyond multiple choice items, which focus mostly on recall of factual information. Learning-oriented assessments ask students to construct their responses rather than select a right answer and to apply their knowledge to solving problems in the real world rather than using their skills in decontextualized ways. For example, students might be asked to display their developing competence through exhibitions or portfolios that include selected products from one or more class project(s), oral presentations of findings from data-gathering activities, oral defense of conclusions reached based on research conducted, and debates. Culturally responsive teachers consistently use such authentic assessments.

In diverse classroom situations, the job of assessing student learning is especially complex. As we discussed previously, children enter school with culturally specific understandings of the appropriate means of displaying knowledge. If the teacher and students do not share this understanding, the instructor could easily misjudge the pupils' competence unless he or she is sensitive to cultural differences. For example, teachers use display questions with frequency (e.g., What is the capital of the United States?) to determine what students know about a given topic. These questions require students to display their knowledge before other students in a public forum. Because many American Indian children are not accustomed to this "spotlighting" method of assessment, their performance in situations that rely on it may not be indicative of what they really know (Au and Kawakami, 1994; Philips, 1983). Culturally responsive teachers are aware of the potential for cultural misunderstanding and thus interpret assessment results for students from diverse backgrounds cautiously.

Culturally responsive teachers also offer students a variety of routes to demonstrate what they know about the topic of instruction (Cochran-Smith, 1999; Oakes and Lipton, 1999; Villegas, 1991; Zeichner, 1992). For example, they conduct informal observations of students in various contexts, examine work products as collected in portfolios, attend closely to answers to oral questions or comments during class discussions, and review written work. This variety is important because reliance on a single type of assessment task is bound to create a disadvantage for some children.

Assessing students who speak native languages other than English is particularly challenging. When assessing bilingual students who appear competent in English, culturally responsive teachers therefore exercise much caution. While children can usually gain a fair degree of oral proficiency in a second language within one or two years of schooling, it generally takes five or more years for these students to master the more demanding, context-reduced language of classroom instruction and written text (Cummins, 1991). Culturally responsive teachers are aware of this natural process of language development and understand that what may appear as an academic problem can actually be a stage of normal language development (Ortiz and Maldonado-Colon, 1986). They look for appropriate assessment tools and seek assistance from colleagues and other professionals with expertise in interpreting results.

In brief, culturally responsive teachers break away from conventional testing traditions. This calls for an understanding of the uses and limitations of standardized tests, a commitment to using assessments that both give insight into students' thinking and promote their learning, an ability to design authentic tasks that are consistent with the learning goals and appropriate to the students, and the skills to interpret and use the assessment results. Underlying this set of dispositions and skills must be a will to serve as an agent of change, a belief that all students can achieve to high levels, and a commitment to teaching from a constructivist perspective.

Making the Culture of the Classroom Inclusive of All Students

To succeed in school, children must be academically knowledgeable. But this is not enough. Equally important and often overlooked, students need to know the culturally appropriate ways of participating in learning events and of displaying what they know (Mehan, 1979; Villegas, 1991). It is useful to think of the classroom as a community with its own culture or patterned way of life. While some variation in the culture of the classroom exists, certain features have prevailed over time and persist today despite ongoing efforts to reform teaching and learning. In many classrooms, for example, the dominant form of interaction is the teacher-directed lesson in which the instructor is in full control of the event, determining the topics of discussion, allocating turns at speaking, and deciding what qualifies as a correct response. Verbal participation is required of students; implicitly, teaching and learning are equated with talking, and silence is interpreted as the absence of knowledge. Students are questioned in public and required to bid for the floor by raising their hands. Speaking in sequential turns is the rule. Display questions prevail. Individual competition is valued over group cooperation. However, the home socialization of many children from nonmainstream backgrounds clashes with many of the sociocultural demands of this type of classroom (see Villegas, 1999; Wong-Fillmore, 1990). Such cultural incompatibility between home and school is a major source of the problems many children who are poor and of color experience in school, particularly in the early grades. Those problems are compounded even further when teachers lack an awareness of the potential for such cultural clashes.

Culturally responsive teachers understand that the classroom is not a neutral setting where all students can participate in instructional events equally and display what they know freely. They further understand that embedded in their own teaching are implicit rules that govern what counts as knowledge, how questions are used, how stories are told, how access to the floor is gained, how knowledge is demonstrated, how space is organized, and how time is used. To gain awareness of the specific sociocultural demands of their classrooms, culturally responsive teachers reflect on their teaching. Then they use the insight gained through such reflection to create inclusive classroom communities in which all students understand the appropriate ways of participating in the various learning events. This includes making explicit to children the socio-cultural expectations built into different learning activities, whenever needed.

For example, instructional projects involving small groups of children collaborating to devise solutions to problems could be culturally challenging to many students. Children who have been brought up to value the individual above the group are apt to experience difficulties—at least initially—when expected to collaborate with peers. Similarly, children who have been socialized at home to defer to authority are likely to resist seeking their own answers to questions, preferring instead for the teacher to give them those answers. To enable these students to participate effectively in collaborative problem-solving projects, the culturally responsive teacher helps them understand not only how to participate in this type of instructional event, but also why it is important for them to adopt ways of learning that are culturally unfamiliar, perhaps even clashing. Needless to say, these discussions demand considerable knowledge of and sensitivity to cultural differences on the part of teachers. We want to make clear that we are not proposing that teachers replace the cultural patterns students bring from home in order to "fit into" the culture of the school and classroom. Rather, we are suggesting that teachers help students add new patterns to their cultural repertoire, thereby expanding the children's ways of participating in the world.

While culturally responsive teachers stretch students beyond that which is familiar to them, they also find ways of incorporating into their teaching cultural patterns that are known to the children from their home and community experiences. Marva Collins, a highly acclaimed teacher of African American students, illustrates this strategy clearly. Collins's teaching was documented by Hollins (1982), on whose work we draw. According to Hollins, Ms. Collins often corrected her students' grammar, thereby signaling to them the importance in U.S. society of mastering standard English. However, she also encouraged the use of community language patterns in the classroom. For example, analogical comparisons often used in traditional African American speech were evident in Ms. Collins's teaching. Jive talking, based on improvisation with language, was accepted as a viable means of communication in her classroom. Interaction patterns commonly found in the African American church—including choral reading, audience participation, and use of analogies—were also used frequently. Hollins concluded that Marva Collins's teaching success was due, in large part, to her ability to make learning culturally relevant to the students.

Because the culture of the classroom is so pervasive, even the most attentive teachers find it impossible to become conscious of its

many different manifestations. Cognizant of this, culturally responsive teachers make it a point of monitoring the sociocultural dynamics of their own classrooms to identify problems and facilitate their
solution. Such teachers do not assume that students who do not follow classroom procedures are purposefully misbehaving. Instead,
they first rule out the possibility of a cultural misunderstanding. For
example, students who learn at home to use overlapping turns at talk
(in which more than one person in the exchange has the right to speak
at the same time) are likely to have difficulties with the one-speaker-
at-a-time approach to turn taking that is used with frequency in
schools. Instead of raising their hands and waiting to speak until the
teacher awards them the floor, they might call out. In doing so, the
children are merely complying with the rules of interaction that are
valued in their homes. Rather than automatically interpreting such
behavior as a conscious breach of discipline, culturally responsive
teachers verify the students' familiarity with the turn-taking rule
being enforced. Such precaution could prevent serious miscommunication in culturally diverse classrooms.

In brief, making the culture of the classroom inclusive of all students
is a delicate task that requires considerable knowledge and competence
in a multicultural society. Culturally responsive teachers know that
learning, whether in or out of school, occurs in a sociocultural context.
They understand that the instructional events they organize (e.g., group
projects, peer centers, teacher-directed lessons) can—and often do—
clash with the ways in which some of their students are socialized at
home. They are aware that cultural disjunctures between home and
school can make students appear academically incompetent, even when
the students actually know the subject matter well. They also have the
ability to reflect on their teaching and, from such reflection, glean
insight into the hidden cultural expectations built into the learning activities used. Equally important, they have knowledge of their students' cultures, especially the discourse patterns and interaction styles valued in
the children's homes and communities.

Figure 3.6 provides an overview of the salient responsive teaching
practices discussed above. As our discussion suggests, the job of a culturally responsive teacher is demanding and complex. It involves engaging all students—not just some—in learning for understanding; creating
instructional experiences that build on students' individual and cultural
knowledge, while supporting them in reaching beyond the known; helping students view the themes of the curriculum from the perspectives of
different groups, not just the dominant viewpoint; using assessments
that support learning and provide opportunities for students to demonstrate their competence in ways that are familiar to them; and molding

FIGURE 3.6
Culturally Responsive Teaching Practices

- *Involving all students in the construction of knowledge*
  > Inquiry projects
  > Having students working collaboratively in small groups of mixed ability
  > Authentic dialogues
  > Having students assume increasing responsibility for their own learning

- *Building on students' personal and cultural strengths*
  > Helping students access prior knowledge and beliefs
  > Building on students' interests
  > Building on students' linguistic resources
  > Using examples and analogies from students' lives
  > Using appropriate instructional materials
  > Tapping community resources
  > Creating different paths to learning by using varied instructional activities

- *Helping students examine the curriculum from multiple perspectives*

- *Using varied assessment practices that promote learning*

- *Making the culture of the classroom inclusive of all students*

the culture of the classroom to make it inclusive of all students.

It is unrealistic to expect teachers-to-be to become the type of culturally responsive teachers described in this strand during their preservice preparation. The extensive knowledge and sophisticated skills of culturally responsive teachers develop only with experience. In fact, becoming a culturally responsive teacher is a lifelong process. Even those of us who are farther along than beginning teachers continue to grow, never reaching a finished state of cultural responsiveness. It is realistic, however, to expect prospective teachers to come away from their preservice teacher education programs well on the way to becoming responsive educators. Specifically, those completing preservice programs of teacher education could be expected to have a vision of what culturally responsive teaching entails and an understanding of what culturally responsive teachers do. They could also be expected to demonstrate an initial ability to tailor their teaching to particular students within particular contexts—the salient quality of a culturally responsive teacher. Equally important, they could be expected to have the disposition to reflect on their own practice in order to glean from experience insights that will help them make their teaching increasingly responsive.

To develop these understandings and abilities, prospective teachers need exposure to culturally responsive teachers—by reading about them, analyzing teaching cases featuring them, and watching them in action. They also need practice in diverse classrooms themselves with feedback from experienced responsive teachers. Such practice is most productive when it is accompanied by guided reflection. In the next chapter, we discuss these and other strategies that teacher educators can use to promote the development of responsive teaching practices among preservice teachers.

CHAPTER 4

Modeling the Practice of
Culturally Responsive Teaching

Up to this point, we have concentrated on the teacher education curriculum. In this chapter, we shift our attention to the pedagogy needed to successfully carry out that curriculum. We contend that because teachers tend to teach in the ways they were taught (Floden, 1991; Feimen-Nemser and Melnick, 1992; Howey, 1996; Korthagen and Kessels, 1999; Shaw, 1991; Tom, 1997), those of us who teach them during their preservice preparation need to model for them the practice of culturally responsive teaching. In programs that have a vision of culturally responsive teaching similar to the one we advocate, that means involving preservice teachers actively in the construction of knowledge, building on their strengths while challenging their misconceptions, helping them examine ideas from multiple perspectives, using varied assessment strategies, and making the culture of our classrooms inclusive of all. To do this, we will need to move away from the transmission-of-knowledge approach that prevails in higher education (Korthagen and Kessels, 1999; McDiarmid, 1990b; McDiarmid and Price, 1990; Tom, 1997).

In college and university classes, faculty typically do almost all the talking, while students sit and listen. The lecture predominates, as we are driven to "cover" the curriculum. We typically present students with a body of information that they are expected to report back exactly as they "learned" it. In so doing, we present ourselves as the unquestioned authority in the classroom and place students in a largely silent role as recipients of course content and passive followers of classroom procedures that have been determined mostly by us.

This transmission approach is inappropriate for preparing culturally responsive teachers. Clearly, it does not model the type of teaching we are advocating. It also is not likely to inspire the conceptual change our curriculum proposal demands. Upon entering teacher education, aspiring teachers are far from being "empty vessels." Instead, they bring beliefs regarding the nature of schools, diversity, knowledge, learning, and teaching derived from years of education and life experiences (Feiman-Nemser and Melnick, 1992; Harrington and Hathaway, 1995; Lortie, 1975; McDiarmid, 1992; McDiarmid and Price, 1990; Paine, 1989; Richardson,

1995). Because they have typically been socialized to see schools and other social institutions as equitable and meritocratic, to view departures from mainstream culture as problematic, to accept school knowledge as objective and neutral, to take a passive role in learning, and to see the teacher as the only legitimate source of knowledge in the classroom, many prospective teachers are bound to resist the curriculum we are proposing in this book. Simply telling them about alternative ways of thinking is not likely to change their views (Feiman-Nemser and Melnick, 1992; Feiman-Nemser and Remillard, 1996; Kennedy, 1998).

Despite these shortcomings, transmission pedagogy has a strong foothold in higher education. For one thing, just as prospective teachers have developed their transmission views through years of experience in schools, so too have higher education faculty—through even more years of schooling. Like our students, those of us who teach at colleges and universities have been socialized to hold transmission views of knowledge, learning, and teaching. Even if we know the literature on constructivism, we may not have taken the next step to apply it to our own teaching. In addition, our preparation for becoming faculty members— that is, our graduate education—has typically focused on academic content. Even degree programs that have prepared us to become faculty in schools or colleges of education have generally given little attention to pedagogy in the higher education classroom. This focus on content promotes a transmission view of education. To become constructivist teachers, then, we face the challenge of overcoming our own socialization, which has privileged the transmission of content. In chapter 5, we discuss the types of professional development that will enable us do so.

In the remainder of this chapter, we examine classroom-based and field-based pedagogical practices that teacher educators can use to create constructivist classrooms and model culturally responsive teaching for prospective teachers. We want to emphasize that these practices are applicable not just in education courses, but throughout the undergraduate curriculum in such fields as anthropology, sociology, history, literature, biology, and mathematics. Our discussion is not all-inclusive, however. We highlight a sample of practices that are described in the literature on multicultural teacher preparation and that invite learners to construct knowledge. Figure 4.1 provides an overview of the practices we will consider.

CLASSROOM-BASED PRACTICES

We begin this section with a discussion of the importance of organizing the classroom as a community of learners in which students actively

FIGURE 4.1
Practices That Promote the Development
of Culturally Responsive Teachers

Classroom-Based Practices

- Creating classroom communities of learners
- Developing dispositions, knowledge, and skills of culturally responsive teachers
  - > Reflective writing
  - > Simulations and games
  - > Exploring family histories
  - > Articulating sociocultural affiliations
  - > Exploring personal history and development
  - > Learning about the history and current experiences of diverse groups
  - > Accounts of successful teaching and learning in diverse settings
  - > Teaching cases

Field Experiences

- School and community visits
- Service learning
- Studies of students, classrooms, schools, and communities
- Practica in diverse contexts with responsive teachers

---

engage in the construction of knowledge. We then describe more specific activities and strategies that foster prospective teachers' awareness of their own beliefs and assumptions and help them move beyond awareness to develop the dispositions, knowledge, and skills of culturally responsive teachers.

Creating a Community of Learners

The way a classroom is organized has profound implications for the type of learning that takes place there. In the traditional classroom we described above, the professor directs activities, and the students simply follow his or her lead. The professor is assumed to have knowledge, and the students are expected to gain access to that knowledge by listening to the professor and reading texts written by other experts. They are then expected to display what they have learned by producing various products, primarily papers and tests, that are evaluated by the professor. While some interaction may take place among students, learning is assumed to be an individual act that occurs within each learner. Students in a class are seen mostly as individuals who happen to be sitting in the same room at certain times during the day or week but who "learn" separately. A classroom that encourages the construction of knowledge requires a different sort of organization, however. As we discussed in chapter 3, learners construct meaning individually, through cognitive processes, and socially, through "a collective participatory process" involving interactions with others (Salomon and Perkins, 1998, 2). In fact, the two processes go hand in hand, each supporting the other. Teachers at all levels in the educational system who take seriously the social dimension of learning establish classroom communities in which learners play active roles in their own and each other's learning.

Classrooms organized as communities of learners engage students in purposeful activities. In such classes professors aim to make course content meaningful to students rather than allowing concepts and ideas to remain abstract and decontextualized. Students pose problems and questions that are of interest to them and are relevant to the world beyond the college/university classroom, and they devise ways to explore them. They engage in activities involving hypothesizing, predicting, comparing, evaluating, integrating, and synthesizing. They examine how principles and theories play out in particular contexts through individual and collaborative projects involving data collection, analysis, and interpretation.

Through inquiry projects, for example, students attempt to answer a question or to more fully understand an issue or phenomenon of concern to them. In an educational foundations course focusing on the education of diverse student populations that one of the authors teaches, students carry out such a project. They are encouraged to see the activity not as a class exercise but as an opportunity to develop an understanding of an issue that has perplexed them. The students first articulate a question they want to answer. Then they gather information from various sources to help them answer their questions. In addition to conducting library and Internet research, they interview educators, parents, students, and community members who have insights about the issue they are studying. They might also collect school and community documents. At the end of the class, they present what they have learned to their classmates. One student who was hoping to teach in a district with a large number of immigrants, for instance, was eager to find out what schools and teachers can do to help English language learners be successful once placed in mainstream classes. In addition to reading a number of articles, she interviewed several ESL and mainstream teachers, mainstreamed ESL students, and the course instructor, who has done research on the education of English language learners and on the transition process in particular (Lucas and Wagner, 2000). She also observed several mainstream classes that enrolled ESL students. From the data she gathered, she identified a variety of strategies that support the transition of ESL students into mainstream classes.

While inquiry projects make course content meaningful to students and help them see connections between theory and practice, they can still remain largely intellectual activities unless students are asked to put what they learn into action (Christensen, 1991; Osajima, 1995; Tatum, 1992). Developing action plans can give students hope in the possibility of change and empower them to become agents of change (Tatum, 1992). When students develop action plans to accompany projects, they must also consider the real-world implications and applications of their ideas. The projects for the class described above end with a plan to take some action, however small, based on what students learned. The prospective teacher who learned about strategies for supporting main-streamed ESL students sent a letter to the educators she interviewed describing her findings and suggesting resources of potential interest to them. In another class, a student who had studied about Ebonics wrote a letter to the editor of a local newspaper refuting inaccurate statements in a recently published article. This, in turn, encouraged other students in the class to read newspaper articles focused on education more criti-cally than they had done before. The final project for a course on race and education taught by Osajima (1995) also requires students to write a paper analyzing a problem they identify and to develop an action plan. One group developed a video for use in future classes in which students talked about how racism affected them. Another group wrote letters to the editors and publisher of a fifth-grade social studies text presenting their critique of the book's treatment of Native Americans. Two other students developed and conducted an antiracism workshop for white students.

Wijeyesinghe, Griffin, and Love (1997) describe a module in a course focused on racism in which participants identify ways to take action against racism and develop their own plans for interrupting racist practices. Participants examine the characteristics of allies in the strug-gle against racism, discuss "costs and benefits of interrupting racism," explore ways of combating racism in different dimensions of their lives, complete an action planning worksheet that prompts them to be explicit and reflective about actions they can take, and develop an action plan that includes a "change contract" (102–3). They are encouraged to develop realistic plans and to help each other refine their proposals. To better prepare them to carry out their plans, they spend some time exploring factors that might hinder and support their implementation.

Young (1998) describes activities other than inquiry projects and action plans that she used in a social foundations course in which she set out to foster a community of learners. The students participated in discussions, debates, storytelling, role plays, and real conversations about their experiences and ideas related to the transformation of schools for social justice. They posed questions and interpreted and clarified each other's ideas on the relationship between social phenomena and schooling. They led class discussions. They engaged in ongoing interaction with her through their journals. They articulated their positions on such issues as race and racism to one another and then pushed one another to critically examine those positions. According to Young, they "questioned . . . idiosyncratic and subjective explanations" (111). In a journal, one student wrote that an "honest" conversation she had with two other students outside class about "blaming the victim" was "a wonderful way to learn" (111). Students credited changes in their value systems, personal beliefs, perceptions of themselves as future teachers, and ways of thinking about their future students to their participation in the classroom community.

Like inquiry projects, action plans, debates, storytelling, and other purposeful activities, dialogue is essential to classrooms organized as communities of learners. In contrast to the closed teacher-student interactions of transmission classrooms in which teachers know where they want the interactions to end up, dialogue is open, "following the argument where it leads" (Lipman, 1997, 7). The goal of classroom dialogue is discovery and understanding. It tends "toward a decentered and nonauthoritarian view of learning" (Burbules, 1993, 9) and takes an "exploratory and interrogative" tone (Burbules, 1993, 8). Dialogue values the voices of all participants and seeks to involve everyone in the community in discussing issues of common concern (Burbules, 1993; Fernández-Balboa and Marshall, 1994). It opens up students' beliefs, worldviews, and assumptions to critical inspection and simultaneously values multiple worldviews (Harrington and Hathaway, 1995). Freire (1968) saw dialogue as central not only to learning but also to human liberation and transformation. He described it as "a horizontal relationship of which mutual trust between the dialoguers is the logical consequence" (80). Collaborative dialogue among equals, which departs considerably from traditional pedagogical approaches, is needed if we want prospective teachers to learn for understanding (as distinct from memorizing) and to modify fundamental views that contradict the practice of culturally responsive teaching.

In a dialogic classroom community, the class members spend most of their time engaging each other in substantive exchanges about issues of importance to them. The classroom is arranged so they can see each other, thus making dialogue possible. The participants, including the instructor, share the floor, show interest in each other's ideas, take responsibility for moving the dialogue forward, ask and answer authentic questions, listen to each other, ask for clarification, and provide and seek examples and counterexamples (Sharp, 1991). The instructor guides discussions but does not dominate them (Griffin, 1997a).

The members of the classroom community establish class procedures for interaction and dialogue, just as they later take responsibility for seeing that the community follows the procedures—or for modifying the procedures if they are found not to be workable. Explicit ground rules are developed to make the class safe enough for participants to openly discuss their beliefs and assumptions (Adams, 1997; Griffin, 1997a). A fundamental aspect of a safe environment is respect for all members of the class regardless of where each is in the process of addressing the issues raised. Tatum (1992) suggests four specific guidelines for creating a safe climate for discussion. First, students honor the confidentiality of the group and refrain from identifying any of their classmates in discussing the class with anyone outside. Second, students do not use put-downs, which often serve to provide comic relief from the anxiety provoked by a discussion. Third, students speak from their own experience rather than make generalizations. Fourth, students address their questions and comments to one another rather than focusing primarily on the professor. Andrzejewski (1995) also includes "honest and respectful dialogue" in her class ground rules (p. 6) and gives students a chance to express their fears about the class by having them share in small groups and then with the whole class rumors they have heard about the course.

In addition to establishing ground rules, facilitators of communities of learners make the classroom climate safe by incorporating such reflective practices as processing, debriefing, and feedback (Adams, 1997; Griffin, 1997a). These activities allow participants to express their own feelings and reactions, reflect on what they have learned and what they still want to learn, develop personal meanings, understand their impact on others, and clarify miscommunications (Bell and Griffin, 1997). These reflective activities might consist of sequenced questions that guide participants "from individual reflection, to dialogue in pairs, to smaller or larger group conversations" (Adams and Marchesani, 1997, 268). Such a sequence can reduce anxiety that might arise if participants are expected to share their reactions with the whole group.

Through dialogue in classroom communities, learners engage in meaning making, critical analysis, and democratic practice that affirms diverse views and experiences. Dialogue between white students and students of color, for example, can help broaden participants' understanding of themselves and of each other as they give serious consideration to multiple beliefs, values, and experiences. In this process, "respect across differences" can be fostered (Burbules and Rice, 1991, 21). The differential power of the teachers and students in a classroom community can itself serve as rich material for a critical examination of power differentials (Fernández-Balboa, 1999a).

However, in communities of learners, teachers do not present themselves as authoritarian experts. While they are clearly more knowledgeable of course content than the students, and they guide classroom activities and facilitate student learning, they are also participants in the community. They share their experiences and insights when relevant, modeling for students the self-disclosure involved in the struggle for social justice (Bell et al., 1997). Koppleman and Richardson (1995), for example, describe how they share personal anecdotes about their own upbringing and experiences to show their university students their own past and present work to overcome prejudices. Richardson describes his father's negative reaction when they both learned that Richardson's college freshman roommate was African American. This "confession" made it easier for their university students to reveal the messages they had received from their own parents when growing up (150). Faculty members can also participate more extensively by carrying out the same activities as their students, such as writing autobiographical pieces that they share with the class (see Rosenberg, 1993; Vanett and Jurich, 1990). When instructors participate in the community rather than simply leading it, they send powerful messages to students. For one thing, students are likely to feel safer in disclosing personal experiences, asking questions, and raising concerns that might cause discomfort if the professor is doing so as well (Griffin, 1997a). When instructors present themselves as learners along with students, they also show future teachers that learning continues throughout one's professional life.

In a classroom community that promotes the construction of knowledge, students are given a variety of ways to display what they have learned. They show their knowledge by applying it rather than recounting it. They might show what they have learned through class discussions, debates, oral defense of conclusions reached from research or inquiry projects, actions they take outside the classroom, and exhibitions or portfolios that include selected class products. In addition, the students might participate in developing the criteria for assessing their learning and applying those criteria to their own work. They could also have a choice in determining how much emphasis is given to different aspects of their work in the overall assessment. Such self-evaluation is important for future teachers, in particular, forcing them to grapple with the complexities of assessment from the learner's point of view— an experience that few teachers have had before they become responsible for making evaluative decisions about their students.

In sum, a classroom community of learners provides a context in which educators of teachers can model culturally responsive teaching. In such a community, learners become actively engaged in constructing their own knowledge through collaborative and purposeful activities, including inquiry projects and dialogue. Because these activities take place in the company of others, participants see that learning is not a solitary activity, that knowledge is interpreted and understood differently by different knowers, and that knowledge changes over time. They not only develop an ability to think critically but also refine their understanding of knowledge and of learning as socially constructed. A community of learners is also inclusive, promoting recognition of and affirming attitudes toward diverse perspectives and ways of thinking. Because it is open and supportive, engendering trust and mutual respect among participants, it tends to be a safe place for students to examine their beliefs and assumptions (Young, 1998). While resistance is bound to arise in classes where issues of social justice and equity are openly addressed, such resistance is minimized by the inclusiveness and respect for differences, the explicit ground rules, and the varied opportunities for dialogue, reflection, and expression of thoughts and feelings provided in a classroom community of learners (Griffin, 1997a). Such a community also offers various opportunities for students to display their learning and involves them in assessing their own growth. Unless prospective teachers have direct exposure as students to culturally responsive practices such as these throughout their undergraduate studies, they are not likely to become culturally responsive teachers.

Developing Dispositions, Knowledge, and Skills of Culturally Responsive Teachers

In chapters 2 and 3, we presented the dispositions, knowledge, and skills needed by prospective teachers to teach a changing student population. We described culturally responsive teachers as those who

- understand that a person's location in the social order influences how he or she sees the world;
- are favorably disposed to diversity;
- see themselves as active agents of change in educational institutions;
- understand and embrace constructivist views of knowledge, teaching, and learning;
- understand the necessity to learn about their students and have strategies for doing so; and
- design instruction to draw on students' strengths and address their needs.

Because the assumptions embedded in this vision of culturally responsive teaching are apt to clash with those that many prospective teachers bring to teacher education, future teachers will likely need to undergo a fundamental resocialization to become culturally responsive. Educators of teachers can support such resocialization by helping teachers-to-be gain awareness of and critically examine their own beliefs and assumptions, become dissatisfied with those that are inconsistent with the practice of culturally responsive teaching, and embrace conceptions that support it. Below, we describe a variety of activities and strategies that can facilitate this process.

Reflective Writing   Because it gives time for thought in the process of formulating ideas, writing lends itself to introspection. Through reflective writing, prospective teachers can gain awareness of their beliefs and assumptions. Journal writing, for example, can be a powerful tool for discovering and exploring one's beliefs (Arends, Clemson, and Henkelman, 1992; Beyer, 1991; Carter and Anders, 1996; Fernández-Balboa, 1999b; Lucas, 1991, 1992; Olmedo, 1997; Pajares, 1993). When it is treated as an unevaluated, nonthreatening component of classes, journal writing serves as a medium through which students can "frame the tentative first drafts of ideas" (Britton et al., 1975, 82) and can give shape to previously unarticulated thoughts and feelings. The private nature of the communication between student and instructor in journal writing makes it a less risky medium than whole-class discussions for examining issues that may be associated with guilt, anger, and discomfort. If ungraded, it can also be a safer medium for expressing these ideas and feelings than are graded papers in which students are more apt to say what they think the professor wants to hear.

Through responses to students' journals, professors can encourage critical reflection on beliefs and assumptions (Ladson-Billings, 1991; Zeichner, 1996a). When they respond to journal writing as authentic communication rather than as a classroom exercise, they engage in an instructional dialogue through which they can push students to examine issues more deeply and to reconsider assumptions. This interaction also expands the opportunities for one-on-one communication between the professor and each student, a precious commodity in higher education that allows the professor to gear his/her responses to students' particular levels of awareness. Because it is individualized, journal writing can help the instructor pinpoint individual students' misconceptions more easily and give more tailored feedback to help them address and work through those misconceptions. In a class that one of us teaches, the students are asked to keep a weekly log in which, responding to classroom discussions and readings, they trace the development of their theories as to why poor students and students of color tend to perform less well in K–12 schools than their white, middle-class peers. The professor collects these logs three times during the semester and writes lengthy responses, encouraging students to go further in their analyses, challenging some of their assumptions and interpretations, asking them for clarification of their ideas (which they provide in later logs), and expressing her own ideas, perceptions, and experiences.

Like journal writing, autobiographical writing can help future teachers clarify and examine their perceptions (Cochran-Smith, 1995a; Fernández-Balboa, 1999b; Ladson-Billings, 1991, 1994; Sleeter, 1995a). For example, Cochran-Smith (1995a) has student teachers write "personal narrative essays about their lives and the experiences that have shaped their views of race, culture, and diversity" (501). She has found that, through their writing, these prospective teachers examine the ways they construct diversity in their lives and in their teaching. The activity helps them not only to better understand their own worldviews but also to recognize the active roles they can play in promoting or obstructing the success of individual students and groups of students and to consider ways they might act toward these students in the future. Thus, it takes them beyond awareness of their assumptions, engaging them in critical examination of the influence of those assumptions on their behavior. Autobiographical writing is also a productive means for encouraging future teachers to explore their beliefs about teaching and learning. They can write their educational histories or create short vignettes about specific educational experiences. In the process, they can see how their experiences in schools and the messages they received from family and teachers have shaped their views of what knowledge is, what teaching entails, and how learners learn.

Autobiographical writing should not occur in a vacuum; ideally, it should be accompanied by dialogue with and opportunities to learn about people who hold different views. In fact, if prospective teachers tell their own stories without a well-informed understanding of the experiences of others, they are likely to assume commonalities that do not exist and that obscure the reality of social inequalities (Rosenberg, 1993). For example, white, middle-class women who recognize the impact of sexism on their own lives may equate their experience of sexism with the experience of racism by people of color, diminishing their ability to understand the impact of racism. This is a special concern with regard to students who have had little contact with oppressed people. At the same time, however, members of oppressed groups may be unable to acknowledge the oppression of other groups whom they perceive as less oppressed than themselves. Thus they too need opportunities to learn about people different from themselves.

Simulations and Games   Participating in simulations and games can reveal prospective teachers' assumptions and prompt scrutiny of them. Such activities can be especially effective in bringing those who have never been the targets of oppression face to face with their unexamined worldviews. For example, BaFa BaFa, Star Power (Shirts, 1969, 1977; cited in Sleeter, 1992, 1995a), and Barnga (Thiagarajan, 1990) simulate experiences with different cultural rules and the power differentials associated with them. In BaFa BaFa, participants are divided into groups, each of which receives a different set of cultural rules and customs. They are given time to learn the rules and customs by interacting with others in their group. Then they are brought together with other groups and told to interact. What they do not know is that many of the customs of the different groups are in direct conflict. For example, men in one group are not allowed to speak to women first, while men in another group always initiate conversations with women; in one group, touching is a highly valued behavior, while in another group, it is considered extremely rude and always provokes the other person to turn his/her back on anyone who touches another person. In debriefing sessions, participants inevitably express anger and frustration and frequently make comments that stereotype other groups. The role of the facilitator is to help participants make connections between their experiences in the game and real-life cross-cultural interactions.

Barnga and Star Power also set up different rules for different groups that result in feelings similar to those evoked by BaFa BaFa. In Barnga, participants play a card game for which they are given different rules, so some people think they have legitimately won a hand, while others think they are not playing fairly. Star Power is a trading game that is rigged so that one group always wins, believing their success to be a result of their skill. As different groups are allowed to change the rules, they rig the game in their favor, thus provoking feelings of power and powerlessness among the different groups. These activities provide firsthand experiences of sociocultural differences and power differentials, which result in the perception of being treated rudely and of feeling angry, confused, and powerless. These experiences and subsequent guided reflections have an especially strong impact on many members of dominant sociocultural groups.

Another classroom exercise is a "power walk." In this exercise, people line up across the middle of a room. The facilitator instructs them to take steps forward or steps backward if they have had certain experiences or have certain attributes, which the facilitator calls out. For example, he/she might say: "If you had your own bedroom when you were a child, take one step forward." "If you are gay, take 3 steps back." "If you are an African American male, take 3 steps back." "If you are European-American, take 3 steps forward." "If you went to private elementary and/or high school, take 2 steps forward." When the facilitator ends the exercise, everyone in the room is asked to consider where they are and where others are and think about the differences in power related to the various aspects of our lives and experiences. The facilitator then leads the group in exploring their reactions to this experience. This activity is more challenging for the facilitator and the participants than the simulations described above in that it requires some degree of personal revelation (though one always has the option of not moving if the attributes/experiences are not visible). For that reason, it is best used only after a sense of trust and confidentiality has been clearly established, as we have previously discussed.

A variation on the power walk is described by Yeskel and Leondar-Wright (1997). The purpose of this activity is to help students get to know each other and find common ground rather than to highlight power differentials related to sociocultural differences. Participants stand in a circle, and the facilitator calls out categories or descriptive phrases similar to those used in the power walk. In the common ground activity, those who fit the category or description step into the center of the circle. They then look around to see who else in the group has shared their experiences. The participants can contribute categories as well. Yeskel and Leondar-Wright have used this activity in a class devoted to exploring classism. Categories they suggest include those who grew up in rented apartments, have credit cards their parents pay for, have traveled internationally, shared a bedroom as a child, and have shopped with food stamps (237).

Exploring Family Histories   Given the extent to which individuals' worldviews are shaped by those of their families, investigating family histories can be enlightening for prospective teachers (see Murray, 1992; Nichols, 1992; Walters, 1992). Interviewing family members can be particularly instructive. Many white, middle-class people tend to view their family histories as sociopolitically neutral. When they probe about events and motivations, they often find out differently. In a course that one of the authors teaches, the students, the majority of whom are white and have lived most of their lives in the suburbs, are asked to conduct an informal interview with their parents or other older relatives about when and why the family originally moved to the suburbs. Before the interviews, most of the students hypothesize that their families moved because of job availability. Several students typically return to class the following week surprised to have discovered that, instead, the increasing racial diversity of the cities was the primary reason for the move. This discovery provides an opportunity for a class discussion about spacial segregation, through which cities have become populated largely by people of color and suburbs by white people, which we discussed in chapter 2. Students are shocked to learn, for example, that policies of the Federal Housing Administration in the 1940s and 1950s made mortgage loans for suburban houses easily available to white people but not to people of color (Kantor and Brenzel, 1992). While inequalities may be more apparent to prospective teachers of color than to those who are white, they too can expand their sociocultural consciousness through family studies, which can facilitate articulation and subsequent scrutiny of beliefs and assumptions they may not have made explicit before.

Articulating Sociocultural Affiliations   To help prospective teachers gain awareness that their views of the world are not universal but are shaped by social factors, teacher educators can engage them in exploring and articulating their sociocultural affiliations. One activity is for prospective teachers to locate themselves as members of different communities. Gollnick and Chinn (1986) discuss microcultures within the United States, which they define as "subsocieties" characterized by "cultural elements, institutions, and groups" that are not shared by the larger macrosociety (16). Everyone identifies with a number of microcultures defined by such factors as race/ethnicity, socioeconomic status, national origin, primary language, gender, sexual orientation, age, religion, and geographic region. Each of us also identifies more strongly with some microcultures than with others. For example, one working-class African American woman may identify more strongly as a woman, while another may identify more strongly as a person of African American heritage, and yet another as a member of the working class. When prospective teachers are pushed to reflect on the differential social status of the various microcultures to which they belong, they recognize that differences among microcultures are not neutral and that some microcultures are accorded greater status than others.

Jackson (1995), for example, asks students in her comparative education courses to situate themselves within the different communities with which they identify and examine how these affiliations have influenced their attitudes and practices toward people in other communities. They then write an essay exploring how their racial/ethnic identities have influenced their educational experiences. Griffin (1997b) has students complete a social group membership profile indicating their membership in different groups identified by race, gender, class, age, sexual orientation, religion, and ability/disability. They share their profile with one other person in the group, whom they can choose. They then identify whether they are agents or targets of oppression within each group and, with a partner, answer questions about how difficult it was for them to identify their status as agents or targets, which statuses they are most and least aware of on a daily basis, what surprises them about their profile, and what they would like to learn more about. Such reflection can help prospective teachers gain sociocultural consciousness. By articulating their affiliations with different sociocultural communities, they can see that their everyday lives—as well as their values, perspectives, and interpretations of the world—reflect their location in the social order.

Exploring Personal History and Development   To extend the exploration of family history and the articulation of sociocultural affiliations, prospective teachers can explore their personal history and development, especially as these relate to diversity and social justice. Wijeyesinghe, Griffin, and Love (1997) suggest that students explore their early memories of socialization as part of the process of understanding their racial heritage and socialization, developing a racial identity, and understanding the role of racism in their lives. Participants reflect on each of a series of questions and talk with a partner about their reflections, moving from one partner to the next to discuss each new question. The questions might ask when they were first aware of themselves and others as members of racial groups, when they first recognized that others or they themselves were being treated differently because of race, and when was a time they were proud of their racial identity (90). After this process, the facilitator leads a discussion of what the participants learned from the discussion, highlighting similarities among the different experiences. Then he or she draws students' attention to a model of socialization that illustrates "how we are systematically socialized by individuals, culture, and the institutions of society to accept a system of racial dominance and racism" (91). A similar process could be used to heighten students' awareness of their personal history with regard to ethnicity, social class, and other socially constructed categories.

It is also beneficial for students to see the development of their awareness of their personal history with regard to sociocultural categories. One productive way for prospective teachers to trace the development of their beliefs and assumptions is by completing questionnaires and interviews related to class themes. Tatum (1992) has her students audiotape an interview with themselves about their racial attitudes at the beginning of a teacher education course and then listen to it at the end of the course and reflect on ways their perceptions have changed. This process has resulted in increased self-awareness, as participants uncover prejudices, and has also allowed them to "consciously observe their own development" (22). Similarly, we designed a questionnaire and administered it during the first and next-to-last class sessions in a teacher education course that one of us teaches. One portion of the questionnaire asks the students to indicate the extent to which their race, ethnicity, gender, native language, and socioeconomic backgrounds have influenced their lives and educational experiences. While many of the white and mostly female students in the class initially recognize that these factors influence the lives of people of color, they do not perceive themselves as similarly affected, except perhaps by gender. By the end of the semester, however, many of their perceptions have changed. One white female student explained why she rated the influences of these factors higher the second time she filled out the questionnaire: "I didn't think it influenced me at first because it didn't trouble me. The first time, I thought none of it was a problem. By the end of the semester I realized it put me in a position of privilege. I was enjoying privileges but not realizing they were privileges . . . before I took the class." While clearly it was the class and not the questionnaire that led this student to develop an awareness of her privileged social position, the activity of filling out the questionnaire gave her a vehicle for gauging the development of her sociocultural consciousness. By the end of the class, many students have recognized that these factors are never neutral, and the questionnaire brings this recognition to a greater level of awareness.

Learning about the History and Current Experiences of Diverse Groups   Learning about the lives of others inevitably leads us to reflect on and compare our own lives, "as we contemplate seeing ourselves in them: mirrors of otherness" (Jackson, 1995, 33). Thus, learning about people different from themselves can heighten prospective teachers' awareness of their own views and lead them to recognize that those views are not universal. When they encounter ways of thinking, talking, and behaving other than their own and are guided to examine the differences, they also become more acutely aware of the variability of experiences within and across groups and of the impact of this variability on people's perspectives. Typically, the teacher education literature focuses on the need for white prospective teachers to learn about people of other racial/ethnic backgrounds. We agree that this is a critical aspect of the education of teachers, especially given the high proportion of teachers and teachers-to-be who are white. However, prospective teachers of color also need to develop a greater understanding of the experiences and perspectives of people of different cultural backgrounds since they too are likely to teach children from backgrounds different from their own (Villegas, 1997).

One way future teachers can begin to develop a greater understanding of others' experiences and worldviews is to learn about other people in their classes. Optimally, future teachers should engage in ongoing interaction and dialogue with peers who are different from themselves in various ways, including racially/ethnically, socioeconomically, and linguistically. Institutions that are committed to giving future teachers the best opportunities to learn about and from the perspectives and experiences of people different from themselves make it a priority to recruit teacher candidates from culturally diverse backgrounds. We discuss recruitment strategies in chapter 5. If a classroom community promotes trust and respect, students can share their experiences and perspectives in formal and informal discussions and dialogues, as we have already discussed. For example, they might share what they learn from interviews with family members, as did the students in the urban education class who interviewed their parents about why they moved from the city to the suburbs. Jackson (1995) has her students write a series of reflective autobiographical pieces examining their affiliations with ethnic, gender, and language groups and how gender and class have affected their educational experiences. They then share these pieces in small groups and select one to share with the whole group. In this process, the class members discuss multiple perspectives and "examine structures of domination and oppression in various manifestations" (38). This allows prospective teachers to see alternative views and to consider their own views in relation to those alternatives.

Even when a class is largely homogeneous, we can help our students gain access to different perspectives. By learning about the histories of people from diverse backgrounds, students can develop some understanding of the differential impacts of social, economic, and political factors on different individuals and groups, including the groups with which they identify, and of the different meanings people make of events and ideas. While it is not feasible for all students to develop extensive historical knowledge about many different groups, gaining insight into key historical experiences from the perspectives of some groups (e.g., colonization, slavery, the conquest of the Southwest, immigration of particular groups) allows prospective teachers to draw some telling connections between history and current events. Students can learn about these histories through various means—such as viewing documentaries and films; reading books, articles, and newspaper accounts; and interviewing older people. For example, Sleeter (1995b) recommends having students view *Eyes on the Prize*, which informs them about legalized racial discrimination, white racism, African American "struggle and persistence," and the radically different historical experiences of blacks and whites (24). A documentary, *¡Chicano!* presents the history of the struggle for civil rights among U.S.-born Mexican Americans, about which most prospective teachers have quite limited knowledge (National Latino Communications Center, 1997). Learning about the struggles of

European groups such as Irish and Italian immigrants can also expand awareness of the complexities of oppression. While fictional films must be carefully selected to ensure that they are historically accurate and that they do not simply perpetuate stereotypes, such commercially available films as *El Norte, Farewell to Manzanar, The Ballad of Gregorio Cortez, The Color Purple,* and *The Dollmaker* can have a powerful impact on the viewers. By drawing viewers into the events portrayed and prompting them to identify with characters involved in those events, such films can lead to significant shifts in perspectives as well as provide insight into the experiences of different groups.

Through published autobiographies, memoirs, and biographies, readers learn about the experiences of real people in different historical contexts and, in the first two of these three genres, they learn about the authors from their own points of view and in their own voices. This practice is especially relevant for courses in English, history, or sociology. To give students access to first-person accounts of the experiences of people of diverse backgrounds, Yeskel and Leondar-Wright (1997) suggest having students read aloud from autobiographical excerpts and then engage in a discussion that might address such issues as advantages and limitations related to the authors' backgrounds, similarities and differences in their experiences, and ways the accounts challenge stereotypes.

As part of a multicultural education course in which the focus is on differential access to resources by different groups, Sleeter (1995a) has her predominantly white teacher education students read *The Education of a WASP* by Lois Stalvey (1988), an autobiography that describes a white woman's learning about racism in the 1960s. She asks them to list what Stalvey learned about the ways in which African Americans were denied access to resources and then to identify the beliefs that whites used to justify their actions vis-à-vis African Americans. To help students better understand the historical context of the book, Sleeter shows her students excerpts from *Eyes on the Prize.* Drawing from these experiences, the students then come up with questions about current racism that they can investigate (e.g., how many people of color have served on the local city council, how are inequalities reproduced in schools and classrooms), and they go out and collect data to answer their questions. Stalvey's autobiography thus provides the starting point for a set of activities that not only deepen prospective teachers' awareness and understanding of racism in the past and its impact on others but also lead them to question their own views about racism in the present.

Learning only about the history of diverse groups may unintentionally reinforce the notion that racism and other forms of oppression are of largely historical relevance. Prospective teachers also need to learn about the current experiences and perspectives of individuals and groups to be prepared to work with diverse student populations. Such learning can help them understand people different from themselves and encourage them to examine their taken-for-granted perspectives. Again, various means can be used to build their knowledge and understanding. There is an abundance of autobiographical and biographical literature to choose from. Autobiographers include, for example, Maya Angelou (1971, 1974, 1991), Barney Dews and Carolyn Law (1995; editors of a group of essays about working-class academics), Maxine Hong Kingston (1976), Richard Rodriguez (1982), Lois Stalvey (1988), and Alice Walker (1983, 1996). Relevant biographical works have been written by, for example, Chris Carger (1996), Alex Haley (1965), and Sara Lawrence Lightfoot (1994). Videos also give prospective teachers a way to learn about others. *The Color of Fear*, for instance, is a video prepared from a weekend-long discussion about prejudice and racism among nine men (two African Americans, three Asian Americans, two Latinos, and two whites) (Wah, 1994). The men in the video openly discuss race and racism, persisting even when the issues they raise cause conflicts among them. The men of color directly express their feelings and experiences of racism, which are in turn denied by one of the white men. In fact, throughout most of the video, this man is unable to accept that the men of color really have the feelings and experiences that they say they have. When we have shown this video to prospective teachers, it has had a powerful impact. Many experience considerable discomfort. Some white prospective teachers are ready to hear and accept how the men of color describe their experiences, while others cannot acknowledge that racism is as pervasive as they portray it. Prospective teachers of color, on the other hand, typically respond with recognition of their own perspectives and relief that their perspectives have been accurately presented in class. The video and the discussion of different reactions to it can challenge the perceptions of prospective teachers and illustrate alternative perspectives on race and racism.

While prospective teachers can learn a lot about diverse experiences and perspectives by reading and viewing films, direct contact with people is likely to make a stronger impression. Having members of different communities as guest speakers in class can give experiences and perspectives an immediacy that reading and watching videos cannot. Direct interactions with people whom students would never have a chance to meet otherwise can challenge students' assumptions and stereotypes and present them with alternative ways to interpret experiences. People from different sociocultural groups can give future teachers a sense of the diversity of points of view, priorities, goals, and challenges faced by different communities and by different people within one community.

Guests might come to class individually or as members of a panel (Griffin and Harro, 1997; Yeskel and Leondar-Wright, 1997). Depending on the nature of the course, it might be desirable to invite people from different sociocultural groups who play the same role within a community (e.g., a group of teachers) or who play different roles (e.g., parent, teacher, business person, community leader). A guest speaker who personally experienced forced integration of schools or who was punished for using his or her native language in school gives a human face to these experiences that most prospective teachers typically only read about. Hearing from people of different ages who entered schools speaking languages other than English can highlight the ways in which attitudes toward nonnative speakers of English have and have not changed over the decades. Such activities are most productive when prospective teachers prepare questions to ask the guests beforehand and then engage in follow-up reflection and discussion to interpret what was said in light of the course content.

Accounts of Successful Teaching and Learning in Diverse Settings
Prospective teachers can best envision and embrace culturally responsive teaching practices when they have access to descriptive and narrative accounts of such practices. One way to gain this access is to read accounts of successful teaching and learning in diverse settings (Zeichner and Hoeft, 1996). Such reading provides teachers-to-be with concrete examples showing how theory connects to practice. It can also sow the seeds of hope among prospective teachers who may have such students in their classes in the future, countering the descriptions of failure that are pervasive in the popular press and the educational literature by offering contrasting examples of success. Future teachers can thus begin to develop "visions of success" rather than "rationales for failure" (Delpit, 1995, 178). By analyzing and synthesizing accounts of success, future teachers can begin to develop a repertoire of culturally responsive pedagogical strategies they can use to engage their own future students in the construction of knowledge. As they embark upon field experiences in culturally diverse settings, which we discuss below, they can draw on what they have learned from these accounts to interpret those experiences.

Numerous descriptions of successful teaching and learning in diverse settings are available. Henze and Lucas (1993), for example, describe four high school classes in which Latino language minority students experienced academic success. They provide detailed descriptions of a college preparatory geometry class, a biology class for Spanish speakers, a life science class for speakers of multiple languages other than English, and a low-intermediate ESL class. They also situate the practices in the literature on effective teaching for English language learners, analyzing how each teacher showed evidence of high expectations for students, promoted first- and second-language development, supported the development of content knowledge, promoted the active engagement of students in learning activities, and worked to develop students' self-esteem. Successful instruction of Latino students is also described in Abi-Nader (1990), Garcia (1988, 1999), Lucas, Henze, and Donato (1990), Moll (1988), Nieto and Rolón (1997), and Olsen and Mullen (1990). Ladson-Billings (1990, 1994) documents successful teachers of African American students, as do Foster (1989), Lipka (1991), and Sims (1992).

Teaching Cases   Long used in such fields as law and medicine, cases situate practices within concrete contexts, providing rich narrative and descriptive details (Merseth, 1991; Shulman and Mesa-Bains, 1993; J. Shulman, 1992; L. Shulman, 1992; Sykes and Bird, 1992). Teaching cases, typically five to ten pages in length, usually tell a short story in narrative form, often accompanied by some descriptive information about the context and the participants. The events depicted in the narrative involve a problem, conflict, or dilemma that may or may not be resolved or resolvable. Teaching cases can be used to engage future teachers in examining their own beliefs and assumptions about the roles of schools and teachers in society, about the nature of knowledge, teaching, and learning, and about students from diverse backgrounds. They can also give prospective teachers access to the details and complexities of culturally responsive teaching while they are still in the college/university classroom, helping them connect principles to classroom practice.

Because cases typically require students to reflect on and articulate their own points of view and to try to understand those of their peers, using cases can increase prospective teachers' awareness of their taken-for-granted notions (Guillaume, Zuniga, and Yee, 1998; Kleinfeld, 1989, cited in Zeichner and Hoeft, 1996; Parker and Tiezzi, 1992; Shulman and Mesa-Bains, 1993). Teaching cases can induce prospective teachers to question their beliefs and assumptions by prompting discussion of differing perspectives and alternative interpretations through critical analysis and collaborative problem solving (Grossman, 1992; Kleinfeld, 1992, 1998; Shulman and Mesa-Bains, 1993). For example, one of us uses a case that invites students to examine their views of knowledge, teaching, and learning (McGraw-Hill Primis, 1995). The case describes the thinking of a teacher as she plans and carries out an instructional unit that reflects constructivist views of teaching and learning. The students are asked to consider questions such as the following: What does teaching mean to this teacher? What role does she expect the students to play? Are the students comfortable playing this role? How is this class different from and similar to elementary and secondary school classes in which you were a student? What does the teacher know about her students? How does she use her knowledge of the students? If you were the teacher, what would you do similarly and differently? Subsequent class discussions typically lead students to recognize that their educational experiences have largely reflected transmission views and that those experiences have influenced their beliefs about knowledge, teaching, and learning.

Through analysis of teaching cases, prospective teachers can also examine culturally responsive teaching in practice. They can see what it means for a teacher to get to know his or her students, to involve students in the construction of knowledge, to build on students' strengths, to engage students in examining the curriculum from different perspectives, to use varied assessment practices, and to establish an inclusive classroom environment. In effect, teaching cases can give future teachers exposure to "a slice of life in culturally diverse contexts" (Kleinfeld, 1998, 141) and provide "vicarious experiences in culturally diverse settings" (145; see also Guillaume, Zuniga, and Yee, 1998; Kleinfeld, 1992; Shulman and Mesa-Bains, 1993). For prospective teachers with limited opportunities to conduct field experiences in diverse settings, the opportunity to "see" what teaching in such settings might entail is especially valuable.

Cases thus provide fruitful material for connecting the principles of culturally responsive teaching to classroom practice (Nieto, 1996; Parker and Tiezzi, 1992; Shulman and Mesa-Bains, 1993). "Content and process, thought and feeling, teaching and learning are not addressed theoretically as distinct constructs. They occur simultaneously, as they do in real life" (L. Shulman, 1992, 28). When later faced with the realities of the situation, prospective teachers who have had frequent opportunities to analyze cases are likely to recognize that the relationship between theory and practice is complex and that applying principles to practices is not a simple unidirectional process. In addition, because well-developed cases provide "vivid, moving stories" and "candid, dramatic, highly readable accounts of teaching events," they can give substance and life to concepts and principles that otherwise might remain obscure (Shulman and Mesa-Bains, 1993, v).

The particularity of cases supports the development of sensitivity to diversity while discouraging generalizations and stereotyping (Kleinfeld, 1998; Nieto, 1996). On the one hand, a case is not simply an engaging story; it must exemplify "a larger class of experiences" (Shulman and Mesa-Bains, 1993, vi; L. Shulman, 1992). On the other hand, cases are not intended to represent large groups or classes of people or settings; they are "contextual, local, and situated" (L. Shulman, 1992, 28). The details and narrative quality of cases encourage readers to respond to them as specific instances, not to assume that interpretations can be generalized. In addition, a well-designed case can include different perspectives, actions, and reactions by people from the same cultural background, thus illustrating diversity within cultural groups.

There are other benefits to teaching cases. Without the pressure of actually being in the situation, prospective teachers can step back and analyze the problems, dilemmas, and opportunities presented in cases. Cases give future teachers the opportunity to consider some of the many dilemmas they will face in their future work. For example, they might grapple with the very real dilemma posed by the pressure to assess and rank students according to standardized test scores, on the one hand, and the commitment to preparing all students for fulfilling lives and informed democratic participation, on the other hand (Smylie, Bay, and Tozer, 1999). When cases present problems that potentially have resolutions (rather than dilemmas), prospective teachers can consider the origin of the problem, factors in the larger institutional setting as well as in the classroom that might have contributed to the problem, ethical dimensions of the problem, and strategies that those in the situation might use to solve or avoid the problem (Kleinfeld, 1998).

Teacher educators who use the case method effectively have a thorough understanding of the case being discussed, the issues that it raises or might raise, relevant conceptual and theoretical issues, and relevant pedagogical practices. They know the backgrounds of their students, so they can facilitate the discussion most effectively, and they are skilled at promoting classroom dialogue (Merseth, 1991). They are culturally sensitive (Zeichner and Hoeft, 1996) and able to ensure that various viewpoints are heard (Kleinfeld, 1998). They strike a balance between closing off discussion with "right answers" and leaving participants frustrated with too little closure. Finally, they select cases that are appropriate, relevant, and well designed to elicit fruitful analysis and dialogue (Carter and Anders, 1996; Merseth, 1991). Some publications provide guidance for the use of cases (e.g., Nieto, 1996; J. Shulman, 1992; Shulman and Mesa-Bains, 1993), but there are many rich and detailed cases without such guidance (e.g., CBS News, 1983; Holmes, n.d.; NCREST, 1995–96; Paley, 1981 [all but NCREST cited in Parker and Tiezzi, 1992]). For faculty who have not taught with cases, it is wise to seek professional development that will cultivate skills in doing so.

FIELD EXPERIENCES

Field experiences have long been a part of the education of teachers. Usually toward the end of their professional preparation, prospective teachers carry out an apprenticeship with an experienced teacher during which they have the opportunity to try out what they have learned about teaching and to receive feedback and mentoring from a practicing teacher as well as from a university-based supervisor. However, field experiences can and should be considerably more varied than this traditional form of student teaching. If prospective teachers spend only one semester in one classroom with one teacher before they complete their preservice education, they will not be sufficiently prepared to work effectively with students of diverse backgrounds. Therefore, many of those involved in preparing teachers to teach culturally and linguistically diverse students advocate frequent and varied exposure to classrooms, schools, and communities where the students and their families live and go to school (Farber and Armaline, 1994; Gordon, 1994; Grant, 1997; Ladson-Billings, 1994, 1995; Larke, 1990; Larkin, 1995; Nelson-Barber and Mitchell, 1992; Zeichner, 1990a, 1994; Zeichner et al., 1998; Zeichner and Hoeft, 1996; Zeichner and Melnick, 1996). They argue that the most beneficial field experiences are broadly conceived as encompassing diverse activities in schools and communities.

The types of field experiences prospective teachers need can be brief one-time events, or they can involve an extended period of immersion in a community. They may take place in schools, social service agencies, community centers, health care facilities, day care centers, local government agencies, other community locations, or a combination of locations. These experiences may be part of a course in the college/school of education or in arts and sciences. Prospective teachers may be engaged primarily as learners, for example, in internships or in community studies, or they may act primarily as providers of assistance, for example, as tutors or mentors.

Regardless of these details, field experiences that promote culturally responsive teaching share a number of salient characteristics. The experiences are carefully planned in advance (Larkin, 1995; Zeichner et al., 1998), and their planning is guided by a theoretical framework and clear pedagogical purposes (Grant, 1997). Prospective teachers are also well prepared for the experience before they begin (Noordhoff and Kleinfeld, 1993; Zeichner and Melnick, 1995; Zeichner et al., 1998). This preparation might involve reflection on their expectations, development of a plan of activities, development of questions to ask different people in the community, and practice with ethnographic techniques. Schools chosen as sites for field experiences serve diverse student populations and, to the extent possible, the teachers are already working successfully with culturally and linguistically diverse students or are actively engaged in bringing about changes to increase their success in teaching diverse student populations (Cochran-Smith, 1991; Zeichner, 1992; Zeichner et al., 1998). It is also recommended that field experiences begin early in prospective teachers' education to give them as much exposure as possible to diverse schools and communities and to make it possible to identify and counsel out of teaching those who are not likely to become culturally responsive teachers (Farber and Armaline, 1994; Nelson-Barber and Mitchell, 1992; Tellez et al., 1995).

Finally, to help prospective teachers make sense of their field experiences, teacher educators provide them with ongoing opportunities to engage in critical reflection on those experiences (Armaline, 1995; Farber and Armaline, 1994; Murrell, 1991; Nelson-Barber and Mitchell, 1992; Zeichner and Hoeft, 1996; Zeichner and Melnick, 1995; Zeichner et al., 1998). Reflective activities are designed both to challenge prospective teachers to go beyond their own perspectives and to support them "through the turmoil that these experiences can produce" (Nelson-Barber and Mitchell, 1992, 257). Perhaps the best context for such ongoing reflection, challenge, and support is a seminar that meets regularly during the period of the field experience. Ideally, the seminar is led by a teacher educator who has had experience working with culturally diverse students him- or herself (Grant, 1997; Nelson-Barber and Mitchell, 1992; Zeichner et al., 1998).

Field experiences contribute to the preparation of culturally responsive teachers in a number of ways. Most important, they offer prospective teachers their only opportunity to build a contextualized understanding of culturally responsive teaching by getting them out of the university classroom and into schools and communities. When future teachers spend time in the classrooms of experienced culturally responsive teachers, they see the day-to-day application of principles they have learned in university classes, including how teachers tailor their instruction to draw on the strengths of their particular students. Through field experiences, aspiring teachers can also develop strategies for learning about students and communities that they can use when they become teachers, including those we discussed in strand five.

By learning about communities with which they have had little contact, teachers-to-be can begin to see students from those settings as members of family, community, and cultural groups and become more knowledgeable of and sensitive to values, lifestyles, and cultures other than their own (Zeichner and Melnick, 1996). Through direct contact with people from socio-cultural groups other than their own, prospective teachers can uncover, reflect on, and test their preconceptions, thus increasing their sociocultural consciousness and developing more affirming attitudes toward people different from themselves. They can develop practical knowledge of community agencies and other services as well as of the funds of knowledge in previously unfamiliar communities (Moll et al., 1992; Zeichner and Melnick, 1996). They can also develop social skills for interacting with people of diverse cultural backgrounds (Irvine, 1992). Through guided reflection on instances of oppression and inequity, they can begin to build a commitment to act as agents of change and to remain involved in community service.

Below, we describe four types of field experiences, organized according to the broad purposes they serve:

- school and community visits;
- service learning;
- studies of students, classrooms, schools, and communities; and
- practica in diverse contexts with culturally responsive teachers.

While these categories are useful for our discussion, in reality, the distinctions are not always clear; each type of field experience actually serves multiple purposes. All of them encourage the development of dispositions, knowledge, and skills that can contribute to culturally responsive teaching in the future professional lives of prospective teachers, who will gain most if they have all of these experiences, not just one or two. Visits to schools and communities and service learning might be conducted early in a teacher's education, with more focused studies following, leading to practica that facilitate collaboration with practicing teachers.

School and Community Visits

Prospective teachers need to spend time in schools and communities to familiarize themselves with these settings. Although they are experienced students, most future teachers have not looked at schools from a teacher's perspective—a more radical shift than they may imagine. Visiting schools to observe activities and interactions inside and outside classrooms can help them begin to envision themselves as teachers in a context with real students, teachers, staff, and administrators. Such visits can also give them the opportunity to gain a new perspective on what school is like for students, especially for students different from themselves.

Having teacher education students shadow a veteran teacher for a day, for example, can give them valuable insight into the daily life of teachers in schools. Accompanying a teacher through the day will make a much bigger impression than reading or hearing a description of a "typical" day. Prospective teachers can get a sense of the teacher's daily schedule and varied responsibilities. They can see the extent and nature of record keeping and paperwork that is part of a teacher's job as well as the types of duties teachers have outside the classroom. They can get a feel for the time a teacher has during the day for planning and for interacting with colleagues. By observing different culturally responsive teachers in action in the classroom, future teachers can also extend their understanding of classroom life. Guidelines can help focus these observations on particular aspects of teaching that may go by unnoticed in the midst of multifaceted classroom activities. Prospective teachers might, for example, focus on the use of instructional time, the types of learning activities observed, how these activities are introduced, and the roles of teacher and students in the activities. Helping the teacher out during classroom visits can be another productive strategy for giving future teachers exposure to the work of teachers. They might assist individual students with their assignments or work with a group of learners on a project.

Field experiences of this nature, if carried out early in the teacher education program, give aspiring teachers an opportunity to test their interest in pursuing a career in teaching. While seeing the constraints on teachers' time and activities might discourage some from becoming teachers, it also helps them build realistic expectations of what a teacher's life is like. Lacking such clarity, they are more likely to become discouraged when, as beginning teachers, their idealistic image is not realized.

Prospective teachers can also gain exposure to communities they are unfamiliar with by visiting those communities. They can go to local community centers, agencies, or museums to meet with community members or agency representatives. They might visit an urban health department or attend a city council meeting (Reed and Simon, 1991). They might attend cultural events such as national days of celebration. Zeichner and Melnick (1995) describe community visits that are part of the Urban Education Program of the Associated Colleges of the Midwest, a consortium of fifteen colleges. Students in this teacher education program are placed for one semester in Chicago schools. To help them see the relationships between the schools and communities, they go in teams on "neighborhood walks" in different ethnic neighborhoods in Chicago. Before their walks, they make "concept maps" of what they expect to see in the neighborhoods, study city maps to plan their trips, are given tips on being "walking anthropologists," and are given specific tasks to complete while in the neighborhood (50). They may be asked to gather artifacts, note the physical conditions of buildings, keep records of murals they see, and talk to residents and shopkeepers. After completing their walks, they engage in structured activities to help them make sense of their experiences. They share with their peers what they saw and learned; do reflective journal writing about their experiences;

and, with their team members, develop and teach short lessons using what they learned.

Students in the Teach for Alaska program at the University of Alaska at Fairbanks spend a week in small rural high schools early in the program (Noordhoff and Kleinfeld, 1993; Zeichner and Melnick, 1995). They are completely immersed in these Athabaskan communities for the week, even sleeping in the schools while they are there. During the day, they spend time in the schools; after school hours, they attend community events and participate in social activities. The goals of this immersion experience are to give them a sense of what it would be like to teach in the community, exposure to native schools, and an opportunity to learn about native culture and community life (Zeichner and Melnick, 1995). These field trips are planned, facilitated, and followed up by faculty members and community members, so they can address assumptions and stereotypes that arise among prospective teachers with little prior knowledge of these cultures.

In brief, through visits to schools and communities, aspiring teachers gain early exposure to and familiarity with these contexts. These visits can help them clarify their understanding of the work of teachers, provide them with insight into worlds that are mostly different from their own, and give them experience interacting with people in different contexts.

Service Learning

Another type of field-based experience through which prospective teachers become directly engaged with people in a school or community is service learning. Service learning is a way of organizing the content and pedagogy of a course so that community service is integrated into academic content, thus enhancing it. One of the primary aims of service learning is to cultivate a commitment to civic responsibility among students by engaging them in providing assistance to children and/or adults in a given community. When incorporated into courses for prospective teachers, service learning can increase their awareness and challenge their assumptions by giving them experience in contexts of cultural diversity and poverty, increasing their understanding of and appreciation for the complexities of others' lives. It can also inspire them to examine inequity and serve as a model for experiential teaching and learning (Boyle-Baise, 1998; Stachowski and Mahan, 1998; Wade, 1997b).

Courses in disciplines across the college/university lend themselves to a service-learning approach. While in practice service-learning programs and activities vary considerably, the growing body of literature in the field identifies some characteristics that distinguish service learning from traditional community service. These include collaboration among institutions involved to develop activities that will benefit all participants and structured opportunities for reflection on the service activities and their relation to academic learning (Bringle and Hatcher, 1996; Wade, 1997a; Zlotkowski, 1999).

Montclair State University has a service-learning program that involves courses across the university, including several in the College of Education and Human Services (Lucas, 2000). The university has developed partnerships with more than twenty agencies in the Township of Montclair, including the Board of Education and several individual schools, where university students carry out service activities. A community survey conducted by the United Way identified the literacy and academic development of school-age children, care for the elderly population, substance abuse prevention, and access to computer technology as pressing community issues. Service-learning courses at the university are designed to address one of these issues.

As part of Montclair State University's program, students in a number of courses work with young people in schools and after-school programs to promote the development of their literacy and other academic skills under the supervision of certified teachers. For example, in an education course entitled Reading Theory and Process, prospective teachers spend thirty hours during the semester tutoring elementary school children in reading in an after-school program sponsored by the Montclair Board of Education. As part of the course, they write journals and engage in class discussions about their tutoring experiences. The community and classroom activities enhance their awareness of the lives of children who for the most part are very different from themselves and help them make the connection between what they are learning in class about theories of reading development and their tutoring experiences. Several sections of Freshman Composition, which is in the English department, are also taught as service-learning courses. Students in these courses build their understanding of writing and their own writing skills while they tutor children and adolescents in writing. Some freshmen in these courses tutor children in the Montclair after-school program, while others work with middle and high school students in a program called the "Writer's Room." This long-standing community-based program prepares Montclair students and other community volunteers to coach young people in developing their writing skills.

In some teacher education programs, prospective teachers tutor children early in their course work to gain initial experience in a teacher role (Korthagen and Kessels, 1999). Bondy, Schmitz, and Johnson (1993) describe a teacher education program in which first-semester students tutor young people in local public housing projects for ten weeks to give them experience working with children who are poor and from racial/ethnic minority backgrounds. Before they begin tutoring the children, the future teachers go on a bus tour of the neighborhood and receive an orientation to tutoring. The tutoring is discussed in a course they are taking, and they are encouraged to seek assistance from their instructors whenever needed.

While many of the service-learning experiences for prospective teachers center around schools, there are benefits in having them engage in various types of community activities. They can learn about diverse communities and the agencies and institutions serving them, gain experience and skills in collaborating with people in these agencies and institutions, and develop a sense of various roles they might play in the lives of children. For example, students in service-learning courses at Montclair State University work in senior citizen centers, design and install computer learning centers in community day care agencies, participate in adolescent substance abuse prevention programs, and assist in group homes for adolescents (Lucas, 2000). Tellez and colleagues (1995) describe a field experience for prospective teachers that requires twenty hours of service in a community agency. Participants can choose from a number of agencies, including Chicano Family Centers, urban YMCA after-school programs, community health centers, and homeless shelters. A course in the University of Houston's teacher education program requires twenty-four hours of volunteer work of any sort in a cultural setting unfamiliar to the students (Wade, 1997b). Ladson-Billings (1991) has her students spend a minimum of ten hours working in human service agencies such as homeless shelters, soup kitchens, senior centers, and low-income child care centers. Students in the Cultural Immersion Projects at Indiana University-Bloomington are required to carry out at least one service-learning project in the communities where they are placed for an immersion experience, many of them on Indian reservations (Stachowski and Mahan, 1998). The program asks that the projects be carried out in the community rather than the school, involve community members directly, represent "realistic tasks that serve the community," and "be based on the premise of reciprocal exchange between equals" (159). The projects have included herding sheep, working to clean up lakes and roadsides, helping out in nursing homes, delivering meals to the homebound, and providing adult literacy instruction.

Thus, service learning has the potential to give prospective teachers valuable firsthand experience in communities and schools. Through these experiences, they can develop a greater sensitivity to the issues that are important to the community, to teachers, and to students. Those who work directly with children of diverse backgrounds also benefit from interacting with children in instructional and noninstructional settings. When they have the supervision of qualified and culturally sensitive adults, they can reflect on and critically examine their experiences under the guidance of veteran educators and community activists, a process that can contribute significantly to their development as teachers.

Studies of Students, Classrooms, Schools, and Communities

Studies of students, classrooms, schools, and communities are intended to give prospective teachers opportunities to investigate particular issues and questions by systematically collecting information through observations, interviews, and review of documents (e.g., Armaline, 1995; Cochran-Smith, 1995a; Liston and Zeichner, 1991; McDiarmid, 1992; Sleeter, 1995a; Teitelbaum and Britzman, 1991; Zeichner, 1996a). These studies enable future teachers to develop skills for gathering and interpreting information about students and their communities that can be very useful when they become teachers. This work can also expand prospective teachers' knowledge of sociocultural groups other than their own, give them insight into how inequalities are structured in schools and society, and deepen their understanding of culturally responsive teaching. Once again, guided reflection on the field work is essential. Without it, preservice teachers might interpret problems they observe as deficiencies within the students, their families, and their communities while overlooking how inequitable conditions in schools and society contribute to those problems.

To learn about the day-to-day lives of children, prospective teachers can shadow a student for a day, including observing him or her in non-classroom settings (Noordhoff and Kleinfeld, 1993). By shadowing an English language learner, for example, they can gain insight into how language affects the participation of students in classroom discourse. Prospective teachers can conduct more extensive studies of students as well. At the University of South Florida, teachers preparing to teach linguistically diverse student populations conduct a detailed case study of a child who speaks a language other than English (Grognet, Nutta, and Canton, 1999). In conducting a case study such as this, prospective teachers might interview the child and his/her teachers; visit the child's home to interview his/her parents and other family members; observe the child interacting with other children inside and outside school—for example, at home and at church; and review the child's school work. In this process, the future teachers would get a holistic picture of the child, answering many of the questions we included in our discussion of learning about students in strand five. They would also get practice in gathering this kind of information.

By studying classrooms, future teachers can extend their developing understanding of the practice of culturally responsive teaching. As we have discussed, culturally responsive teaching involves helping students build bridges to learning by drawing on their prior knowledge and experiences—both individual and cultural. This approach to teaching can be introduced in university courses—first as an abstract concept and then as an increasingly contextualized practice. By reading accounts of culturally responsive teaching and by analyzing teaching cases that feature culturally responsive teachers, aspiring teachers can begin to see the practice in action. However, to truly understand the many subtle ways teachers can help their students build bridges to learning, aspiring teachers need to see this scaffolding in real classrooms with real children, and they need access to the thinking behind the instructional decisions that teachers in those classrooms make.

One way to offer this experience to aspiring teachers is by asking them to conduct a long-term study of a classroom taught by a culturally responsive teacher, specifically searching for examples of how the teacher tailors instruction to his or her students. To prepare for this field experience, preservice teachers can be asked to develop a list of different bridge-building strategies they have studied in their coursework to guide their observations. This list might include strategies such as the following:

- activating students' prior knowledge about the instructional topic by asking students a set of questions relative to that topic before beginning an instructional unit;
- giving children opportunities to explore topics of interest to them;
- creating interest in a topic by helping students see its relevance to their daily lives;
- explaining concepts by using analogies that are meaningful to the students;
- selecting instructional materials that are relevant to the students' experiences;
- inviting parents and other members of the community to share their expertise with the students; and
- using a variety of activities to give students with different learning styles access to learning.

Aspiring teachers can be asked to find examples of the above strategies in their observation notes and to identify other strategies they saw the teacher use. They can also interview the teacher about the ways she or he learns about the students and uses the resulting insight in designing instruction. The benefit of this field experience can be maximized by having prospective teachers discuss their findings with peers at the university.

Future teachers could also be asked to familiarize themselves with students in a particular class and then design an instructional unit tailored to those students. Designing a unit on Shakespeare sonnets for a vaguely conceived group of generic students—as is common in methods courses for future teachers—does little to prepare aspiring teachers to teach in culturally responsive ways. Instead, they need the experience of grappling with how to make connections between those sonnets and a particular group of students if they are going to understand the essence of culturally responsive teaching.

By studying schools, prospective teachers can learn about the nature of the school as an institutional culture, exploring ways in which the context outside the classroom influences the lives of students and teachers. They can see the ways in which school policies and practices both support and hinder teachers' efforts to be culturally responsive. They can get a sense of the individual and frequently isolating nature of teachers' work, on the one hand, and the need and potential for collaboration, on the other. If they study schools where equity and social justice are priorities, they might learn about ways that teachers can work collectively to bring about changes in their schools that will increase access to knowledge for all students. This can give them a sense of the possibility for teachers to play leadership roles outside the classroom.

Studies can be focused on any number of school-level issues and practices. School-based studies could examine how textbooks are adopted, how curriculum is developed and revised, and what opportunities are available for teachers to play leadership and decision-making roles. In a school study, for example, prospective teachers might examine the grouping practices in a school, how they came to be developed, and how they affect different groups. This would require that they gather documents related to grouping practices in recent years, including the current course schedule and course descriptions, school policies regarding student placement, and district policy statements. They might interview selected teachers, students, and administrators to understand the subtleties of grouping practices and people's perceptions of them, since there are likely to be informal, unwritten practices. They would need to observe some classes at different levels or tracks to get a sense of what the differences in curriculum and instruction are and how they affect students and teachers day to day.

Another study might examine policies and practices with regard to students who speak native languages other than English. Again, to get a complete picture, the student researchers would probably need to collect documents (including district level policy statements), conduct interviews with key people, and observe some classes and other events and activities. They would want to find out how students are identified as speakers of languages other than English, how their level of fluency in English is determined, what special classes are available, how they are placed in those classes, and what the process is for moving them out of special classes. They might want to explore the nature and extent of the involvement of parents of English language learners and the preparation of faculty who teach them.

Community studies take prospective teachers beyond the classroom and the school to examine aspects of the larger community that are relevant to teaching and learning. Such studies are especially helpful in informing future teachers about communities with which they have had little or no previous contact. Familiarity with a community will reveal the variability within groups, thus challenging aspiring teachers' stereotypes and misconceptions. Future teachers can gain important insights about particular aspects of the lives of the young people who live in the communities and develop skills for communicating with members of communities different from their own. These skills and insights will be quite useful for them once they become teachers.

Prospective teachers can carry out any number of small-scale studies in communities. For example, they might conduct "mini-ethnographies" that require one or two data collection visits to address a focused question (Sleeter, 1995b; Tellez et al., 1995). Such a question might be What are some uses of literacy in the community? Aspiring teachers might go to the different areas in the community and note all the uses of literacy they can find. Another assignment for a mini-ethnography might be to "walk around the neighborhood and observe, then think of twelve ways to link what they saw with academic content" (Sleeter, 1995b, 27). Prospective teachers might also examine two or more ethnic communities to identify and compare key sources of knowledge (Vásquez, 1992) or visit homes and attend community activities to identify funds of knowledge that students bring with them to school (Moll et al., 1992). These funds of knowledge might be evident, for example, in the types of work members of the community do; forms of art and music in the community; skills for making toys, furniture, musical instruments, food, and clothing; and knowledge of healing and medicine. To learn about these funds of knowledge, prospective teachers might interview a few people in the community (e.g., parents, shopkeepers, local government figures) and/or visit and describe community centers, agencies, and institutions, such as libraries and museums (Stachowski and Mahan, 1998).

Martin (1995a) has her students visit two similar institutions in different socioeconomic areas of a community and critically analyze the differences between them "to gauge the impact of each institution's services upon people in the community" (69). One student, for example, visited grocery stores, one serving a low-income inner-city African American community and the other serving a largely white, middle-class suburban community. She was shocked by the differences she found in the quality and variety of the food, the differences in prices, and cleanliness of the stores.

School and community studies can also be combined. Cochran-Smith (1995a) describes how her students work in groups to conduct school and community studies of their student teaching placement sites. They gather demographic and statistical information about the school and community through published documents. They take photographs of the school and surrounding community. They interview school personnel, students, parents, and community members, and read community newspapers. They visit community centers and attend teacher orientations, back-to-school nights, and parent-teacher meetings. They each interview and observe their cooperating teachers. They then pool their information to present an overview of their school and community to their peers in the teacher education course.

Practica in Diverse Contexts with Culturally Responsive Teachers

The student teaching practicum is an important aspect of the socialization process of novice teachers into the teaching profession (Cochran-Smith, 1991; Levine, 1996). It involves placing prospective teachers in classrooms with experienced teachers for an extended period. To contribute optimally to the development of culturally responsive teachers, the experience should not be limited to activities in a single classroom; prospective teachers need opportunities for contact with people other than their cooperating teacher at the school and with people and organizations outside the school, as we have previously discussed. Therefore, we prefer to use the term *practicum/-a* to refer to this apprenticeship, which takes place at the end of the teacher preparation program. Practica need to be considered an important part of the work of teacher educators—both those at the university and those in the schools. Too often, university faculty consider student teaching peripheral to the teacher education curriculum, and cooperating teachers in the schools do not receive sufficient support for the time and effort required of them (Zeichner, 1996a). In addition, practica need to be conceived as an opportunity for future teachers to learn rather than simply to apply and display what they have learned in their teacher education courses (Liston and Zeichner, 1991; Zeichner, 1996a). Instead of being treated as a largely bureaucratic process of matching schedules on the basis of convenience, practica that prepare culturally responsive teachers are carefully planned to ensure that prospective teachers will have certain kinds of experiences (Zeichner, 1996a).

University faculty and cooperating teachers who prepare culturally responsive teachers work together in all aspects of the practicum experience—including planning the curriculum (Cochran-Smith, 1991; Goodlad, 1990b; Liston and Zeichner, 1991). In addition, as in all aspects of their teacher education program, practica that help aspiring teachers become culturally responsive educators engage them in ongoing reflection and offer continuing support from university supervisors as well as school-based faculty (Armaline, 1995; Farber and Armaline, 1994; Murrell, 1991; Nelson-Barber and Mitchell, 1992; Zeichner et al., 1998; Zeichner and Hoeft, 1996; Zeichner and Melnick, 1996).

Careful selection of placement sites and of experienced teacher-mentors is a high priority for those committed to preparing culturally responsive teachers. To the extent possible, student teachers should be placed in contexts where they can gain experience with culturally diverse students. Exposure to a diverse student population, however, does not ensure that they will develop culturally responsive teaching skills. The choice of teacher-mentors is critical to the learning of prospective teachers. Programs that aim to prepare culturally responsive teachers seek mentors who have high degrees of sociocultural consciousness and affirming attitudes toward diverse students, are actively engaged in working toward equity and social justice, and practice culturally responsive teaching in their own classrooms.

Cochran-Smith (1991) argues convincingly that to prepare future teachers to be agents of change, student teaching should go beyond placement of individual student teachers with individual cooperating teachers. As we discussed in strand three, she believes that the only way to instill and maintain the abilities and commitment of new teachers to work toward the equitable reform of schools is through collaborative work with experienced educators who are themselves involved in educational reform. Student teaching built on this model of collaboration gives prospective teachers opportunities to spend time in experienced teachers' classes, observing, assisting, and teaching. But at the same time they work jointly with university and school-based faculty to pose questions and discuss problems related to teaching and learning, conduct action research focused on particular schools and classrooms, analyze teaching cases, and plan curriculum.

Cochran-Smith (1991) has documented a number of these collaborations and has found that they provide future teachers with a variety of learning experiences that would be impossible for student teachers in traditional contexts. One group examined underlying assumptions about and consequences of school policies such as labeling and categorizing children. In another school, prospective teachers had firsthand experience with the complexities of developing curriculum that was not fully compatible with the district's philosophy. Yet another group confronted moral dilemmas involved in the schooling of boys and girls from racially and socioeconomically diverse backgrounds. Specifically, they grappled with the contradictions inherent in the "possible advantages for minority children of going to school with children of their own race or gender groups versus the clear disadvantages of being segregated from the culture of power" (298). The ongoing interaction with practicing teachers who are struggling to become ever more responsive to diverse learners allows prospective teachers to see up-close the difficulties and rewards of being fully engaged culturally responsive educators. This process constantly challenges future teachers to articulate, reflect on, and refine their views of schools, students of diverse backgrounds, teachers, knowledge, teaching, and learning. It also helps them develop skills they will need for collaborating with their future colleagues.

In this chapter, we have argued that pedagogy in higher education is a vital element in the preparation of culturally responsive teachers. If those of us who prepare future teachers want them to actively involve their future students in the construction of knowledge, build on students' personal and cultural strengths, help students examine the curriculum from multiple perspectives, use varied assessment practices, and make the culture of the classroom inclusive of all students, then we must model these practices for them. We have offered examples of classroom-based activities and strategies as well as field experiences that we believe will provide such modeling. The pedagogical practices we have described call for new ways of thinking about teaching and new teaching skills on the part of many faculty members. If practices such as these are to be widely used across the university, higher education institutions must have strong infrastructures in place to support them. In the next chapter, we discuss the role that the larger institution must play in bringing about the changes in pedagogy and curriculum that we are advocating.

CHAPTER 5

The Institutional Context
Needed to Educate Culturally
Responsive Teachers

Reform in higher education does not occur in a vacuum. Institutional values, norms, and processes shape all aspects of campus life, including the education of teachers (Mills and Buckley, 1992; Price and Valli, 1998; Tom, 1997; Villegas, 1995; Zeichner et al., 1998; Zeichner and Hoeft, 1996). Curricular and pedagogical changes such as those we advocate in this book are not likely to occur in the absence of broad institutional support for diversity. Institutions committed to preparing culturally responsive teachers and to diversifying the teaching force would do well to acknowledge that colleges and universities, like elementary and secondary schools, were not traditionally designed to promote the value of diversity or to serve a racially/ethnically diverse student population. Such an admission spares the institution the waste of valuable time and resources rationalizing policies and practices that contradict the goal of diversity. It is then free to transform itself into a setting where cultural differences are affirmed rather than viewed negatively as something to be corrected or merely tolerated.

An institution that makes issues of diversity central to its mission is more apt to support the transformation of teacher education we advocate than one whose mission is silent on this theme. Broadly speaking, the mission of an institution refers to its goals and purposes, which are often expressed as formal statements but can also take the form of informal understandings (Chesler and Crawfoot, 1997). While mission statements alone are insufficient to bring about change, they serve as a mandate for action that members of the organization cannot readily ignore. The power of such statements was illustrated in the study of a small private liberal arts college located in the heart of a Midwestern urban community (Villegas, 1995). A few years before data were collected, the Board of Trustees and the president at this institution had agreed on two goals relative to diversity—to have the student population reflect the diversity found in American society and to develop the students' ability to live meaningfully in a multicultural world. These two goals prompted a series of actions on the part of the institution, as faculty and administrators set out to achieve them. A minority recruitment counselor was hired to work in the Admissions and Academic Services Department. He networked with departments in the college and with agencies and groups in the local community to increase the responsiveness of the college to people of color and to increase the confidence of the community in the college's programs and their relevance for the community. The institution also developed a precollege program to prepare students who otherwise would not meet entrance requirements. The admissions criteria were modified to include performance in an interview in addition to test scores and previous academic records. The Office of Multicultural Services was created to lead and support efforts to revise the college's curriculum to better reflect the multicultural makeup of the United States. Intensive professional development on issues of diversity was provided to faculty. A standing committee was given responsibility for reviewing retention statistics for different student groups and making recommendations for improving the retention of those groups with low rates. While many of these actions might have been taken without the statement of goals, its existence gave institutional authority and official sanction to those efforts.

The existence and impact of institutional goals and related policies is inextricably linked to those who develop and carry them out. Such statements do not materialize on their own, nor do they lead to change without the support and involvement of institutional leaders and administrators, such as chancellors, presidents, provosts, deans, and department chairs. Institutions that are evolving into multicultural sites have leaders who are committed to establishing and enacting consistent goals and policies with regard to issues of diversity. Those leaders are willing to depart from well-established practices and to support changes that are responsive to the growing diversity in the country in general and in the communities served by the institution more specifically. Without the support of institutional leaders, diversity efforts are likely to fail. At best, they will be temporary initiatives that will wane with time (Larkin and Sleeter, 1995; Price and Valli, 1998).

A mission that is supportive of diversity, while essential, is not sufficient to enable an institution to achieve the goals of preparing culturally responsive teachers and increasing the representation of people of color in the teaching profession. Organizations that embrace these goals develop a solid infrastructure of policies, programs, and practices that will sustain efforts toward those ends. In the remainder of this chapter, we discuss four salient aspects of this infrastructure: (1) commitment to increasing the diversity of the college/university community, as reflected in efforts to recruit and retain students and faculty of color; (2) careful recruitment and selection of students into teacher education; (3) collaboration among the college of education, the college of arts and sciences, and local school districts where prospective teachers carry out field experiences under the supervision of practicing teachers; and (4) strong investment in faculty development.

COMMITMENT TO INCREASING THE DIVERSITY OF THE COLLEGE/UNIVERSITY COMMUNITY: RECRUITING AND RETAINING STUDENTS AND FACULTY OF COLOR

Since the 1960s, access to higher education has broadened substantially for people of color in this country, largely as a result of the civil rights movement. In 1996, members of racial/ethnic minority groups accounted for 21 percent of enrollments in four-year colleges, up from about 13 percent twenty years earlier (Chronicle of Higher Education, 1999). While this gain represents a sizeable growth in the fraction of students of color attending four-year colleges, disparities in enrollment patterns continue. The underrepresentation of racial/ethnic minority students is especially evident in programs of teacher education, where they comprise only about 12 percent of total enrollments in the nation (AACTE, 1997). Also disturbing is the fact that regardless of the field of study, students of color are less likely to receive a bachelor's degree than their white peers (Miller, 1995), and those who do complete degree requirements typically take longer than white students (NCES, 1996b). The lack of diversity among college/university faculty is more marked than in the student population. In the fall of 1995, for example, people of color constituted only 12 percent of full-time faculty in this country (Chronicle of Higher Education, 1999). Institutions of higher education striving to transform themselves into multicultural settings actively recruit and retain students and faculty of color.

There are sound educational reasons for creating a racially/ethnically diverse college/university community. The intellectual diversity arising from different perspectives and life experiences enriches everyone involved. When different voices are respected, members of the community learn from one another through dialogue. By hearing different views on racism from students and faculty, for example, students are better able to grasp that reality reflects the knower's location in the social order rather than being a singular entity to be "objectively" discovered. This perspective on knowledge, which we discussed in chapter 3, is difficult to cultivate in the absence of diverse viewpoints. Because white students generally live in racially/ethnically segregated communities and typically have little direct contact with people of color, they stand to gain considerably from ongoing interactions with students and faculty of color. Direct experience with racial diversity has been shown to bolster cultural sensitivity, interracial understanding, and social responsibility on the part of white students (Alger, 1997; Astin, 1993; Humphreys, 1998). Students of color also benefit from an inclusive college/university community, but in somewhat different ways. If their views are genuinely valued, participation in the institutional discourse can help them overcome the feelings of marginalization and alienation that many experience in colleges and universities. Faculty of color can serve as cultural brokers for students of color, facilitating their further integration into the institution. The presence of a critical mass of students and faculty of color also promotes the retention and graduation of this population of students, particularly in predominantly white institutions (Feagin, Vera, and Imani, 1996; Irvine, 1992; Kraemer, 1997; Moses, 1990; Robertson and Frier, 1994).

Like all college students, prospective teachers gain by being educated in a diverse learning community. In the absence of racial/ethnic diversity, it is unlikely that they will develop the dispositions and skills that characterize culturally responsive educators. Because most white teacher candidates have lived their lives within white communities and have lacked opportunities to learn firsthand about the cultures of people of color, they derive special benefit from a racially/ethnically diverse learning environment. Such a setting enables them to learn about diversity through direct interactions with people who are racially/ethnically different from themselves, rather than through decontextualized academic exercises (Zeichner, 1992; Zeichner and Hoeft, 1996). Similarly, dialogue with people of diverse backgrounds enables prospective teachers of color to expand beyond their particular cultural experiences to learn about the experiences of other cultural groups. The presence of a substantial number of students of color also enhances an institution's capacity to increase the diversity of the teaching force by widening the pool of potential candidates of color for teacher education.

Clearly, diversity enhances the quality of the learning environment of a college/university in significant ways. Yet efforts to achieve diversity at colleges and universities are often seen as undermining institutional commitment to educational excellence. Until colleges and universities openly confront this type of thinking that pits diversity and excellence against each other as competing values, efforts to diversify the student population and the faculty are bound to have little payoff.

Recruiting and Retaining Students of Color

Predominantly white institutions that seek to increase their minority enrollments use a multifaceted recruitment approach. This involves reaching out to racial/ethnic minority communities in order to attract college-bound students of color. It also entails helping more students from racial/ethnic minority communities qualify for college.

Outreach to Minority Communities   Institutions of higher education that have an intensive and sustained outreach to minority communities are more likely to attract college-bound students of color than those lacking such outreach. One productive approach is for colleges and universities to work collaboratively with key organizations in the communities—including local schools, churches, and after-school centers—for recruitment purposes. When recruitment efforts involve people from the community who are well respected by other community members, they tend to be taken seriously (Feagin, Vera, and Imani, 1996).

Institutions that are interested in recruiting college-bound minority students ensure that potential candidates and their parents/guardians receive accurate and useful information about the college/university, the application and admissions process, and available scholarships and other forms of financial aid (Gándara, 1995). Strategies that have been found useful in disseminating this information include mail campaigns, information hotlines, and presentations at various community forums (AACTE, 1989; Anderson, 1989). Involving students of color from the college/university in recruitment activities can be highly effective. These students can speak about their experiences at the institution as part of recruitment presentations in high schools and other community settings. If they present a favorable view of the college/university, young people of color from the community are likely to become interested in the institution.

The college application and admissions process is overwhelming to all students and their families. For many young people of color, particularly those who are the first in their families to go to college and/or are immigrants, it can be even more daunting. Colleges and universities committed to recruiting from this population, therefore, make it a priority to give these students a clear sense of what to expect throughout the process, thus demystifying it for them. They also help students identify different sources of financial assistance for which they might qualify and complete application forms required both for admission to the institutions and for financial aid (Gándara, 1995; Lucas, 1997).

While community outreach plays a critical role in getting students of color to consider studying in a predominantly white college/university, such efforts yield maximum results only when the institution has an established record of service to minority communities and a genuine commitment to diversity. The reputation of the institution in the community, therefore, is a critical factor to consider in designing outreach initiatives. If the institution is perceived negatively by community members, considerable work will be needed to overcome that image. As Feagin, Vera, and Imani (1996) point out, "Recruitment plans are burdened by the weight of insincere practices of the past" (140). Ultimately, if outreach strategies are to succeed, those who are targeted for recruitment must feel that the institution's interest in having them on campus is based on respect for their unique strengths and experiences, not on a need to fill quotas.

Expanding the Pool of Potential College Students   It is not sufficient, however, to recruit students of color who are already headed for college. Because many children of color receive an inadequate education in elementary and secondary schools, as many of them are currently structured, the college-bound pool is not likely to augment minority enrollments in colleges and universities in an appreciable way. A more promising way to alter the composition of the student population is to expand the pool of potential college entrants. One way to do this is by implementing early recruitment programs (Clewell, 1995; Contreras and Nicklas, 1993; Villegas and Clewell, 1998a). Such initiatives identify likely college candidates before their senior year in high school—possibly as early as the middle grades—and involve them in interventions designed to enhance their preparation for college. Early recruitment programs use a variety of strategies to prepare students for postsecondary education. Typically, a battery of diagnostic tests is first administered to determine participants' academic needs. Structured tutorial assistance is then provided throughout the school year, usually during after-school hours and on Saturdays, to address identified needs. A central element of this assistance is the development of test-taking, study, and time-management skills. Summer enrichment programs, also designed to expand students' academic preparation, supplement the services offered during the school year. Students are sometimes enrolled in introductory college courses during their junior and senior years in high school. They may receive guidance on course selection to ensure that they take the academic courses needed to qualify for college admission. Preparation for college entrance examinations is provided as well. Field trips and tours to the college/university campus are organized to help the students develop familiarity and comfort with the setting.

A collaboration between San Francisco State University (SFSU) and several high schools in San Francisco Unified School District—called "Step-to College/Mission-to-College"—incorporates several of the early recruitment strategies described above (see Westat, 1992). Begun in 1985, the program provides extensive support to underrepresented students to facilitate their enrollment in the university. Features of this initiative include a college preparatory program beginning in ninth grade, college-level courses taken for university credit in eleventh and twelfth grades, tutoring, counseling, instruction in study skills, field trips and orientation to the university, and assistance in applying for the university and for financial aid. Students also receive counseling, tutoring, and a college success skills course during their freshman year at SFSU. High school faculty collaborate with university faculty in planning the program, and both receive professional development for working with diverse students. As part of the collaboration, high school faculty teach courses at the university, and college faculty teach courses at the high schools.

Community college students constitute another nontraditional pool from which four-year colleges can recruit candidates of color (Gándara, 1995). Community colleges enroll more than half of all students of color in higher education (Chronicle of Higher Education, 1999). Yet, disappointingly low proportions of them transfer into four-year colleges (NCES, 1996a). Four-year institutions that aim to diversify their student populations can greatly advance this goal by establishing partnerships with two-year colleges. These collaborations generally involve a dual-admissions system that virtually guarantees community college students entry into the partner four-year college, as long as they satisfactorily complete a specified program of general studies. Because course requirements for admission into different programs at four-year institutions vary widely, transfer agreements with community colleges are tailored to each program involved. Below we discuss partnerships that aim specifically to recruit students from community colleges into programs of teacher education at four-year institutions. The principles illustrated in this discussion, however, apply to other programs as well.

To effectively tap the pool of minority students in community colleges, considerable programmatic coordination is needed between the four-year college and its partner two-year college. Central to these partnerships is an articulation agreement that outlines the framework for the transfer of credits from the two-year to the four-year institution. Also needed is a comprehensive set of guidelines for use in the evaluation of transcripts. These guidelines serve another practical purpose; they enable counselors and students at the community college to select the courses that apply to the teacher education programs at the four-year institution. Typically, transfer programs require some curriculum development at the community college to ensure that the students will meet requirements for admission into teacher education at the four-year institution. For many community college students, this involves taking additional courses to strengthen their academic skills. To effectively identify students' academic needs and assign them to appropriate courses, the partner community college has in place a strong academic assessment and placement system. Transfer programs also offer participants a variety of support services to increase their chances of success (AACTE, 1989; Anderson and Goertz, 1995; Anglin, 1989; Haberman, 1988; Terzian, 1991).

According to Anderson and Goertz (1995), several factors facilitate the success of community college/four-year college transfer programs for future teachers. These include strong leadership and commitment to preparing teachers at both institutions, including a competent liaison at each institution who assumes responsibility for coordinating program-related efforts at their respective sites and a key person at the community college who oversees the transfer process for students. Program participants are carefully selected to ensure that they will meet admission requirements at the four-year institution in general and the teacher education program in particular. A set of support services is designed to meet participants' academic needs and facilitate their integration into the teacher education program at the four-year institution once the transfer occurs.

The Teaching Leadership Consortium (TLC) Project of Kent State University and Cuyahoga Community College in Ohio illustrates many of the elements of transfer programs described above (see Anderson and Goertz, 1995). Established in 1989, TLC was designed to select twenty community college students from underrepresented groups each year and prepare them for careers as teachers. A planning committee, comprised mostly of faculty from both institutions, was formed to develop the pre-education curriculum. By comparing courses offered at Cuyahoga Community College to courses required for admission into teacher education at Kent State University, the committee was able to identify applicable community college courses and suggest other courses needed to facilitate the transfer for program participants. Selected faculty from the two institutions worked together to develop those courses. The primary source of support for TLC participants at Cuyahoga Community College was their counselors, who were responsible for helping the students plan a program of study that ensured transferability. To carry out this critical task, counselors received ongoing information and support from Kent State staff. Once the students transferred to Kent State, they were required to attend a series of advisement sessions designed to ensure their ongoing success in upper-level courses at that institution. To successfully transfer to Kent State University's teacher education program, TLC participants had to have completed their associates degree—

including all approved pre-education courses—with a minimum grade point average of 2.75. They also had to convince a selection committee of their genuine commitment to teaching.

Regardless of the recruitment approach used—outreach to college-bound students of color, early intervention programs, or transfer agreements with community colleges—two factors profoundly affect the capacity of a college/university to attract students of color: the criteria used to select students into the institution and the availability of financial resources. Admission into colleges and universities depends largely on traditional criteria such as GPA and scores on standardized tests. Because traditional academic measures have been shown to underpredict the potential of nontraditional students, applicants of color are seriously disadvantaged in the admissions process (Haney, Madaus, and Krietzer, 1987; Smith, 1989). Colleges and universities that rely strictly on traditional predictors of success inevitably exclude large numbers of students of color. In so doing, they ignore the valuable contributions this population makes to the institution by adding different perspectives for learning.

If colleges and universities are to become multicultural communities, admissions criteria need to be expanded to include not only past academic achievement but also nontraditional indicators that give a fuller picture of applicants' strengths. Among such indicators are the quality of writing samples, performance in individual or group interviews, leadership skills, motivation to succeed, evidence of persistence when faced with obstacles, maturity, residency and involvement in a minority community, and orientation toward social and community concerns (Clewell and Villegas, 1999; Contreras and Nicklas, 1993; Phillips, 1991; Villegas, 1997; Villegas and Clewell, 1998a). This broadening of conventional admissions criteria does not represent a watering down of standards. On the contrary, the expansion strengthens the conventional view of excellence by adding to it a component that is sorely missing—diversity of experiences. Such a redefinition of excellence is needed if the institution is to evolve into a truly multicultural community.

The extent to which financial incentives are available is the second major factor influencing the capacity of colleges and universities to recruit students of color, the overwhelming majority of whom are from low-income backgrounds. The cutback in federal financing of postsecondary education that began in the early 1980s has made it more difficult for students of color to attend college. For example, Pell grants covered over four-fifths of college costs at public institutions in 1980. By 1995, those grants covered only about one-third of the cost (Chandler, 1997). Increased reliance on loans, combined with the higher cost of a college education, inevitably leave students with large debts to pay after graduation. The pressure of having to pay back a large sum of money after college deters many candidates of color from going on to postsecondary education. And those who do go on are less likely to choose a career in a relatively poorly paid profession such as teaching (Earley, 1987). Financial incentives help attract people from racial/ethnic minority backgrounds into higher education in general and teacher education more specifically (Chandler, 1997; Clewell and Villegas, 1999; Gándara, 1995; Tomás Rivera Center, 1993; Villegas and Clewell, 1998a, 1998b). These incentives might include scholarships for highly talented students, loan forgiveness programs for capable students who are willing to commit to working in minority communities for a given period of time after graduation, and work study programs that place minority college students in elementary and secondary schools or other community settings to work with younger students of color.

Retention of Students of Color through Graduation   Once students of color are admitted into a college/university, the institution must assume responsibility for helping them succeed. Unfortunately, predominantly white institutions have a poor minority retention record, particularly with first-generation college students from low-income backgrounds (Brown et al., 1994). For reasons we have discussed already, many students of color come to higher education with gaps in their academic preparation. Many also lack familiarity with the college experience and faith in colleges and universities, which have traditionally excluded people of color. These factors render students of color vulnerable in postsecondary institutions. If left on their own to maneuver the maze of institutional demands, many from this group are apt to drop out of college. A strong network of support services, however, can make the difference for these students between completing a degree or not (Arends, Clemson, and Henkelman, 1992; Dandy, 1998; Feagin, Vera, and Imani, 1996; Gordon, 1994; Kraemer, 1997; Phillips, 1991; Villegas and Clewell, 1998b). Elements of this system of support include an orientation to the institution, a strong academic advisement system and ongoing monitoring of progress toward completion of a degree, academic support services, counseling, mentoring, and the use of a cohort structure. Also central to the retention of students of color is a multicultural curriculum.

All students who are new to higher education need to develop familiarity with the setting before they can feel some comfort in it. For reasons noted above, this need is especially strong among racial/ethnic minority students attending predominantly white institutions. One way institutions can help students develop such familiarity is by giving them *a formal orientation* to the campus. Orientations can be as brief as several hours, or they might extend over a longer period of time. The overriding goal of these orientations is to integrate the new students into the college/university community, a process begun during recruitment. Orientations are most useful to the students when held prior to the beginning of the academic year or shortly afterwards. These sessions provide an opportunity for faculty and others to welcome the students to campus and give participants a chance to begin forming relationships with peers. To acquaint participants with student services at the institution—such as financial aid, academic advisement, academic tutoring, counseling, and mentoring programs—staff from these offices and programs can be invited to make brief presentations about their services. Written materials describing the various services in more detail can be distributed to the students for future reference. Faculty representing different academic and professional programs, including teacher education, can also be introduced. Effective orientations foster as much interaction as possible among those who are present and allot sufficient time for students to ask questions. By the end of the orientation, all students know where they can go for help with problems they might have.

Nontraditional students, including students of color, also benefit from *assistance in planning their academic programs* and staying on track to completing them. For many students of color, the unfamiliarity of the system can interfere with their planning and progress. They might need help negotiating the complex system of credit requirements and course sequences that challenge all students, traditional and nontraditional alike. It helps to hold one person responsible for providing academic advising and for monitoring a student's progress over time. This continuity makes it easier for the advisor and advisee to develop a relationship of trust. Ongoing monitoring also enables advisors to identify students who are experiencing difficulties and intervene on their behalf. At one site studied by Villegas and Clewell (1998a), the education advisor sent out a midterm memorandum to all faculty teaching her advisees asking for feedback on the students' performance in class. Using this information, she immediately referred students who were not doing well to specific sources of assistance at the institution. At the end of each semester, the advisor automatically received copies of the students' grades from the office of the registrar. We do not mean to imply that all students of color will need such tight monitoring. Our point is that those students who are experiencing academic difficulties should not be left to deal with the problem on their own.

Students of color who enter the college/university with academic lags should be held responsible for meeting established academic standards. Not to do so would be a tremendous disservice to those individuals. Institutions that take this responsibility seriously give these students sufficient *academic support* to enable them to complete degree requirements satisfactorily. According to Clewell and colleagues (1995), such support includes

- noncredit courses in reading, writing, and mathematics to strengthen basic skills;
- academic assistance labs or centers that provide learning support on a drop-in basis;
- peer tutoring to provide one-on-one assistance;
- course-based study groups organized by professors or teaching assistants; and
- special workshops or seminars focused on a specific area of need, such as writing term papers.

Availability of support services does not guarantee their use, however. It is helpful, therefore, to prescribe individual support plans for those students known to have academic gaps and to hold them responsible for completion of the plans (Coley and Goertz, 1991; Villegas, 1995; Waters, 1989).

In addition to providing academic support, institutions of higher education can promote the retention of nontraditional students by offering *personal support*. Because the higher education environment can be confusing and alien to students of color, they can experience considerable stress. Formal and informal counseling can ameliorate this problem. Colleges and universities that have a multicultural counseling staff are more apt to work effectively with students from diverse backgrounds than those lacking multicultural counseling expertise. Assigning students to mentors, at least through their freshman year of college, is another type of personal support. Mentors—who might be faculty, administrators, or staff—can periodically meet with mentees to discuss the students' ongoing experiences at the college/university and help them develop strategies to address problems that arise.

When nontraditional students enter a college or university as part of a group, they have a built-in support system that can make a big difference in their adjustment to and success in the institution (Arends, Clemson, and Henkelman, 1992; Villegas and Clewell, 1998a; Gordon, 1994; Nelson-Barber and Mitchell, 1992). *A cohort structure* promotes the development of a learning community among students and faculty who work with them. It also facilitates deeper commitments to the students by faculty and encourages them to integrate students' experiences into the curriculum (Arends, Clemson, and Henkelman, 1992). Simply put, a cohort structure ensures that relationships will be a central feature of participants' educational experiences. Institutions that make use of a cohort structure provide multiple opportunities for the group to develop and take advantage of large and small support systems. The cohort may participate in a common orientation, group advising sessions, and workshops on various topics; may take one or more classes together each semester; and may participate in group social activities. Informal groups inevitably develop through which students work together and establish friendships.

While educators and policymakers often speak about the high "drop out" rate among students of color in higher education, it would be more accurate to say that many of the students who leave college are "pushed out" of the institution. The college curriculum, as mediated through interactions among professors and students in classes, can be a major contributor to the lack of persistence of students of color at predominantly white institutions. When the curriculum marginalizes the interests, history, and perspectives of people of color—as has traditionally been the case in higher education, and sadly continues to be so in many institutions—students of color have little recourse but to distance themselves from these settings, first emotionally, then intellectually, and finally physically.

Because issues of diversity are central to the intellectual life of institutions committed to retaining students of color, they have a *multicultural curriculum* that brings the voices and experiences of historically excluded groups from the margins to the center. The curriculum might

- involve students in examining issues of power, stratification, and discrimination in society;
- cultivate a sense of responsibility for dealing with inequalities in society;
- use a comparative approach in the study of U.S. and world history;
- promote the integration of diverse perspectives into analyses and interpretations;
- encourage a willingness to examine one's own assumptions;
- provide opportunities for students to solve problems in diverse groups; and
- foster respect for differences and a willingness to learn from diverse others.

  (Humphreys and Schneider, 1997; Feagin, Vera, and Imani, 1996; Hill, 1991; Price and Valli, 1998; Zeichner et al., 1998)

A multicultural curriculum signals to all students, regardless of their backgrounds, that the institution values diversity. This symbolic message goes a long way toward helping students of color develop trust in the institution. It also legitimates institutional efforts to prepare prospective teachers for diversity. In fact, the preparation of culturally responsive teachers discussed in this book calls for a multicultural perspective across the curriculum, including courses in general education and academic subjects. As we discussed already and elaborate in a subsequent section of this chapter, the extensive cultural knowledge and skills responsive teachers need cannot possibly be developed within the confines of courses in the professional teacher preparation sequence.

In brief, colleges and universities that hope to successfully recruit students of color actively reach out to minority communities to provide information and assistance to college-bound students of color and find creative ways to increase the pool of potential minority college students. The latter involves collaborating with K–12 schools to develop early recruitment programs and collaborating with community colleges to smooth the way for transfer from two-year colleges into four-year institutions. To retain those who are successfully recruited, higher education institutions allocate adequate resources to offer the academic, social, and personal support the students might need to succeed. They also invest in creating a multicultural curriculum.

Recruiting and Retaining Faculty of Color

Institutions of higher education seeking to become multicultural communities work to diversify not only the student population but also the faculty. Issues of diversity are not likely to become a priority for a faculty that is made up overwhelmingly of white people with limited interracial experience and few links to minority communities (Larkin and Sleeter, 1995). The "litmus test" for whether institutions of higher education can recruit and retain students of color, cultivate respect for cultural diversity among all students, and prepare culturally responsive teachers is whether they can provide models of cultural diversity among their faculty (Irvine, 1992, 86). Yet, despite the advantages that can be derived from a diverse faculty, people of color continue to be woefully underrepresented among professors of higher education.

Strategies for Recruiting People of Color for the Faculty   Both short-term and long-term recruitment strategies are needed to diversify the faculty of colleges and universities. Most immediately, institutions need a plan that will ensure the widest possible pool of applicants of color for faculty lines that become available (Bronstein, 1993; Cooper and Smith, 1990). To help guide recruitment activities, committed institutions first establish clear and realistic hiring goals. Such goals are best set by the different academic units based on a review of their respective faculty profiles (Gares and Delco, 1991; Humphreys, 1998). To draw a large applicant pool, the universities describe the positions in broad terms. Position announcements that communicate respect for diversity are more likely to attract people of color than those that merely include a trite line about the institution's adherence to equal employment opportunity practices. One tangible way of communicating this commitment is by specifically inviting applications from individuals who have a scholarly interest in issues of diversity (Arciniega, 1990; National Association of Independent Colleges and Universities, 1991).

The traditional avenues for advertising faculty positions—including the *Chronicle of Higher Education*, disciplinary and professional publications, and mainstream local newspapers—do not typically yield large numbers of applicants of color (Gares and Delco, 1991; Feagin, Vera, and Imani, 1996; Mickelson and Oliver, 1991). Tapping into nontraditional networks and using alternative advertisement strategies are more productive. For example, position descriptions can be distributed to minority professional organizations and doctoral granting institutions known to have a substantial number of students of color (Linthicum, 1989). Faculty of color at the institution can be asked to use their personal networks to contact minority colleagues elsewhere who might be interested in the position and encourage them to apply. Nominations can be invited from local, state, and national minority groups and organizations. Letters can also be sent to faculty of color at other colleges and universities soliciting their nominations of candidates for the position (Gares and Delco, 1991; National Association of Independent Colleges and Universities, 1991; Scott, 1992).

Institutions committed to diversifying their faculty make every effort to ensure a diverse applicant pool before inviting candidates for interviews. The criteria used to screen applications highlight not only teaching experience and publication records but also diversity in perspectives derived from life experiences. The institution thus signals to everyone the depth of its commitment to diversity. If the applicant pool is lacking in diversity, the search committee presses to readvertise the position until a more acceptable pool is secured (Delco and Gares, 1991) or to abandon the search altogether (Tierney and Bensimon, 1996).

When applicants are invited to campus, the search committee uses the interview process to systematically explore their awareness of and sensitivity to diversity issues. All candidates can be asked, for example, how they would demonstrate their commitment to diversity if hired. Their past experiences relative to diversity, or lack thereof, can also be probed. Campus visits can be used to give all candidates clear information about the requirements for tenure and promotion and the support they will receive from the institution to succeed. Minority candidates can also be given opportunities to informally meet with faculty of color, who can give them an insider's view of the institution's commitment to diversity. What candidates hear from faculty of color could be the deciding factor in their decisions to accept or decline an offer.

Support from the highest levels of the university is critical to the success of efforts to diversify the faculty (Haro, 1992; Tierney and Bensimon, 1996; Rosser, 1990). Such support is evident, for example, in statements from the Board of Trustees declaring the hiring of faculty of color an institutional priority. Decisive action from the president of the institution is also important. His or her office can promote progress toward diversifying the faculty by reviewing the work of search committees to ensure that a good faith effort has been made to recruit applicants from racial/ethnic minority backgrounds, closing down searches that result in a short list of white candidates when it is determined that the effort to obtain a diverse pool of applicants was insufficient, monitoring the racial/ethnic makeup of the faculty, and offering incentives and rewards to campus units for hiring qualified faculty of color (Chandler, 1997; Gares and Delco, 1991; Melnick and Zeichner, 1998; Price and Valli, 1998; Rosser, 1990; Tierney and Bensimon, 1996).

The recruitment strategies described above assume that a large enough pool of potential faculty of color already exists. Brown (1994), however, provides convincing evidence to the contrary. Four-year colleges that are genuinely committed to increasing the diversity of their faculty work consistently to expand the number of people of color in the educational pipeline. Such long-term strategies include preparing culturally responsive teachers for elementary and secondary schools to enable more students of color to graduate from high school and go on to college, recruiting more students of color for higher education and giving them the support needed to complete their bachelor's degrees, and encouraging students of color to go on to graduate education. Unless four-year institutions succeed in attracting and graduating larger numbers of students of color, the dearth of minority faculty will continue.

Strategies for Retaining Faculty of Color   An institution's responsibility for diversifying its faculty does not end once minority recruits have been hired. Unless the institution can retain those recruits and help them qualify for tenure and promotion, little progress will be made toward increasing the diversity of the faculty. While the journey to tenure and promotion is demanding for all, it can be even more so for minority faculty. Many predominantly white colleges and universities are inhospitable to people of color, making them feel like outsiders (Carter and O'Brien, 1993; Garza, 1993; Reyes and Halcon, 1991; Turner and Myers, 2000). This is communicated in subtle and not so subtle ways.

For example, the qualifications of minority faculty may be questioned by their white colleagues, some of whom persist in seeing them simply as affirmative action hires. White students, unaccustomed to seeing people of color in faculty positions, may challenge their authority. Minority faculty may be made to feel that issues of diversity are their responsibility, not the obligation of the entire faculty. Those who arrive at the institution eager to address issues of racism may run up against the resistance of their white peers. Experiences such as these can be profoundly demoralizing to faculty of color.

Another major barrier that faculty of color often contend with is the burden of "cultural taxation" (Padilla, 1994; Tierney and Bensimon, 1996). This burden manifests itself in a variety of ways, including the obligation to serve on an inordinate number of committees and task forces as a result of diversity requirements; to spend considerable time advising students of color and helping them deal with problems they are experiencing at the institution or at home; and to assume a heavy load of other services to the institution, such as helping to recruit minority students and being the minority representative at numerous college/university activities. While all these tasks are important and deserving of attention, the fact that they are not central to the reward structure of most institutions leaves minority faculty vulnerable in the tenure and promotion process.

Exposed to such pressures, faculty of color can quickly become dissatisfied with an institution. And as the dissatisfaction grows, their level of engagement and productivity is likely to decline. Ultimately, some will seek employment in other institutions they perceive to be more supportive of diversity. Thus, institutions that want to both attract and retain minority faculty work diligently to ensure that the value of diversity permeates the day-to-day experiences of members of the campus community rather than remaining nothing more than an empty mission statement.

Making a college/university an inclusive community is not possible without a comprehensive professional development initiative for faculty, administrators, and staff regarding issues of diversity. In a subsequent section of this chapter, we discuss elements of such an initiative. The goal of inclusiveness also calls for the institution to help all students understand the many benefits that can be derived from exposure to people whose life experiences are very different from their own. This message needs to be communicated consistently throughout their coursework and reinforced through special campus workshops and seminars. The institution must also make it clear to everyone that racial/ethnic or any other form of discrimination will not be tolerated.

If the institution's reward system does not support the value of diversity, there will be little incentive for members of the college/university community to engage in the hard work involved in transforming the institution to reflect this value. Even those in the community who are personally committed to issues of diversity will eventually become discouraged when their efforts are neither acknowledged nor rewarded. As we discussed above, this is true of minority faculty when they are expected to advance the institution's diversity agenda at their own expense. Thus, colleges and universities that are striving to become multicultural settings align their reward structures with this goal. This means, for example, counting toward tenure and promotion diversity-related services rendered by faculty of color (Blackwell, 1988; Frierson, 1990).

Two strategies that have been found particularly effective in retaining faculty of color are assigning a mentor and creating a collegial campus atmosphere (Blackwell, 1989; Granger, 1993; Turner and Myers, 2000). Mentoring pairs a junior faculty member with a senior faculty member for support purposes. The scope of mentoring relationships is determined by the mentor and mentee and can range from occasional conversations to more extended interactions. Having a person who is designated as a mentor provides a ready resource to new faculty members for information and support as varied as help with teaching, insight into the institutional culture, suggestions for how to prioritize the use of their time, information about the committee structure, help with publications, and introductions to others on campus. According to Brinson and Kottler (1993), a mentoring relationship is the single most important way in which institutions can help faculty of color develop career goals and attain professional success. Equally important, if not more so, supportive associations with senior faculty can help junior faculty of color break through the oppressive walls of isolation many experience (Turner and Myers, 2000).

While a good relationship with a mentor can be of tremendous assistance to a new faculty member, she or he also needs a broader network of colleagues with whom to collaborate on various professional activities (National Association of Independent Colleges and Universities, 1991). By creating a collegial atmosphere on their campuses, colleges and universities can promote such networking. Institutions can, for example, offer opportunities for faculty to share research and other interests, to team teach, and to observe each other teaching. A collegial campus culture can reduce the stress on individual faculty to meet expectations for tenure and promotion. For minority faculty, having a strong sense of community with their minority peers on campus can be especially helpful not only in facilitating their own professional growth but also in integrating them into the institution as a whole (Tierney and Bensimon, 1996).

To summarize, we have argued above that a diverse faculty and student population yields considerable educational benefits to all members of the college/university community and that without this diversity, institutions are not likely to succeed in preparing culturally responsive teachers. In creating diverse learning communities, higher education also contributes to society in another significant way. Specifically, it helps in building consensus about the need for diversity in all aspects of our lives and thus in overcoming the fear, ignorance, and stereotypes that often result from the racial and ethnic isolation that is so pervasive in this country.

Careful Recruitment and Selection
of Students into Teacher Education

Within teacher education itself, a clearly articulated framework for recruitment and selection of students can help to ensure that those who enter the program have the potential to become successful teachers of diverse students. Such a framework promotes two separate but related lines of action—identifying prospective teachers of all racial/ethnic groups who are culturally sensitive and attracting more people of color into teacher education. We discuss both types of action below.

Recruiting and Selecting Culturally Sensitive Teacher Candidates   Teaching requires more than content knowledge and pedagogical skills. As we have already discussed, a person's belief system profoundly influences his or her expectations for student learning and how he or she treats students. For example, in chapter 2, we reviewed research showing that teachers who see children of racial/ethnic minority backgrounds through a deficit lens tend to expect little of those children; once low expectations are formed, they expose the children to a watered-down curriculum, give them less instructional time, and provide them with less encouragement to learn and less praise for good work. A deficit mindset, which is derived from a lifetime of experiences, is not easy to change. In fact, by now there is considerable evidence that preservice teacher education programs, as they are typically organized, have a limited effect on the perspectives of those who enter with little or no sensitivity to diversity (Grant and Secada, 1990; Haberman, 1989, 1991; Haberman and Post, 1998; Larkin and Sleeter, 1995; Paine, 1989; Ross and Smith, 1992; Zeichner, 1992; Zeichner and Hoeft, 1996).

On the basis of the mounting evidence, many scholars argue that it makes more sense to select people for teacher education who are already favorably disposed to issues of equity and diversity rather than to try to change those who are not (Foster, 1993; Gomez, 1994; Haberman, 1991; Haberman and Post, 1998; Sleeter, 1992; Tabachnick and Zeichner, 1993). This calls for an expansion of traditional criteria used to select students into teacher education, which rely largely on academic indicators such as GPAs and test scores, to include indicators of sensitivity to diversity and concern for equity. Such indicators include experience working with children and adults of diverse backgrounds; experience with community service; favorable views of children from racial/ethnic minority backgrounds; competence in more than one language or variety of English; awareness of racism and other forms of discrimination; and interest in and commitment to working in urban areas and with students of different racial, ethnic, and linguistic backgrounds (Gordon, 1994; Guillaume, Zuniga, andYee, 1998; Ladson-Billings, 1994; Larkin, 1995; Zeichner et al., 1998).

In addition, Haberman (1991) has argued that young people tend to be too immature to be effective teachers of diverse students. According to him, they are still in the process of identity formation themselves and cannot serve as confident and competent role models for urban and minority children. Similarly, Kagan (1992) points out that to handle the cognitive dissonance that accompanies changes in attitudes and beliefs, prospective teachers need considerable maturity and self-confidence. This suggests that an applicant's level of maturity is another critical factor that should be attended to in making decisions regarding admission into teacher education.

At the same time, however, screening out teacher education candidates who are not considered culturally sensitive raises difficult issues. For example, Valli (1995) points out that because attitudes are difficult to ascertain, and the screening process can never be perfect, some candidates who, with the right preparation, could develop into culturally responsive teachers will inevitably be screened out. Such exclusionary practice is difficult to reconcile in the context of programs that specifically aim for greater inclusion in education. Valli also fears that "the quest for ideal candidates" will divert attention away from the need to restructure other aspects of teacher education for diversity, such as the curriculum (1995, 128).

While we acknowledge the problems raised by the prospect of screening out some candidates on the basis of cultural sensitivity, we nevertheless believe there is a need for such an institutional policy. The evidence of the intractability of prospective teachers' attitudes and beliefs—given the limits of existing pedagogy and the relatively short time spent in professional preparation—cannot be ignored. To continue to do so is bound to perpetuate the crisis in education experienced by the overwhelming majority of children of color in elementary and secondary schools. However, such an exclusionary policy should not be instituted until criteria, processes, and instruments that can validly and reliably identify candidates who have the potential to become culturally responsive teachers have been developed. Needless to say, this will involve a substantial research and development effort. The interview developed by Haberman (1987) to screen candidates for teaching in urban schools provides a starting point for this work.

In the meantime, the "selecting in" approach proposed by Jacobowitz (1994) and used by Montclair State University, in New Jersey, provides a useful framework for admitting students into teacher education who are open to exploring issues of diversity and social justice. In this approach, applicants play a central role in selecting themselves into or out of teacher education, based on an understanding of the core values that underpin the program to which they have applied. At Montclair State University, those values are articulated in the *Portrait of the Teacher*, a statement that outlines the dispositions and habits of mind that students completing the teacher education program are expected to have. These include a belief in the educability of all children; a commitment to the principles of equity, social justice, and democracy; an attitude of respect for diversity; a view of teachers as agents of social change; and an understanding of teaching as a moral and political activity. Applicants not only receive a copy of this statement but are also asked to refer to its content at various points in the admissions process. For example, to be considered for teacher education, a person must complete a pre-admissions field experience, a portion of which is spent working with children from diverse backgrounds in urban schools. In that course, students are helped to analyze their experiences through the framework provided by the principles inherent in the *Portrait of the Teacher*. Students are also asked to submit an essay in which they cite past experiences they have had that indicate commitment to those principles. During the interview with a selection committee, applicants are again reminded of the mission of the teacher education program, and questions are asked to probe the depth of their understanding of this mission and their commitment to it. Incompatibilities between the applicants' personal views and the program's philosophical orientations, where noted, are discussed openly with the applicant. These discussions have led some candidates to withdraw their applications. More often, however, candidates whose views do not seem to align with the program's principles are admitted on a probational basis until it becomes clearer to those students and the faculty whether or not the program is appropriate for them. While this process does not guarantee that all who are selected for preservice teacher education are indeed sensitive to issues of equity and diversity, it at least puts students on notice that insensitivity to these issues will not be tolerated.

While we believe that people who see little or no value in diversity ought to be screened out of teacher education, we nonetheless recognize that such action will not eliminate the need to help those who are admitted gain clarity about their views toward diversity, acknowledge aspects of those views that might compromise their teaching effectiveness, and make adjustments when needed. People do not enter teacher education programs having either the "right" attitudes or the "wrong" attitudes. Such dichotomous thinking about the nature of attitudes toward diversity is counterproductive. As we discussed in chapter 2, perspectives on diversity fall along a continuum from more deficit-oriented views to more affirming views. Thus, in addition to investing resources in refining the selection of candidates for teacher education, programs designed to prepare culturally responsive teachers invest in devising more powerful pedagogies to help all future educators develop more affirming attitudes toward diversity. Without this institutional commitment, teacher education is not likely to succeed in preparing the cadre of culturally responsive teachers needed to significantly improve the quality of education for the growing number of students of color in this country.

Recruiting and Selecting Prospective Teachers of Color

Throughout this book we have argued that culturally responsive teachers need extensive cultural knowledge to help students from diverse racial/ethnic backgrounds build bridges to learning. Unfortunately, this cultural expertise is sorely lacking in the teaching force (ACE, 1995), just as it is lacking in the population of preservice teachers, the overwhelming majority of whom are white. The knowledge that people of color have about the lives of students of color holds promise for improving the education of these students. Because people of color are a potential asset to the teaching profession, preservice teacher education programs dedicated to preparing culturally responsive teachers actively recruit from this population.

To avoid misinterpretation, we want to make it clear that in advocating for the racial/ethnic diversification of the teaching force, we are not suggesting that teachers be assigned to students on the basis of race and ethnicity. The segregating effect of such a strategy would undermine the vision of schools and society we promote. Instead, we are arguing that the teaching profession as a whole stands to gain from the infusion of expertise about minority cultures, perspectives, and experiences that people of color bring to it. Limited understanding of the life of minority children continues to hamper the ability of many white teachers to develop the types of bridges between home and school that facilitate learning for students of color, even when those teachers understand the principles of culturally responsive teaching. People of color can help white colleagues expand their understanding of the cultural backgrounds of students of color. They can also extend current thinking about culturally responsive teaching by suggesting specific ways in which general principles translate into practice. Equally important, they can add alternative perspectives to solving recurrent problems that students of color experience in schools.

While recruiting more people of color into the teaching force holds considerable promise for improving the quality of teaching in elementary and secondary schools, this potential cannot be realized unless those recruits are helped to understand the principles of culturally responsive teaching and to translate their cultural insight into pedagogy. It is foolish to think that recruiting more people of color into teaching, alone, will improve the education of students of color in any significant way. More to the point, it would be unfair to hold people of color accountable for becoming culturally responsive teachers without the benefit of professional growth experiences to support this. Similarly, it is unrealistic to expect that without explicit preparation, future teachers of any ethnic background will know how to orchestrate the types of interactions that can enable the teaching profession to benefit from the cultural expertise that people of color bring to it. Productive conversations about issues of race and ethnicity are difficult to get started, and even more difficult to sustain over time. If these conversations are to take place among teachers in schools, teachers-to-be must learn the value of such interactions and develop the skills required to talk across racial/ethnic lines. Programs of teacher education cannot provide this type of preparation to prospective teachers unless they enroll a critical mass of students of color.

Programs of teacher education that strive to augment their minority enrollments use an aggressive recruitment strategy that targets different pools of potential candidates. College-bound students of color constitute one pool from which to recruit future teachers. As we discussed above, predominantly white colleges and universities need strong community outreach to attract such students. Even if an institution succeeds in enrolling a sizeable number of college-bound students of color, its teacher education program is likely to experience difficulties interesting those recruits in pursuing a teaching career. There are many reasons for this. Competition for this population from other programs within the institution—such as engineering, business, and health professions—will deplete the numbers available for teacher education (Hawley, 1986; Kirby and Hudson, 1993). The challenging conditions of teaching, particularly in urban schools, will discourage many of those students from choosing a career in teaching (AACTE, 1987; Zimpher and Yessayan, 1987). The low salaries of the teaching profession relative to other fields is another disincentive (Archer, 2000). Also problematic are the increasing parental pressures on many of the students—particularly African Americans—to choose professions that are perceived to have higher status than teaching (Gordon, 1994). Without a compelling argument, teacher education will have little or no success recruiting college-bound students of color. Such an argument might appeal to the students' sense of social justice and responsibility to give back to their communities (Villegas, 1997). To secure parental support, teacher education programs also need to disseminate information within minority communities about the current shortage of teachers of color and the critical role these individuals can play in solving the crisis in education those communities face. Ultimately, without community support, teacher education programs are bound to make little headway in diversifying their enrollments (Smith, 1989).

Even if teacher education could attract a sizable share of the pool of college-bound students of color, this population is not large enough to substantially change the racial/ethnic makeup of preservice programs. To truly increase their representation of students of color, teacher education programs must work to expand the pool of potential candidates beyond those who are likely to attend college. The strategies discussed above for recruiting students of color for higher education in general also apply to recruiting prospective teachers of color. For example, early recruitment programs can be designed not only to provide the academic support and guidance that middle and high school minority students might need to enter college, but also to interest them in a teaching career. "Teacher cadet" programs, as these specialized initiatives are called, use a variety of strategies to motivate participants to want to become teachers, including Future Educators clubs, introductory teacher education courses offered for college credit to juniors and seniors in high school, mentor teachers who talk to participants about the teaching profession, summer programs that give students both academic support and intensive teaching experiences, and programs in which students in the upper high school years tutor younger children in the community (Clewell, 1995; Irvine, 1988). Transfer agreements between two- and four-year colleges, which we described above, are also a productive strategy for recruiting people of color into preservice teacher education.

Paraprofessionals employed in local school districts constitute another untapped source of racial/ethic minority candidates for teacher education (Hidalgo and Huling-Austin, 1993; Joy and Bruschi, 1995; Villegas and Clewell, 1998a). In urban schools, in particular, many paraprofessionals are people of color who live in the same neighborhoods as their students and are knowledgeable about their life circumstances (Haselkorn and Fideler, 1996). Colleges and universities that have succeeded in attracting paraprofessionals into teacher education have programs that address their needs while building on their strengths. In these "career ladder" programs, paraprofessionals continue their salaried positions while they enroll in courses each semester toward completing the requirements for teaching certification and, in most cases, a bachelor's degree as well. Because paraprofessionals work full time during the day, courses are offered during evening hours, weekends, and summers. To make the program more accessible to the students, some of the courses can be taught on site at partner school districts or community agencies. This alleviates travel complications for participants, particularly when the college/university is not easily accessible by public transportation. Such programs work out a strategy to allow paraprofessionals, most of whom bear considerable financial responsibilities for their families, to continue receiving an income during the student teaching period. They also offer a variety of supports, including tuition assistance, to enable participants to make it through graduation and certification (Clewell and Villegas, 1999; Villegas and Clewell, 1998a; 1998b).

School districts employing paraprofessionals who are targeted for program participation are well positioned to play a central role in their recruitment. The districts can publicize the program to potential participants through flyers, newsletters, and electronic mailings. Principals and experienced teachers in the districts can nominate likely candidates from their schools for participation in the program. The districts can also hold a series of information sessions for interested parties as part of the recruitment process. If districts see paraprofessionals as a strong population from which to draw future teachers, they are likely to provide tangible support for the program, such as giving participants release time to attend important program-related activities and offering space for courses to be taught on site (Villegas and Clewell, 1998b).

The Pathways to Teaching Careers Program at Armstrong Atlantic State University (AASU) is a good example of a career ladder program for paraprofessionals (Dandy, 1998). Begun in 1994, the program aims to increase the number of certified teachers—especially members of minority groups—by recruiting paraprofessionals and giving them tuition assistance and other support to complete their bachelor's degrees and teacher certification requirements. The program involves a collaboration between AASU and the Savannah-Chatham County Public Schools. During recruitment periods, the school district sends out information about the program to all paraprofessionals. Principals also encourage potential applicants to apply to the program. Only those applicants who have an exemplary work record at the partner district and a minimum of sixty college-credit hours with an overall GPA of 2.0

or higher are selected for the program. In addition, applicants must be willing to teach at least three years in inner-city schools, preferably in the partner district, after completing the program. To help participants obtain their bachelor's degrees in a timely fashion, the partner institutions worked out an agreement by which twenty-five paraprofessionals per year are allowed to take professional leave on Fridays to attend classes at the university. On that day, students enrolled in the teacher education program at AASU substitute for the paraprofessionals as part of a practicum required for their degree. The program also restructured the student teaching experience to enable participants to fulfill this requirement without losing salary or benefits. Student teaching is extended over a longer time period than usual, thereby allowing the participating paraprofessionals to carry out this practicum on a part-time basis while taking professional leave.

In sum, preservice teacher education programs that aim to diversify enrollments expand recruitment efforts beyond the pool of college-bound students of color. Above we discussed three strategies they can use to broaden the sources of potential candidates—recruiting pre-college students into teacher cadet programs, working out agreements with two-year colleges to facilitate the transfer of junior college students into teacher education at senior colleges, and establishing career ladder programs for paraprofessionals. Regardless of the pool targeted, recruitment efforts will have limited payoff if the process of selecting students into teacher education continues to rely almost exclusively on GPAs and test scores, the customary predictors of success. While such traditional indicators provide important information about applicants' academic backgrounds, they can seriously underpredict the future performance of applicants of color (Haney, Madaus, and Krietzer, 1987). Without some flexibility in what counts as evidence of potential, the fairness of the selection process is compromised. Moreover, a narrow focus on academic indicators of potential for success ignores the unique strengths that applicants of color bring to teacher education, including their personal knowledge of racial/ethnic minority communities, first-hand experience of what it is like to be a member of a racial/ethnic minority group, and the more affirming views of diversity that these experiences generally engender. The inevitable outcome of an admissions process that fails to value such cultural expertise while simultaneously emphasizing traditional academic indicators is the exclusion of many applicants of color from teacher education.

We need to rethink the process by which preservice teachers are selected. By privileging GPAs and test scores while devaluing knowledge about and attitudes toward cultural diversity, programs of teacher education consistently screen out applicants of color who could be admitted while screening in some white candidates who should be excluded. This is another example of how bias is structured into the everyday practices of institutions of higher education.

COLLABORATING TO PREPARE TEACHERS WHO ARE CULTURALLY RESPONSIVE

Traditionally, the education of prospective teachers has been seen as largely the responsibility of faculty in the college of education, from whom these students take professional education courses. Such a view, however, obscures the influential role that faculty from the arts and sciences and from local public schools play in the preparation of teachers. After all, prospective teachers typically take about two-thirds of their undergraduate courses in the arts and sciences. What they learn in these courses about philosophy, history, English, science, mathematics, the arts, anthropology, linguistics, sociolinguistics, and other fields will influence their future teaching as much as or more than what they learn in education courses. Similarly, teachers in elementary and secondary schools who mentor preservice teachers during their various field experiences, including student teaching, exert a powerful influence on their mentees' developing understanding of the teaching profession, approaches to teaching, and views of children and parents of diverse backgrounds. Yet the key participants in the education of teachers too often work in isolation from one another, a condition that leads to fragmentation between pedagogy (the turf of education faculty) and subject matter (the turf of arts and sciences faculty) and between theory (what is learned at the university) and practice (what is learned in schools). Below we argue that to prepare prospective teachers to be culturally responsive, the faculty from colleges of education, colleges of arts and sciences, and local schools need to coordinate their efforts and work collaboratively toward that goal.

Collaboration between Education and Arts and Sciences

The task of preparing culturally responsive teachers is complex and demanding. It involves supporting future teachers in developing a set of fundamental orientations, including an awareness that their worldviews are apt to be dramatically different from the worldviews of children who are racially, culturally, socially, and linguistically different from themselves; an appreciation of and respect for cultural diversity; and a willingness to teach in ways that challenge existing inequalities and promote social justice. Preparing the type of culturally responsive teachers we envision also entails cultivating among teacher candidates a view of teaching and learning that breaks with tradition, the skills for learning about their future students, and the ability to use their knowledge about students to engage them in the construction of knowledge. This type of teaching demands a deep understanding of subject matter, extensive cultural expertise, well-developed cross-cultural communication skills, and a commitment to social justice. Clearly, this comprehensive preparation cannot possibly take place within the scope of courses in the professional education sequence.

One central way in which faculty from the arts and sciences have traditionally contributed to the preparation of teachers is by helping them develop competence in the subjects they will teach. If they are to become the type of teacher we envision, such competence involves developing a profound and generative understanding of the key concepts in those disciplines and the connections among those concepts, the underlying structures and modes of inquiry in those fields, and the uses of the subject matter in society (Ball, 1991; Darling-Hammond, Wise, and Klein, 1995; Kennedy, 1991; Murray and Porter, 1996). Without this disciplinary foundation, it is doubtful that prospective teachers will be able to help their future students make sense of subject matter. They will not be prepared, for instance, to use fitting examples and counterexamples to illustrate key concepts, select appropriate analogies to represent complex ideas, and ask insightful questions to extend students' understanding of the instructional topic (Shulman, 1987).

A second way that faculty from the arts and sciences can support the development of skills in culturally responsive teaching is by engaging preservice teachers in a critical examination of concerns relevant to a multicultural society (Gomez, 1994; Gordon, 1994; Larkin and Sleeter, 1995; Rodriguez and Sjostrom, 1995). Specifically, the courses preservice teachers take in the arts and sciences can

- guide them through an analysis of issues of power, discrimination, stratification, and segregation;
- involve them in an investigation of how inequalities are structured into the institutions of American society;
- cultivate a commitment to the principles of social justice and equality;
- promote an understanding of the nature of culture, including the recognition that individual differences exist within any cultural group;
- cultivate knowledge of the culture of groups other than those in power;

- engage them in self-examination about how their biographies and past experiences shape their perceptions of the world, attitudes, beliefs, and identities;

- engender an understanding of the nature of language variation and of the fact that varieties of English are complex, rule-governed, and valid systems of communication;

- provide an overview of first- and second-language acquisition;

- develop an understanding of history that includes multiple perspectives; and

- give exposure to multicultural literature.

In most colleges and universities, these types of activities are not likely to take place until faculty rethink the content of general education courses and electives taken by preservice teachers. Such rethinking is not apt to happen unless the institution is consciously working to become a multicultural setting and has made the education of teachers central to its mission.

Even when efforts are made to ensure that preservice teachers receive the type of arts and sciences preparation they need to become culturally responsive, some coordination will be needed between the courses they take in arts and sciences and those they take in education. Otherwise, learning can remain fragmented, and students will be left to make the necessary connections among concepts as well as between pedagogy and content on their own. Faculty from across the college/university can facilitate this type of integration in a variety of ways. For example, a team-teaching arrangement in methods courses that involves a professor from education and a faculty member from arts and sciences can be a powerful strategy for helping teacher candidates translate their knowledge of subject matter into engaging learning experiences for children in elementary and secondary schools. Linking two separate courses can serve a similar conceptual bridging function (Cross, 1993; Tiedt, 1993). For instance, an anthropology course with a field-based component designed to develop the students' skills for learning about a community can be linked with a pedagogy course in which students are expected to use knowledge of that community to design instruction.

Still another way faculty from the arts and sciences can contribute to the education of prospective teachers is by modeling culturally responsive teaching practices. We have made the point already that teachers-to-be learn powerful lessons in how to teach by observing their professors in action. As we discussed in chapter 4, professors who model respect for different learning styles, perspectives, and talents in their classrooms are more likely to convey to prospective teachers the value of diversity than those who merely tell them that diversity is important but do not illustrate this principle in their own teaching. If prospective teachers are to learn to engage their future students in the construction of knowledge, they themselves must experience learning as the active construction of knowledge. In keeping with this principle, effective arts and sciences faculty complement the lecture—the typical mode of instruction in colleges and universities—with methodologies that engage students more actively in learning. These include establishing a class-room community that values and promotes dialogue and exploration; using inquiry projects that have personal meaning to the students and that are accompanied by plans of action; engaging students in varied classroom-based activities such as reflective writing and exploration of their family and personal histories; using a variety of assessment strategies to ensure that students are able to demonstrate what they know in ways that are familiar to them; and inviting students to spend time in the field learning about diverse communities through visits, studies, and community service.

There are, however, numerous obstacles to having the arts and sciences faculty become involved in the education of teachers. One fundamental barrier is the devaluing of teaching and of preparing teachers (Gross, 1993; Patterson, Michelli, and Pacheco, 1999). Faculty in arts and sciences have been socialized to think of the content of their disciplines as the heart of what they do. Teaching is typically not central to their identities as academics; rather, it is the means for conveying their disciplinary content to students. This view is reinforced by a system that rewards faculty largely for their contributions to their disciplines, while ignoring or giving only minimal attention to how effectively and responsively they teach. It is not surprising then that many arts and sciences faculty give little time or energy to thinking about teaching and that they do not see themselves responsible for preparing those who are going to become teachers. We suspect this will not change unless the institution as a whole comes to value good teaching and makes the education of teachers a priority, changes that need to be reflected in the institution's system of rewards, as we discuss below.

A related set of obstacles to the involvement of arts and sciences faculty in the education of teachers is inherent in the structure of higher-education institutions. The rigid boundaries between schools/colleges and departments deter any type of collaboration (Dittmer, 1999; Gross, 1993; Liston and Zeichner, 1991; Tom, 1997). The institutional structure encourages a sense that each discipline has its own special body of knowledge and set of responsibilities. Since pedagogical knowledge and the responsibility for preparing teachers is now seen as belonging to the college of education, it cannot also belong to other colleges or departments. The departmental structure, through which faculty generally answer to their department chair and school/college dean, also encourages loyalty to the department over loyalty to the institution. Thus, one's colleagues might view a faculty member as disloyal if he or she became involved in activities that do not directly promote the department. Finally, the rigid boundaries between departments simply make it difficult to find opportunities to collaborate. Other than universitywide committees, processes for collaboration are typically rare. Yet we must bridge the gaps across structural boundaries in order to ensure the best education for prospective teachers. We believe that the concept of a center of pedagogy proposed by Goodlad (1990a, 1990b, 1994) offers one promising approach for bringing together not only arts and sciences faculty and education faculty but also educators from school districts. We next discuss the need for collaboration between the university and school districts and then examine the center of pedagogy as a means for facilitating both types of collaboration.

Collaboration between Colleges/Universities and School Districts

Just as the task of educating culturally responsive teachers cannot be accomplished by the college of education alone, it also cannot be accomplished by the university without the involvement and collaboration of professionals from school districts. Efforts to reform teacher preparation are inextricably linked to life in elementary and secondary schools. In fact, the powerful socialization into the profession that occurs during student teaching can overshadow the socialization preservice teachers receive during their entire professional preparation at the university (Morine-Dershimer and Leighfield, 1995; Zeichner, 1996a). For many years, however, the role of schools in the education of teachers was seen largely as a matter of providing sites for field work. Typically, once prospective teachers began student teaching, most of their connections with university-based educators came to an end (Goodlad, 1994). More recently, attention has been focused on the need to create strong school-university partnerships for purposes of educating teachers-to-be. While much has been written on this topic, our discussion focuses on collaborative relationships in which resources are used to prepare teachers who can successfully teach students from culturally diverse backgrounds.

Practicing teachers can contribute to the complex process of preparing prospective teachers to teach a diverse student population by helping them bring together theory and practice. As we discussed in chapter 4, by observing culturally responsive teachers in action, prospective teachers can see the application of responsive pedagogical practices, and with guidance from their mentors, they can begin to apply those practices themselves. Guided experiences in schools can help prospective teachers deepen their understanding of how to design instruction that builds on students' personal and cultural strengths, how to create varied paths to learning in order to accommodate differences in learning styles and engage students in the construction of knowledge, how to use var-ièd assessment practices that are appropriate to the students they teach, how to create a classroom culture in which all students feel valued and capable of learning, and how to establish and maintain trusting rela-tionships with students. When clinical experiences of this nature are accompanied by opportunities for broad collaboration with experienced teachers, prospective teachers can also develop a strong sense of efficacy and learn to see themselves as active agents of change who are working toward the equitable reform of schools. As we have explained, while these practices can be introduced in college/university courses, their meanings are most clearly grasped in the context of working with real students, in real classrooms, in real schools. Herein lies the value of field experiences in schools, which are most effective when integrated throughout the sequence of professional preparation courses, not just in student teaching at the end of the program.

To support the development of culturally responsive teaching prac-tices, field experiences need to be carefully planned and carried out in settings where children of diverse backgrounds are successful or where teachers and others are actively engaged in reform efforts to improve their success with diverse students (Cochran-Smith, 1991; Grant, 1994a; Zeichner, 1992; Zeichner et al., 1998; Zeichner and Hoeft, 1996; Pugach and Pasch, 1994). Teachers who supervise field experiences need to be committed both to the principles of culturally responsive teaching and to the continuous improvement of their own practice. This is espe-cially true of those teachers who mentor student teachers. When men-tors lack commitment to and skills in responsive teaching, their mentees experience dissonance between what they are learning at the university and what they see and are expected to do in schools. Such dissonance deprives prospective teachers of the support they need to merge theory and practice. Left to fend for themselves, they often see no other option but to adopt the nonresponsive approaches of their mentors. And upon taking over their own classrooms, these novice teachers replicate the practices they learned during student teaching. Thus, inequitable teach-ing practices are perpetuated.

University faculty who want to ensure that prospective teachers have access to school sites where they can observe and participate in practices that will support their development as culturally responsive educators make it a priority to identify and cultivate relationships with teachers and schools that are actively working toward becoming culturally responsive. However, collaborations do not only serve the purpose of providing sites for field experiences; they also give university-based educators opportunities to learn from educators in elementary and secondary schools who are engaging in culturally responsive practices. Involvement with these educators can inform the programs at the university, keeping them vital and relevant to the contexts in which university graduates will become teachers. Practicing teachers, for example, can assist in developing appropriate courses and clinical experiences for prospective teachers, can either team teach courses with college/university faculty or teach courses themselves as clinical faculty, and can serve as guest speakers in selected classes and seminars. Further, reciprocal relationships between university- and school-based faculty can inform and strengthen school-based educators, keeping them engaged in current thinking about culturally responsive teaching.

Both school-based and university-based educators who are agents of change constantly reach out to other teachers and schools to engage them in developing culturally responsive practices. We cannot emphasize the importance of this work enough. The fact is that in the absence of a broad network of schools with a critical mass of educators who are committed to the principles of culturally responsive teaching, our ability to educate future teachers to be responsive themselves is compromised. As Goodlad (1994) has reminded us, the improvement of teacher education and the improvement of elementary and secondary schools are interconnected. Better teachers are needed to make our schools better, and better schools are needed to prepare better teachers.

Developing collaborative relationships between universities and schools is no less difficult than building connections between schools/colleges of education and arts and sciences. As Patterson, Michelli, and Pacheco (1999) point out, differences in the cultures and structures of these two institutions often result in antagonistic relationships. Universities move slowly and emphasize inquiry, while school districts are more likely to act to meet immediate needs. University faculty have considerable flexibility in their use of time, while school faculty must follow rigid schedules. There is also a history of distrust between university faculty and school personnel. University faculty may be perceived as out of touch with the life in schools by those in them, while school faculty may be seen as not keeping pace with current thinking by their colleagues at the university. Making matters even more complex, collaboration demands persistence as participants work to overcome the boundaries of traditional turf and learn to create new roles for themselves. They also require patience because the benefits of partnerships do not materialize quickly.

Facilitating Collaborations among Education, Arts and Sciences, and School Districts through a Center of Pedagogy

We have identified numerous institutional barriers that keep education, arts and sciences, and school district faculty from working collaboratively to educate prospective teachers. In our view, the concept of a center of pedagogy proposed by Goodlad (1990a, 1990b, 1994) represents one promising approach to making these collaborations happen. As envisioned by Goodlad, the center of pedagogy is a formal structure; that is, it has its own staff, including a director whose primary responsibility is to coordinate the center's activities, it has a set of articulated procedures for carrying out its functions, and it has a governance structure that involves the three partners equitably in decision making. The center of pedagogy can be located inside or outside a school/college of education. Regardless of its location, its overall mission is to work simultaneously for the renewal of teacher preparation and the renewal of elementary and secondary schools. A critical element of such work is to develop a shared vision of what this renewal involves. To carry out this mission and realize this vision, the center of pedagogy is given the authority and responsibility for coordinating all aspects of the preparation of teachers, including professional preparation courses, general studies, and field experiences. A center of pedagogy also makes inquiry a central aspect of its work. It provides financial and other types of support for inquiry about teaching, the purposes of education, and the preparation of teachers.

Montclair State University's Center of Pedagogy, described by Patterson, Michelli, and Pacheco (1999), illustrates the concept in practice. Established in 1995, the Center of Pedagogy at Montclair is "responsible for conceptualizing, planning, and carrying out teacher education" (93). It includes the Office of Admissions (into teacher education), the Office of Teacher Education and Placement (which oversees the placement of preservice teachers in student teaching sites), the Curriculum Resource Center (a curriculum library and technology resource center), the Agenda for Education in a Democracy (an office that keeps track of renewal efforts), the National Education Association/Teacher Education Initiative (which manages the evaluation of the renewal efforts in teacher education), the Teacher Education Advocacy Center (which recruits, counsels, and supports students of color in teacher education), and the New Jersey Network for Educational Renewal (NJNER; which coordinates school-university partnerships). While Montclair's Center of Pedagogy is housed in the building with the College of Education and Human Services, it is distinct from all three constituent groups. The director, who also has a faculty appointment, has a dual reporting responsibility. As director of the Center of Pedagogy, she reports to an advisory board consisting of twenty to twenty-five members, evenly distributed among the three constituent groups; as a faculty member, she reports to the academic dean of the college in which she has a faculty appointment (which for the current director is the College of Education and Human Services). All policy decisions are made by the advisory board, whose chair rotates among the three partner groups.

In addition to this jointly constituted advisory board, other mechanisms at Montclair State University foster collaboration across institutional boundaries. The process by which students are admitted into the teacher education program serves to break down the barriers that have traditionally existed between the college of arts and sciences and the college of education. Students who are planning to teach in secondary schools—the majority of teacher education students at Montclair—major in an academic department, not in education. A committee consisting of faculty in the department to which a student is applying and faculty in education meet to consider each application. They jointly interview the candidates and make decisions about acceptance. Once admitted into the program, students are assigned advisers in the academic departments rather than in education. Arts and sciences faculty thus have more ownership of teacher preparation than their peers in many other higher-education institutions.

The primary organizational bridge between the university and school districts is the NJNER. More than six hundred teachers and administrators from twenty-two partner school districts have been granted clinical faculty status, which entitles them to serve as cooperating teachers, on-site education supervisors, co-teachers of student teaching seminars, and adjunct faculty of other university courses. Upon joining the NJNER, school districts agree to give priority to Montclair State's preservice teachers for field placements and student teaching. They also agree to work with the university and other NJNER partner districts to effect change in schools and in teacher education.

Under the auspices of the Center of Pedagogy and the offices and programs it coordinates, opportunities are provided for engaging faculty in education, the arts and sciences, and the public schools in ongoing dialogue. A critical function of these conversations is to support the development of a shared vision among the three groups regarding the purposes of schooling and the ways to prepare prospective teachers. One of the principal vehicles for creating a shared vision as well as for solidifying the collaboration across the three groups is the Leadership Associates Program, modeled on a program developed by the National Network for Educational Renewal and the Agenda for Education in a Democracy at the University of Washington in Seattle (Jacobowitz and

Michelli, 1999). For six years, approximately twenty educators, in roughly equal numbers from each of the three constituent groups, have come together each summer at Montclair State University for two weeks to read about and discuss issues related to John Goodlad's vision of educational renewal. Participants are expected to deepen their understanding of the moral dimensions of teaching in a democracy, collaborate in the renewal of schools and the preparation of teachers, and become agents of change in their own institutions. Four themes—adapted from Goodlad (1994)—guide these discussions: enculturating the young into a social and political democracy, providing access to knowledge for all children and youth, practicing pedagogical nurturing, and ensuring the stewardship of schools. Participants also develop inquiry projects, which they carry out in the coming academic years and then report on in subsequent summers to current and former leadership associates. Inquiry projects have included an exploration of ways to increase the number of people of color in teaching, an examination of how service learning can prepare students to be active participants in a democracy, and identification of factors that support and hinder teachers in becoming change agents. Throughout the academic year, leadership associates come together for meetings, presentations, and discussions on topics such as urban education and critical pedagogy.

In addition to the Leadership Associates Program, the Center of Pedagogy offers a number of other opportunities for dialogue among faculty from the arts and sciences, education, and the schools. Every January, an "advance" (similar to a retreat) focusing on a theme related to education in a democracy is held for two to three days and is well-attended by members of all three partner groups. The advance is jointly planned by a committee consisting of representatives from each of the three groups. In 1999 and 2000, respectively, the themes of the advances were *Beyond Multiculturalism: Confronting Prejudice, Privilege, and Power in Ourselves and Our Students,* and *Educating Other People's Children and Ourselves about Race and Racism: Working Together and Communicating across Racial Lines.* The NJNER also provides small grants of five hundred dollars to Network participants and university faculty to purchase books and materials for study groups to engage in inquiry on topics of mutual interest. Through a grant from a private foundation, the NJNER awards grants of up to five thousand dollars to teams of educators from Network districts. For example, a team from Paterson, New Jersey, studied effective strategies for teaching science to students of limited English proficiency. To receive these grants, interested educators write a brief proposal that is reviewed for its compatibility with the Center of Pedagogy's evolving vision of educational renewal for schooling in a democracy.

Three schools are involved in more intensive collaboration with the university through their status as professional development schools (PDSs). PDSs are schools that work in close collaboration with universities to improve teacher preparation and elementary and secondary schooling (Darling-Hammond, 1994a; Holmes Group, 1990; Patterson, Michelli, and Pacheco, 1999). To become a PDS with Montclair State, a school needs to have a strong commitment to the Center of Pedagogy's evolving vision of schooling and teacher preparation. A faculty member from the university spends one quarter of his or her time in each PDS and receives credit toward tenure and promotion through the Faculty Scholarship Incentive Program (FSIP), which allows Montclair State faculty to receive a course release each semester to pursue scholarship in one of three areas—pedagogy; application of knowledge; or discovery, integration, or aesthetic creation (adapted from Boyer, 1990). Thus, the university PDS liaisons are formally rewarded for concentrating their efforts on building, maintaining, and strengthening the school-university partnership—an example of application of knowledge in the FSIP system. Other faculty may also have relationships with a PDS. For example, they may teach courses for prospective teachers on site at the school, organize professional development activities for and with school personnel, or spend time working directly with teachers in classes. Conversely, teachers from the PDSs may serve as clinical faculty at the university, team teaching seminars for student teachers or serving as adjunct faculty for other university courses.

The existence of the Center of Pedagogy at Montclair State University greatly enhances the ability of the institution to foster the types of collaborative relationships we discussed above by sending the message that all three groups share responsibility for the preparation of teachers. The fact that the school districts are involved in all decisions and activities builds trust among school district personnel that the university is serious about including them as equal partners in the education of teachers. The fact that arts and sciences faculty are also involved in center decisions and activities and that they have primary responsibility for the academic programs of prospective teachers creates some ownership of teacher preparation. Most important, by fostering the development of a common vision among the three groups, the Center of Pedagogy promotes coherence in the education of prospective teachers.

However, simply having a center of pedagogy will not result in the preparation of culturally responsive teachers. To successfully prepare teachers for diversity, teacher educators associated with the center must spend time developing a conception of culturally responsive teaching and integrating that conception into the evolving vision of the simultaneous renewal of teacher preparation and of K–12 schools. This is what teacher educators at Montclair State University have been working on during the past two years. While that work is still at an early stage, a review of what has been accomplished illustrates how a teacher education program can move toward coherence in preparing culturally responsive teachers.

For some time, many of us who work with preservice teachers at Montclair State have known that preparing teachers for an increasingly diverse student population is critically important for our multicultural society and especially for the highly diverse region we serve. Many of us have also acknowledged that our program needs to do a better job of preparing such teachers. Acting on this need, the director of the Center of Pedagogy convened a task force—comprised of faculty from education, arts and sciences, and the partner school districts—with the charge of recommending a curriculum to prepare preservice teachers to teach culturally diverse students. The task force, of which the two of us were members, adopted the conception of the culturally responsive teacher described in chapters 2 and 3 as a preliminary curriculum framework to be used in discussions with faculty in different colleges and departments at the university and in the partner school districts. The task force proposed that the initial phase of this discussion involve faculty from the three departments that offer the courses comprising the professional education sequence—Curriculum and Teaching, Educational Foundations, and Reading and Educational Media.

The representative to the task force from each of these departments presented the preliminary framework to members of their respective departments. Department faculty reviewed the framework and discussed its implications for the courses they teach. After considerable discussion, these departments agreed in principle to adopt the six curriculum strands in the framework on the condition that faculty would be free to engage students in discussions of viewpoints that differ from those promoted by the strands. The faculty also developed a plan for systematically infusing the diversity strands across the courses comprising the professional education sequence, as shown in figure 5.1.

To widen faculty involvement in the infusion work beyond those who regularly teach courses in the professional development sequence, the Center of Pedagogy has supported several initiatives. The Leadership Associates Program described above has been used to this end. In recent summers, culturally responsive teaching has been a central topic of discussion. In 2000 and 2001, in particular, the associates engaged in an in-depth exploration of the six diversity strands. They also developed strategies for use in coursework and fieldwork to help prospective teachers cultivate the identified qualities of the culturally responsive teacher.

FIGURE 5.1
Proposed Distribution of Curriculum Strands across Courses in the
Professional Education Sequence at Montclair State University

Courses	Curriculum Strands						Over-view
	1	2	3	4	5	6	
Educational Psychology [distribution of strands to be determined]							
Initial Field Experience (CURR 200)	✗	✗					*
Teacher, School, and Society (CURR 400)	✓	✓	✗		✓		*
Philosophical Orientations (EDFD 220)	✗	✓	✗	✗			
Teaching for Critical Thinking (EDFD 409)	✗	✓	✗	✗		✓	
Reading Course [distribution of strands to be determined]							
Intermediate Field Experience (CURR 410)	✓	✓			✗	✓	
Methods Course [distribution of strands to be determined]							
Effective Teaching/ Productive Learning (CURR 435)				✓	✓	✗	
Professional Seminar (CURR 402)			✓	✓	✓	✓	*
Supervised Student Teaching (CURR 411)			✓	✓	✗	✗	

✗ = To be addressed in course (central theme)
✓ = To be addressed in course
* = Overview of all six diversity strands

The Center of Pedagogy has also used the annual "advance," mentioned above, to promote the curriculum infusion work. For example, the diversity strands were the focus of discussion during the January 2001 advance. As part of this advance, participants were given opportunities to explore their own sociocultural consciousness.

Mini courses sponsored by the NJNER, housed in Montclair's Center of Pedagogy, constitute another aevenue for involving K–12 educators in discussions of what it means to be a culturally responsive teacher. In recent years, a mini course on culturally responsive teaching has been offered on a voluntary basis to network educators. The Center of Pedagogy is currently considering making this mini course a requirement for school faculty seeking clinical status at Montclair.

As this discussion illustrates, the pursuit of coherence in the preparation of teachers for a diverse student population is not a simple process. Developing and refining a conception of culturally responsive teaching, reaching consensus on that conception, and reconstructing the teacher education curriculum to reflect it is a disjointed enterprise, subject to a host of individual and institutional distractions as well as moments of inspiration and breakthroughs. The process also takes a long time and demands patience. While we at Montclair State have accomplished a lot during the last two years, we still have a long way to go. Our experience is another reminder that the work of renewal requires a long-term commitment because it never really ends.

Our discussion may suggest to some that institutions without a center of pedagogy cannot achieve the coherence we advocate. This is not the case. Even without a formal structure such as a center of pedagogy, an institution can work toward coherence in the preparation of culturally responsive teachers. We do believe, however, that having a center of pedagogy gives an institution a head start in the process. As we have said, a center of pedagogy provides a structure for bringing together the key parties responsible for preparing prospective teachers. Perhaps more important, the existence of a center of pedagogy indicates that many of those associated with the institution have already acknowledged the need for coherence in teacher education. If such a foundation is not already in place, the process of transforming teacher education for diversity must start there. Teacher educators need to recognize the value of offering prospective teachers a set of seamless learning experiences, and they need to understand that a shared vision of culturally responsive teaching can help them do so.

A task force could be a vehicle for convening a core group of faculty to take the lead in developing such a vision. But, to make an impact, the task force must have institutional recognition and responsibility. In the absence of a center of pedagogy, the appointment of this task force by the president or provost would give it that recognition. Once the task force has generated a preliminary conception of culturally responsive teaching to guide the reform of teacher education, the next challenge is to reach out to other faculty. The details of strategies for involving others will vary, depending on the history and culture of each institution. The ultimate goal, however, is the same—to get as many faculty members as possible to buy into the evolving vision and to become committed to the process of transforming the preparation of teachers.

STRONG INVESTMENT IN FACULTY DEVELOPMENT

As important as they are, shared vision and commitment to institutional change are not sufficient to bring about the transformation of teacher education that we are advocating. Even if the organization and content of the curriculum are revised, most of us who educate teachers are not adequately prepared to address issues of diversity in our own practice or to model culturally responsive teaching (Cochran-Smith, 1995b; Grant, 1994b; Larkin and Sleeter, 1995; Melnick and Zeichner, 1998; Shade, 1995; Zeichner, 1992). Even those of us who specialize in issues of diversity benefit from ongoing professional development designed to deepen our understandings of ourselves and of people different from us, to broaden our knowledge of diversity, and to hone our skills in responsive teaching. As we have said, the process of becoming a culturally responsive educator never ends. Institutions committed to preparing responsive teachers, therefore, make a strong investment in professional development related to issues of diversity (Grant, 1994b; Haberman, 1991; Larkin and Sleeter, 1995; Melnick and Zeichner, 1998; Zeichner, 1992; Zeichner and Hoeft, 1996).

Professional development needs to reach beyond faculty to include staff and administrators as well. Noninstructional personnel, secretaries, and other staff come into frequent contact with students. If inclusiveness is a priority across the institution, staff need access to learning opportunities so they can become aware of institutional goals, enhance their sensitivity to issues of diversity, and develop competence in interacting with students of different racial, cultural, and linguistic backgrounds. To provide leadership in establishing an inclusive community and bringing about the changes needed to prepare culturally responsive teachers, administrators as well as faculty and staff need to build relevant understandings and skills. By seeking and engaging in professional development themselves, they will not only be better leaders but will show that institutional statements promoting inclusiveness are not simply hollow platitudes but a serious institutional commitment. While institutions need to offer professional development for all personnel, the remainder of our discussion focuses specifically on professional development for university- and school-based faculty—those most directly involved in the preparation of teachers.

The content of a faculty development initiative focused on issues of diversity depends, to a large extent, on the conception of culturally responsive teaching adopted by the institution. An institution that adopted the conception we have presented in chapters 2 and 3, for example, would give priority to faculty development related to the six curriculum strands detailed in those chapters and to modeling the practice of culturally responsive teaching. To illustrate, we will highlight types of dispositions, knowledge, and skills that faculty would need in a teacher education program grounded in our conception. As the discussion will make clear, most of us would benefit from opportunities for development in a number of these areas.

If we as teacher educators are to help prospective teachers develop the fundamental orientations to teaching diverse students discussed in chapter 2, we ourselves need to understand the influence of factors such as race, ethnicity, social class, and language on our own and others' identities and worldviews; the role of schools in society; and differential access to power and privilege in schools and society. We need to be aware of our attitudes about and have a deep knowledge of people from diverse racial, ethnic, and linguistic groups. We need affirming attitudes toward diverse students. We also need to understand the role of teachers in bringing about educational change and see ourselves as agents of change.

To teach prospective teachers and model for them the skills of culturally responsive teaching discussed in chapter 3, we need to understand and embrace constructivist views of teaching and learning. Rather than simply accepting the traditional knowledge base in our area of expertise, we need to be able to critique and supplement this knowledge base in order to reduce racism and ethnocentrism and incorporate multicultural perspectives (Banks, 1993a). Like the future teachers we are preparing for elementary and secondary schools, we teacher educators also need skills for learning about our own students so we can adjust our teaching to foster their construction of knowledge (Richardson, 1999). For example, we need strategies for uncovering our students' beliefs about diversity and about young people from diverse backgrounds, about the roles of teachers and schools in society, and about the nature of teaching and learning. Once these beliefs are revealed, we must then be able to use that awareness to guide our students toward greater sociocultural consciousness; more affirming attitudes toward diversity; conceptions of teachers and of themselves as agents of change; and constructivist views of knowledge, teaching, and learning.

We need to use the type of pedagogy we discussed in chapter 4 to support conceptual change. We need to establish communities of learners in which our students actively engage in purposeful learning activities. We need to be flexible and varied in our teaching style, lecturing sparingly and instead using such activities as reflective writing, inquiry projects, problem-solving activities, authentic discussions, storytelling, role play, simulations and games, and teaching cases. This approach to teaching requires that we guide discussions without dominating them. We need to be skilled at selecting materials—videotaped documentaries, fictional movies, articles, and books—that reflect different perspectives on issues addressed in class rather than simply presenting the received wisdom from those considered experts, most of whom are white males.

Further, we need skills that will enable us to facilitate collaboration and dialogue among students of different racial/ethnic groups and establish safe classroom environments where students can engage in these activities across racial/ethnic lines. To this end, we need strategies for responding when students express conflict, anger, and frustration. This includes being able to ask difficult questions and to address discomfort that is likely to arise from the inclusion of multiple perspectives in classes. We need to recognize the potential for students of color to be silenced, especially when there are few of them in a class. We also need strategies for monitoring our interactions with students of diverse backgrounds in order to prevent such silencing (Shade, 1995). We need skills for dealing with racially segregating classroom patterns and with racial incidents when they occur in class.

We also need to expand our knowledge and skills to successfully prepare our students for various types of field experiences in culturally diverse settings beyond our own classrooms and to engage them in reflection on those experiences. If we are to support our students in their field experiences, we need to be familiar with diverse schools and communities and to know how to collaborate with teachers, families, and community members in those settings. We need to be able to conduct the kinds of observations and information gathering activities we ask our students to do. We need skills in cross-cultural communication and sensitivity to cultural differences in order to prepare our students for their fieldwork in multicultural schools and communities.

We should not be expected to have all these dispositions, knowledge, and skills without the benefit of professional development. Faculty development initiatives can best support us in this endeavor if they are characterized by flexibility, variety, and frequency of learning opportunities. For example, lecture series that feature the work of different researchers and practitioners can expose us to current thinking on a variety of topics related to diversity. Workshops—which typically involve some combination of formal presentation, discussion, and interactive activities—can help us not only build knowledge but also develop strategies for applying that knowledge in our own work. Retreats, longer and more intensive than workshops or lectures, can offer more opportunities for reflection on our dispositions as well as for knowledge building. Ongoing seminars and study groups foster even more sustained engagement with particular issues while building community among participants.

The professional development initiatives we envision engage faculty at colleges and universities as well as in the schools in projects to make the curriculum more multicultural and inclusive (Brawer, 1990; Price and Valli, 1998). These initiatives vary considerably in their details, as their designs reflect particular community and institutional contexts. Some initiatives might involve us as individuals or in groups in evaluating and revising courses to reflect the conception of culturally responsive teaching adopted by our institution. We might also conduct action research to examine and reflect on what happens in our own classes with regard to cultural diversity and responsive teaching. We could then engage in dialogue on these issues by sharing our findings with colleagues.

Team teaching and peer coaching are two other ways in which we can develop knowledge and skills related to culturally responsive pedagogical practices. These activities engender intensive collaboration, dialogue, and self-reflection, as we observe and are observed by colleagues and then discuss these observations. When a university faculty member team teaches with a school-based faculty member, the opportunities for growth and new insights can be enhanced by the different perspectives and experiences with students that each partner brings to the task. Having our classes videotaped provides another means for analyzing and reflecting on our practices as a way to improve our teaching. Using such videos to examine the responses of students from different cultural backgrounds to our instruction can give us valuable insights about the impact of our teaching. For those of us who teach at the university, one other avenue for professional development regarding issues of diversity is to spend more time in schools that serve diverse student populations and with teachers who are actively working to become more culturally responsive. PDSs provide the opportunity for university faculty to become engaged with such teachers and students and to expand our understanding of the day-to-day workings of schools.

Institutions that seek to involve a critical mass of faculty in professional development related to issues of diversity must actively support such involvement. One way of doing this is to build time for professional development into our regular responsibilities rather than treating it as peripheral to our work. For example, school districts can give faculty release time to attend organized activities and carry out related projects, can schedule time for collaborative planning and peer coaching, and can approve sabbaticals for diversity-related projects. Higher education institutions can provide faculty with course releases and sabbaticals for similar purposes. Institutions can also provide educators of teachers financial support in the form of funds for conference attendance and internal grants for various types of projects (Brawer, 1990). Ultimately, however, the strongest incentive for faculty to seek professional development on issues of diversity is to make such issues central to the institutional reward system. This might involve offering awards, formal recognition, and credit toward salary increases for those of us who show a commitment to using culturally responsive strategies in our own teaching. When such a commitment is considered in making tenure and promotion decisions, faculty have an even stronger incentive to seek opportunities to grow in these areas.

Making professional development an institutional priority and offering a full spectrum of opportunities will not ensure that educators participate, however. Many of us are reluctant to admit that we may need further professional development (Dittmer, 1999). Especially at the university but also in public schools, we faculty are seen as experts. We may find it difficult to expose our uncertainties and lack of knowledge because we do not want to be seen as less than competent by our peers. We might also fear that we will not be able to handle the conflict, anger, frustration, and confusion of our students surrounding issues of race, class, and language (hooks, 1994). Since most of us have had little experience openly discussing these issues ourselves, we may be uncertain about how best to facilitate such dialogue. Another challenge we face is having to change our basic values and beliefs (hooks, 1994; Shade, 1995). Because issues of stratification and inequity are especially loaded, some of us may be reluctant to critically examine our own attitudes regarding these and related issues. We may fear uncovering some discomforting attitudes and perceptions if we dig too deeply into our values and beliefs (Tatum, 1992). Thus, the challenge we face in participating in professional development focused on diversity is both personal and professional, raising profound questions about ourselves and our professional lives. If we have opportunities to directly address fears and discomfort related to issues of diversity, we are more likely to overcome our resistance and to engage in the hard work involved in becoming culturally responsive educators.

As we hope this chapter has made clear, the institutional transformation we advocate is neither simple nor linear. The different actions described in this chapter need to occur simultaneously. Evaluations and self-studies can be vital in monitoring the process of institutional change (Brawer, 1990; Price and Valli, 1998). Institutions need to systematically track their efforts to enroll and retain students of color and to hire and retain faculty of color, assess the success of their approaches to selecting culturally sensitive candidates for teacher education, document and evaluate collaborative activities across institutional boundaries, and monitor the participation in and impact of professional development. They can devise strategies for determining the extent to which teacher education graduates feel prepared to teach students from diverse backgrounds and how successful they are in teaching them. Part of the complexity of this work is that institutions and the individuals who constitute them are inextricably linked. In fact, it is through engagement in transforming institutions that individuals transform their own consciousness, and it is through the transformation of individual consciousness that institutions are truly transformed. This process is undoubtedly challenging, but we see it as the best opportunity to reach all of our nation's students. The struggle is more than worth the effort.

CONCLUSION

We began this book by demonstrating how changes in the demographic makeup of the student population have made it imperative that all who enter the teaching profession be prepared to address issues of diversity. We further argued that the typical approach to preparing teachers for a changing student population—adding a course or two on multicultural education without altering the established teacher education curriculum—cannot meet this goal. While special courses on multicultural education contribute to the preparation of teachers for diversity, they are insufficient. Their impact is limited unless the ideas introduced in those courses are reinforced and expanded throughout the preservice teacher education curriculum—which we see as including the various learning experiences teachers-to-be are exposed to in education courses, arts and sciences courses, and fieldwork in schools and communities. We have contended that without coherence in the experiences offered across these settings, prospective teachers are not likely to make the necessary connections among key ideas, nor are they apt to integrate theory with practice.

A central point we make in this book is that to move beyond fragmentation and facilitate coherence, programs of teacher education need to articulate a vision of the role of schools and of the processes of teaching and learning in a multicultural society. Such a vision, we think, is what lends conceptual coherence to the ongoing work of teacher educators—faculty in education, arts and sciences, and elementary and secondary schools—to prepare prospective teachers for diversity. The vision we have proposed is anchored in the belief that a primary role of schools is to promote a more equitable and just society and is informed by constructivist views of teaching and learning. We embrace constructivist thinking for several reasons that are worth reiterating. First of all, from a constructivist viewpoint, all students are seen as capable learners who continuously strive to make sense of new ideas. Their ways of thinking, talking, interacting, and learning are considered resources for further development rather than problems or barriers. Second, in contrast to the hierarchical and authoritarian tendencies of transmission-oriented teaching, constructivist teaching fosters critical thinking, problem solving, collaboration, and the recognition of multiple perspectives.

It is thus well-suited for preparing students to become active participants in a democracy. Third, constructivist classrooms support academic rigor to a greater extent than transmission classrooms through
their emphasis on higher-order thinking and problem solving rather
than memorization. By extending the opportunity to develop these abilities to all learners, constructivist classrooms have the potential to promote academic excellence for all students.

To give focus to their work, teacher educators at each institution
need to do more than articulate the philosophical underpinnings of the
vision of schools and of teaching and learning in a multicultural society
they aim to promote; they must carve out an image of the type of educator they want graduates to be. The image we advance is this book is
that of a culturally responsive teacher. Drawing on empirical and theoretical work in the field of multicultural education, we identified six
salient characteristics of teachers who are culturally responsive. As we
see it, culturally responsive teachers are those who

- understand that their students may see the world differently than
  they do and accept that worldviews are not universal but are shaped
  by each person's individual, social, and cultural experiences;
- recognize that all students bring resources to learning and show
  affirming attitudes toward students of diverse backgrounds;
- see teaching as a political and ethical activity and see themselves as
  agents of change who are skilled at identifying inequitable school
  practices and challenging them;
- understand and embrace constructivist views of teaching and learning;
- know their students well; and
- use what they know about their students to support their learning
  through practices such as engaging all students in the construction
  of knowledge, building on their interests and strengths while
  stretching them beyond what they already know, helping them
  examine ideas from multiple perspectives, using varied assessment
  practices, and making the culture of the classroom inclusive of all.

These six constructs—each of which blends particular dispositions,
knowledge, and skills—serve as the organizing framework that gives
coherence to our curriculum proposal. They represent the conceptual
strands to be woven throughout the learning experiences of preservice
teachers in coursework and fieldwork so that collectively those experiences cultivate the qualities of culturally responsive teachers. No doubt,
teacher educators who adopt this framework will need to spend time

coordinating how the courses they teach and the field experiences they supervise contribute to the development of the desired responsive teaching qualities. The existence of an organizing framework, however, renders this complex task of coordination more manageable.

While we believe that our curriculum proposal reflects the most current thinking on preparing teachers to teach a diverse student population, we also acknowledge that it is not value free. Those who do not share our views that a salient role of schools is to promote a more equitable and just society, that diversity is worthy of affirmation, that teaching is a political activity, or that learning involves the construction of knowledge are likely to take issue with our curriculum proposal. Even those who accept the basic premises of this proposal might conceptualize culturally responsive teaching somewhat differently than we do. Such differences might result in the rearrangement and/or relabeling of the curriculum strands. Our overall intent has not been to present a rigid prescription for all teacher education programs to adopt but to show how a curriculum framework can give coherence to the preparation of teachers for a multicultural society. We are convinced that in the absence of such a framework, the fragmentation that characterizes the preparation of teachers for diversity will continue. While we recognize that a vision for education in a multicultural society cannot be imposed, we nonetheless believe that those who take the time to review the existing literature will find our vision of culturally responsive teaching persuasive.

Aligning the curriculum content with the methods used to teach preservice teachers is the second dimension of the coherent approach to teacher preparation we advocate. Because teachers tend to reproduce pedagogical practices they experience as students, those of us who teach prospective teachers at the university, whether in education courses or arts and sciences courses, need to model for them the practices we want them to use in their future teaching. In institutions whose vision of culturally responsive teaching approximates the one we advocate, such modeling calls for a shift in the predominantly transmission-oriented pedagogy of higher education. As we have explained, if we expect prospective teachers to engage their future students actively in learning, we must create learning experiences that give them an active role in their own learning. If the teachers we envision are those who involve learners in purposeful and meaningful activities, we ourselves must involve prospective teachers in purposeful activities that have meaning for them. If we want teachers to help their students examine ideas from multiple perspectives, we too must engage future teachers in examining ideas from different viewpoints. If we expect teachers to make the culture of their classrooms inclusive of all students, prospective teachers must experience inclusive classrooms in their preservice courses.

Similarly, teachers in elementary and secondary schools who mentor future teachers in field experiences and practica, including student teaching, need to model for their mentees the qualities of responsive teaching. They can play a critical role by showing teachers-to-be, for example, how responsive educators involve their students actively in learning, create purposeful activities that are of interest to students, engage learners in the study of historical events from different points of view, and make the culture of their classrooms inclusive of all students. They can also help prospective teachers understand that cultivating the skills of responsive teaching involves hard work and demands a willingness to learn throughout one's career.

The coherence we envision also has an institutional dimension. We have discussed four institutional priorities and accompanying actions that support the preparation of teachers for our multicultural society. First, institutions committed to preparing culturally responsive teachers strive to become diverse learning communities. In order to develop the cross-cultural sensitivity and skills required to teach students from diverse backgrounds, prospective teachers need direct contact with people who are culturally different from themselves. To establish such diverse learning environments, colleges and universities make the recruitment and retention of students and faculty of color a priority and develop a systematic plan for acting on this priority.

A second way colleges and universities show their support for preparing culturally responsive teachers is by focusing attention on the recruitment and selection of students into teacher education. Because attitudes are so difficult to modify, institutions need to seek out teacher education candidates who are already favorably predisposed to diversity. Such action involves expanding traditional selection criteria, which emphasize past grades and test scores, to include indicators of cultural sensitivity. In addition, institutions need to make it a priority to recruit into teacher education students of color, who bring much-needed cultural expertise to the teaching profession. To expand their minority enrollments in teacher education, colleges and universities develop both short- and long-term recruitment strategies and allocate sufficient resources to carry them out successfully.

A third important priority of institutions that support the preparation of culturally responsive teachers is the recognition that faculty who teach arts and sciences as well as education courses and faculty in elementary and secondary schools who supervise fieldwork all play critical roles in the preparation of prospective teachers. As we have explained, these three groups need to collaborate to develop a shared plan for making culturally responsive teaching a reality. We have argued that one promising way institutions of higher education can facilitate such collaborations is by creating a center of pedagogy, an organizational structure (distinct from a college/school of education) that is formally assigned the responsibility for teacher preparation and in which the three partners are involved equitably in decision making.

Finally, institutions need to make a strong investment in faculty development related to issues of diversity. As we have discussed, the majority of us who are teacher educators—whether in colleges of education, colleges of arts and sciences, or elementary and secondary schools—are not prepared to be culturally responsive. While most of us have developed some knowledge about how to teach a diverse student population on our own, we continue to need professional development to expand our understandings in this area. Even those of us with expertise on issues of diversity recognize that we stand to benefit from opportunities to expand our understanding of culturally responsive teaching. As we have stated, without a willingness on our part to engage in faculty development focused on topics of diversity and an openness to the personal and professional transformation such engagement can promote, we will be limited in our ability to transform teacher education for diversity.

The project we have outlined is an ambitious one. It involves rethinking the role of teacher education in our institutions and our individual roles as teacher educators within those institutions. It requires us to let go of hope for simplistic solutions to the educational problems we face and, instead, to grapple with the complexities of institutional and personal change. It also demands that we make our vision of education explicit and that we do so through collaboration with our colleagues across usually rigid institutional boundaries.

The coherent approach to preparing culturally responsive teachers we have proposed in this book is not an instant cure. We are not so unrealistic as to believe that our schools can single-handedly change the inequities that are embedded throughout society far beyond the schoolhouse door. However, there is much that we can and must do, and the time to start is now. We as educators have an essential role to play—in the classroom, on the campus, in school districts, in the community, and in the political process. Every small change that we make alters the overall configuration, but these changes have tended to take place in a piecemeal and unsystematic fashion. The changing demographics of this country make it imperative that our response to diversity be powerfully thought out and undergirded by a commitment to learning for every child in a society that is striving to become more equitable and just.

NOTES

INTRODUCTION

1. Like others, we have struggled with what terminology to use in referring to students and prospective teachers of diverse racial, ethnic, economic, and linguistic backgrounds. All of the options have their limitations. None satisfactorily captures the realities of those referred to, and some have connotations that we would prefer to avoid. We have chosen to use the terms *minority* and *people/students/teachers of color* interchangeably to refer to the large and varied group of people who differ from the dominant group of white middle-class native speakers of English in one or more of the following ways: race, ethnicity, social class, native language, or native variety of English.

2. We use the term *limited English proficient* when citing publications or data sources that use that term. Otherwise, we use *English language learners* to refer to students whose first language is one other than English and who are not yet fully proficient in English. *Language minority* refers to people who are from home backgrounds where a language other than English is spoken, regardless of their own proficiency in English.

3. We understand that teachers need to be able to deal with a multitude of other issues as well, including those related to gender, special needs, and sexual orientation. Our focus in this book, however, is on race/ethnicity, class, and language. We will use the expression *race/ethnicity* in recognition of the fact that for some people race and ethnicity are equivalent, while for others they are not.

CHAPTER 1. THE SHIFTING DEMOGRAPHIC LANDSCAPE

1. We use the term *African American* except when drawing upon other publications that use other terms (e.g., *black*) to refer to Americans of African heritage. We use the terms *Hispanic* and *Latino* interchangeably, since people of Hispanic/Latino heritage use both terms to describe themselves.

2. The census data showed a less dramatic increase between 1980 and 1990 but a higher number of LEP students—2.39 million in 1990. Again, the actual number is less certain than the fact that the number is increasing.

3. We are not reporting achievement levels for Asian American and American Indian students because their numbers were too small at several of the achievement levels to allow for reliable comparisons.

4. NAEP categorizes test scores on the mathematics and reading assessment into three levels of achievement: basic, proficient, and advanced. At the basic

level, students show "partial mastery of prerequisite knowledge and skills that are fundamental for proficient work" for the grade level being assessed (NCES, 1997c, 8). Students attaining the next achievement level (proficient) present evidence of "solid academic performance" at their grade level. This includes "competency over challenging subject matter, including subject-matter knowledge, application of such knowledge to real-world situations, and analytical skills appropriate to the subject matter" (ibid.). At the advanced achievement level, students show evidence of "superior performance" (ibid.). For the sake of simplicity, we have grouped scores into two categories—"below basic" and "basic and above" in figures 1.6 through 1.8.

5. Undergraduates for whom race/ethnicity was not known were not included in this analysis, nor were nonresident aliens.

CHAPTER 2. DEVELOPING FUNDAMENTAL ORIENTATIONS FOR TEACHING A CHANGING STUDENT POPULATION

1. We acknowledge that attention to key areas such as subject-matter knowledge, child development, and language development (of both first and second languages) is not apparent from this conceptualization. While we consider these essential elements of teacher preparation, we have opted to fold them into our discussion of pedagogical issues embedded in strands four through six. A comprehensive treatment of these important topics, however, is beyond the boundaries of this book.

2. Information for other racial/ethnic groups was not available for that year. The economic disparity between the Native American and white populations is also considerable, however.

REFERENCES

Abi-Nader, J. 1990. "'A house for my mother': Motivating Hispanic high school students." *Anthropology and Education Quarterly* 21, no. 1: 41–58.

Adams, M. 1997. "Pedagogical frameworks for social justice education." In M. Adams, L. A. Bell, and P. Griffin (eds.), *Teaching for diversity and social justice: A sourcebook*, pp. 30–43. New York: Routledge.

Adams, M., and L. Marchesani. 1997. "Multiple issues course overview." In M. Adams, L. A. Bell, and P. Griffin (eds.), *Teaching for diversity and social justice: A sourcebook*, pp. 261–75. New York: Routledge.

Adger, C. 1997. "Issues and implications of English dialects for teaching English as a second language." *TESOL Professional Papers #3*. Washington, DC: TESOL.

Ahlquist, R. 1991. "Position and imposition: Power relations in a multicultural foundations class." *Journal of Negro Education* 60, no. 2: 158–69.

Alger, J. R. 1997. "The educational value of diversity." *Academe*, January–February: 20–23.

American Association of Colleges for Teacher Education. 1987. "Minority teacher recruitment and retention: A public policy issue." *Proceedings and background materials at the Wingspread Conference*. Washington, DC: Author.

———. 1989. *Teacher education pipeline III: Schools, colleges, and departments of education enrollments by race, ethnicity, and gender*. Washington, DC: Author.

———. 1997. *Selected data from the 1995 AACTE/NCATE Joint Data Collection System*. Washington, DC: Author.

American Council on Education. 1994. "The foreign-born population of the 1990s: A summary profile." *Research Briefs* 5, no. 6: 1–12.

Anastasi, A. 1988. *Psychological testing*, 6th ed. New York: Macmillan.

Anderson, A. B. 1991. "Teaching children: What teachers should know." In M. M. Kennedy (ed.), *Teaching academic subjects to diverse learners*, pp. 203–17. New York: Teachers College Press.

Anderson, B. T., and M. E. Goertz. 1995. "Creating a path between two- and four-year colleges." In A. M. Villegas, B. C. Clewell, B. T. Anderson, M. E. Goertz, M. F. Joy, B. A. Bruschi, and J. J. Irvine, *Teaching for diversity: Models for expanding the supply of minority teachers*, pp. 48–71. Princeton, NJ: Educational Testing Service.

Anderson, O. 1989. "New directions in preservice teacher education programs in historically black colleges and universities: The challenge of the 1990s." *Action in Teacher Education* 11, no. 2: 51–58.

Andrzejewski, J. 1995. "Teaching controversial issues in higher education: Pedagogical techniques and analytical framework." In R. J. Martin (ed.), *Practicing what we teach: Confronting diversity in teacher education*, pp. 3–26. Albany: SUNY Press.

Angelou, M. 1971. *I know why the caged bird sings*. New York: Bantam.

———. 1974. *Gather together in my name*. New York: Random House.

———. 1991. *All God's children need traveling shoes*. New York: Vintage Books.

Anglin, L. W. 1989. "Preparing minority teachers for the 21st century: A university/community college model." *Action in Teacher Education* 11, no. 2: 47–50.

Anyon, J. 1981. "Social class and school knowledge." *Curriculum Inquiry* 12, no. 1: 3–42.

Apple, M. 1990. *Ideology and curriculum*, 2nd ed. New York: Routledge.

———. 1993. *Official knowledge*. New York: Routledge.

———. 1996. *Cultural politics and education*. New York: Teachers College Press.

Archer, J. 2000. "Competition is fierce for minority teachers." *Education Week: Quality Counts 2000* XIX, no. 18: 32–34.

Arciniega, T. A. 1990. *The challenge of developing strategies to recruit and retain ethnic minority faculty*. Paper presented at the California Community Colleges Faculty and Staff Conference, Los Angeles, CA. (ERIC Document Reproduction Service No. ED 320 516).

Arends, R., S. Clemson, and J. Henkelman. 1992. "Tapping nontraditional sources of minority teaching talent." In M. E. Dilworth (ed.), *Diversity in teacher education: New expectations*, pp. 160–80. San Francisco: Jossey-Bass.

Armaline, W. D. 1995. "Reflecting on cultural diversity through early field experiences." In R. J. Martin (ed.), *Practicing what we teach: Confronting diversity in teacher education*, pp. 163–80. Albany: SUNY Press.

Astin, A. W. 1993. *What matters in college: Four critical years revisited*. San Francisco: Jossey-Bass.

Au, K. H. 1980. "Participation structures in a reading lesson with Hawaiian children: An analysis of a culturally appropriate instructional event." *Anthropology and Education Quarterly* 11, no. 2: 93–115.

Au, K. H., and A. J. Kawakami. 1994. "Cultural congruence in instruction." In E. R. Hollins, J. E. King, and W. C. Hayman (eds.), *Teaching diverse populations: Formulating a knowledge base*, pp. 5–23. Albany: SUNY Press.

Au, K. H., and C. Jordan. 1981. "Teaching reading to Hawaiian children: Finding a culturally appropriate solution." In H. Trueba, G. Guthrie, and K. Au (eds.), *Culture and the bilingual classroom: Studies in classroom ethnography*, pp. 139–52. Rowley, MA: Newbury House.

Ball, D. L. 1991. "Teaching mathematics for understanding: What do teachers need to know about subject matter?" In M. M. Kennedy (ed.), *Teaching academic subjects to diverse learners*, pp. 63–83. New York: Teachers College Press.

Bandura, A. 1977. "Self-efficacy: Toward a unifying theory of behavioral change." *Psychological Review* 84, no. 2: 191–215.

Banks, J. 1991a. "A curriculum for empowerment, action, and change." In C. E. Sleeter (ed.), *Empowerment through multicultural education*, pp. 125–41. Albany: SUNY Press.

———. 1991b. "Teaching multicultural literacy to teachers." *Teacher Education* 4, no. 1: 135–44.

———. 1993a. "The canon debate, knowledge construction and multicultural education." *Educational Researcher* 22, no. 5: 4–14.

———. 1993b. "Multicultural education as an academic discipline." *Multicultural Education* Winter: 8–11, 39.

———. 1994. *Multiethnic education: Theory and practice*, 3rd ed. Boston: Allyn and Bacon.

———. 1995. "Multicultural education: Historical development, dimensions, and practice." In J. A. Banks and C. A. M. Banks (eds.), *Handbook of research on multicultural education*, pp. 3–24. New York: Macmillan.

———. 1996. "The historical reconstruction of knowledge about race: Implications for tranformative teaching." In J. A. Banks (ed.), *Multicultural education, tranformative knowledge, and action: Historical and contemporary perspectives*, pp. 64–87. New York: Teachers College Press.

Barell, J. 1995. *Teaching for thoughtfulness: Classroom strategies to enhance intellectual development*, 2nd ed. White Plains, NY: Longman.

Barnhardt, R. 1982. "Tuning-in: Athabaskan teachers and Athabaskan students." In R. Barnhardt (ed.), *Cross-cultural issues in Alaskan Education*, pp. 144–64. Fairbanks, AK: Center for Cross-Cultural Studies, University of Alaska.

Bartolomé, L. 1994. "Beyond the methods fetish: Toward a humanizing pedagogy." *Harvard Educational Review* 64, no. 2: 173–94.

Barton, P. 1997. *Toward inequality: Disturbing trends in higher education*. Princeton, NJ: Educational Testing Service.

Bass de Martinez, B. 1988. "Political and reform agendas impact on the supply of black teachers." *Journal of Teacher Education* 39, no. 1: 10–13.

Bell, L. A., and P. Griffin. 1997. "Designing social justice education courses." In M. Adams, L. A. Bell, and P. Griffin (eds.), *Teaching for diversity and social justice: A sourcebook*, pp. 44–58. New York: Routledge.

Bell, L. A., S. Washington, G. Weinstein, and B. Love. 1997. "Knowing ourselves as instructors." In M. Adams, L. A. Bell, and P. Griffin (eds.), *Teaching for diversity and social justice: A sourcebook*, pp. 299–310. New York: Routledge.

Bennett, C. I. 1995. "Preparing teachers for cultural diversity and national standards of academic excellence." *Journal of Teacher Education* 46, no. 4: 259–65.

Bereiter, C., and S. Engelmann. 1966. *Teaching disadvantaged children in preschool*. Englewood Cliffs, NJ: Prentice-Hall.

Berger, P. L., and T. Luckmann. 1967. *The social construction of reality: A treatise on the sociology of knowledge*. New York: Doubleday.

Beyer, L. E. 1991. "Teacher education, reflective inquiry and moral action." In B. R. Tabachnick and K. Zeichner (eds.), *Issues and practices in inquiry oriented teacher education*, pp. 113–29. Bristol, PA: Falmer.

————. 1996. "Introduction: The meanings of critical teacher education." In L. E. Beyer (ed.), *Creating democratic classrooms: The struggle to integrate theory and practice*, pp. 1–26. New York: Teachers College Press.

Blackwell, J. E. 1988. "Faculty issues: The impact on minorities." *The Review of Higher Education* 11, no. 4: 417–34.

————. 1989. "Mentoring: An action strategy for increasing minority faculty." *Academe* 75, no. 5: 8–14.

Bondy, E., S. Schmitz, and M. Johnson. 1993. "The impact of coursework and fieldwork on student teachers' reported beliefs about teaching poor and minority students." *Action in Teacher Education* 15, no. 2: 55–62.

Bourdieu, P. 1986. "The forms of capital." In J. G. Richardson (ed.), *Handbook of theory and research for the sociology of education*, pp. 241–58. New York: Greenwood.

Bowles, S., and H. Gintis. 1976. *Schooling in capitalist America*. New York: Basic Books.

Boyer, E. 1990. *Scholarship reconsidered: Priorities of the professoriate*. Princeton, NJ: Carnegie Commission for the Advancement of Teaching.

Boyle-Baise, M. 1998. "Community service learning for multicultural education: An exploratory study with preservice teachers." *Equity and Excellence in Education* 31, no. 2: 52–60.

Brawer, A. 1990. "Faculty development: The literature. An ERIC review." *Community College Review* 18, no. 1: 50–56.

Bringle, R. G., and J. A. Hatcher. 1996. "Implementing service learning in higher education." *Journal of Higher Education* 67: 221–39.

Brinson, J., and J. Kottler. 1993. "Cross-cultural mentoring in counselor education: A strategy for retaining minority faculty." *Counselor Education and Supervision* 32, no. 4: 241–53.

Britton, J., T. Burgess, N. Martin, A. McLeod, and H. Rosen. 1975. *The development of writing abilities (11–18)*. London: Macmillan.

Bronstein, P. 1993. "Challenges, rewards, and costs for feminist and ethnic minority scholars." *New Directions for Teaching* 53: 61–70.

Brooks, C. 1966. "Some approaches to teaching English as a second language." In S. W. Webster (ed.), *The disadvantaged learner*, pp. 515–23. San Francisco: Chandler.

Brown, A. L., and J. Campione. 1994. "Guided discovery in a community of learners." In K. McGilly (ed.), *Classroom lessons: Integrating cognitive theory and classroom practice*, pp. 229–70. Cambridge, MA: MIT Press.

Brown, A. L., and A. S. Palincsar. 1989. "Guided, cooperative learning and individual knowledge acquisition." In L. B. Resnick (ed.), *Knowing, learning, and instruction: Essays in honor of Robert Glaser*, pp. 393–451. Hillsdale, NJ: Lawrence Erlbaum.

Brown, C. E. 1992. "Restructuring for a new America." In M. E. Dilworth (ed.), *Diversity in teacher education: New expectations*, pp. 1–22. San Francisco: Jossey-Bass.

Brown, S. V. 1994. "The impasse on faculty diversity in higher education: A national agenda." In M. J. Justiz, R. Wilson, and L. G. Bjork (eds.), *Minorities in higher education*, pp. 314–33. Phoenix: Oryx.

Brown, S. V., B. C. Clewell, R. B. Ekstrom, M. E. Goertz, and D. E. Powers. 1994. *Research agenda for the Graduate Record Examinations Board minority graduate education project: An update*. Princeton, NJ: Educational Testing Service.

Bruner, J. 1966. *Toward a theory of instruction*. Cambridge, MA: Harvard University Press.

———. 1996. *The culture of education*. Cambridge, MA: Harvard University Press.

Burbules, N. C. 1993. *Dialogue in teaching: Theory and practice*. New York: Teachers College Press.

Burbules, N. C., and S. Rice. 1991. "Dialogue across differences: Continuing the conversation." *Harvard Educational Review* 61, no. 4: 393–416.

CBS News (Producer). 1983. A *60 Minutes* segment on Marva Collins [videotape]. New York: CBS News.

Cabello, B., and N. D. Burnstein. 1995. "Examining teachers' beliefs about teaching in culturally diverse classrooms." *Journal of Teacher Education* 46, no. 4: 285–93.

Calderón, M. E. 1991. "The benefits of cooperative learning for Hispanic students." *Texas Researcher* 2: 39–57.

Carger, C. L. 1996. *Of borders and dreams: A Mexican-American experience of urban education*. New York: Teachers College Press.

Carlson, D. 1997. *Making progress: Education and culture in new times*. New York: Teachers College Press.

Carter, K., and D. Anders. 1996. "Program pedagogy." In F. B. Murray (ed.), *The teacher educator's handbook: Building a knowledge base for the preparation of teachers*, pp. 557–92. San Francisco: Jossey Bass.

Carter, D. J., and E. M. O'Brien. 1993. "Employment and hiring patterns for faculty of color." *American Council on Education Research Briefs* 4, no. 6. Washington, DC: American Council on Education Research, Division of Policy Analysis and Research.

Cazden, C. B., V. P. John, and D. Hymes (eds.). 1972. *Functions of language in the classroom*. New York: Teachers College Press.

Ceci, S. J. 1993. "Some contextual factors in intellectual development." *Developmental Review* 13, no. 1: 1–32.

Chandler, A. 1997. *Access, inclusion, and equity: Imperatives for America's campuses*. Washington, DC: American Association of State Colleges and Universities.

Chang, H. N. 1990. *Newcomer programs: Innovative efforts to meet the educational challenges of immigrant students*. San Francisco: California Tomorrow.

Chapa, J., and R. R. Valencia. 1993. "Latino population growth, demographic characteristics, and educational stagnation: An examination of recent trends." *Hispanic Journal of Behavioral Sciences* 15, no. 2: 165–87.

Chavkin, N. F. (ed.). 1993. *Families and schools in a pluralistic society*. Albany: SUNY Press.

Chesler, M. A., and J. Crawfoot. 1997. "Racism in higher education II: Challenging racism and promoting multiculturalism in higher education organizations." *CRSO Working Paper Series #538*. Ann Arbor: University of Michigan, Center for Research on Social Organizations.

Cherniss, C. 1995. *Beyond burnout: Helping teachers, nurses, therapists, and lawyers recover from stress and disillusionment*. New York: Routledge.

Children's Defense Fund. 2000. *The state of America's children: Yearbook 2000*. Washington, DC: Author.

Christensen, K. 1991. "Teaching undergraduates about AIDS: An action-oriented approach." *Harvard Educational Review* 61, no. 3: 337–56.

Chronicle of Higher Education. 1999 (August). *1999–2000 Almanac Issue* 46, no. 1.

Clewell, B. C. 1995. "Reaching out to schools." In A. M. Villegas, B. C. Clewell, B. T. Anderson, M. E. Goertz, M. F. Joy, B. A. Bruschi, and J. J. Irvine, *Teaching for diversity: Models for expanding the supply of minority teachers*, pp. 24–47. Princeton, NJ: Educational Testing Service.

Clewell, B. C., M. E. Anderson, B. Bruschi, M. E. Goertz, M. F. Joy, and A. M. Villegas. 1995. *Increasing teacher diversity: Current practices of the Ford Foundation Minority Teacher Education Project*. Princeton, NJ: Educational Testing Service.

Clewell, B. C., and A. M. Villegas. 1999. "Creating a non-traditional pipeline for urban teachers: The Pathways to Teaching Careers model. *Journal of Negro Education* 68, no. 3: 306–17.

Cochran-Smith, M. 1991. "Learning to teach against the grain." *Harvard Educational Review* 61, no. 3: 279–310.

———. 1993. " Discussant's remarks: Symposium on race and racism in teaching and learning." Paper presented at the annual meeting of the American Educational Research Association, Atlanta.

———. 1995a. "Color blindness and basket making are not the answers: Confronting the dilemmas of race, culture, and language diversity in teacher education." *American Educational Research Journal* 32, no. 3: 493–522.

———. 1995b. "Uncertain allies: Understanding the boundaries between race and teaching." *Harvard Educational Review* 56, no. 1: 541–70.

———. 1997. "Knowledge, skills, and experiences for teaching culturally diverse learners: A perspective for practicing teachers." In J. J. Irvine (ed.), *Critical knowledge for diverse teachers and learners*, pp. 27–87. Washington, DC: American Association of Colleges for Teacher Education.

———. 1999. "Learning to teach for social justice." In G. Griffin (ed.), *The education of teachers. Ninety-eighth Yearbook of the National Society for the Study of Education*, pp. 114–44. Chicago: National Society for the Study of Education.

Code, L. 1991. *What can she know? Feminist theory and the construction of knowledge*. Ithaca, NY: Cornell University Press.

Cole, B. P. 1986. "The black educator: An endangered species." *Journal of Negro Education* 5, no. 3: 326–34.

Cole, M. 1996. *Cultural psychology: A once and future discipline*. Cambridge, MA: Harvard University Press.

Coleman, J. S., E. Q. Campbell, C. J. Hobson, J. McPartland, A. Mood, F. D. Weinfeld, and R. L. York. 1966. *Equality of educational opportunity*. Washington, DC: U.S. Government Printing Office.

Coley, R. J., and M. E. Goertz. 1991. *Characteristics of minority test takers.* Princeton, NJ: Educational Testing Service.

Collins, J. 1988. " Language and class in minority education." *Anthropology and Education Quarterly* 19, no. 4: 299–326.

Collinson, V., and T. F. Cook. 2000. "'I don't have enough time': Teachers' interpretations of time as a key to learning and school change." Paper presented at the Annual Meeting of the American Educational Research Association, New Orleans.

Comer, J. P. 1993. "The potential effects of community organizations on the future of our youth." In R. Takanishi (ed.), *Adolescence in the 1990s: Risk and opportunity*, pp. 203–6. New York: Teachers College Press.

Contreras, G., and W. L. Nicklas. 1993. "Attracting minority community/junior college students to teaching." *Action in Teacher Education* 15, no. 1: 1–7.

Cooper, C. C. 1986. "Strategies to assure certification and retention of black teachers." *Journal of Negro Education* 55, no. 1: 46–55.

Cooper, R., and B. L. Smith. 1990. "Lessons from the experience of the Evergreen State College: Achieving a diverse faculty." *AAHE Bulletin*, October: 10–12.

Council on Interracial Books for Children. 1997. "10 quick ways to analyze children's books for racism and sexism." *Rethinking our Classrooms: Teaching for equity and social justice*. Milwaukee: Rethinking Schools.

Crichlow, W., S. Goodwin, G. Shakes, and E. Swartz. 1990. "Multicultural ways of knowing: Implications for practice." *Journal of Education* 172, no. 2: 101–17.

Cross, B. E. 1993. "How do we prepare teachers to improve race relations?" *Educational Leadership* 50, no. 8: 64–65.

Cummins, J. 1991. "Interdependence of first- and second-language proficiency in bilingual children." In E. Bialystock (ed.), *Language processing in bilingual children*, pp. 70–89. Cambridge, England: Cambridge University Press.

Dandy, E. 1998. "Increasing the number of minority teachers: Tapping the paraprofessional pool." *Education and Urban Society* 31, no. 1: 89–103.

Danielson, C. 1996. *Enhancing professional practice: A framework for teaching.* Alexandria, VA: Association for Supervision and Curriculum Development.

Darling-Hammond, L. 1990. "Participants and teaching: Signs of a changing profession." In R. W. Houston, M. Haberman, and J. Sikula (eds.), *Handbook of research on teacher education*, pp. 268–92. New York: Macmillan.

———. 1994a. *Professional development schools: Schools for developing a profession.* New York: Teachers College Press.

———. 1994b. "Teacher quality and equality." In J. Goodlad and P. Keating (eds.), *Access to knowledge: The continuing agenda for our nation's schools*, pp. 237–58. New York: College Entrance Examination Board.

———. 1995. "Inequality and access to knowledge." In J. Banks (ed.), *Handbook of multicultural education*, pp. 465–83. New York: Macmillan.

———. 1996. "The right to learn and the advancement of teaching: Research, policy, and practice for democratic education." *Educational Researcher* 26, no. 6: 5–17.

Darling-Hammond, L., A. Wise, and S. K. Klein. 1995. *A license to teach: Building a profession for 21st century schools.* Boulder: Westview.

Davis, K. A. 1995. "Multicultural classrooms and cultural communities of teachers." *Teaching and Teacher Education* 11, no. 6: 553–63.

Delgado-Gaitan, C. 1990. *Literacy for empowerment: The role of parents in children's education*. New York: Falmer.

———. 1992. "School matters in the Mexican-American home: Socializing children to education." *American Educational Research Journal* 29, no. 3: 495–513.

Delpit, L. D. 1988. "The silenced dialogue: Power and pedagogy in educating other people's children." *Harvard Educational Review* 58, no. 3: 280–98.

———. 1995. *Other people's children: Cultural conflict in the classroom*. New York: The New Press.

———. 1998. "What should teachers do? Ebonics and culturally responsive instruction." In T. Perry and L. Delpit (eds.), *The real Ebonics debate: Power, language, and the education of African-American children*, pp. 17–26. Boston: Beacon.

Deutsch, M. 1963. "The disadvantaged child and the learning process." In A. H. Passow (ed.), *Education and depressed areas*, pp. 163–79. New York: Teachers College Press.

Dewey, J. 1938. *Experience and education*. New York: Macmillan.

———. 1991. *The child and the curriculum*. Chicago: University of Chicago Press.

Dews, C. L. B., and C. L. Law. 1995. *This fine place so far from home: Voices of academics from the working class*. Philadelphia: Temple University Press.

Dilworth, M. E. 1990. *Reading between the lines: Teachers and their racial/ethnic cultures*. (Teacher Education Monograph: No. 11). Washington, DC: ERIC Clearinghouse on Teacher Education and American Association of Colleges for Teacher Education.

Dittmer, A. 1999. "The daunting task of faculty development." In V. M. Rentel and A. Dittmer (eds.), *Themes and issues in faculty development: Case studies of innovative practice in teacher education*, pp. 25–46. Lanham, MD: University Press of America.

Doll, W. E. 1993. *A post-modern perspective on curriculum*. New York: Teachers College Press.

Donmoyer, R. 1996. "The concept of a knowledge base." In F. B. Murray (ed.), *The teacher educator's handbook: Building a knowledge base for the preparation of teachers*, pp. 92–119. Washington, DC:American Association of Colleges for Teacher Education.

Earley, P. 1987. "State and federal report: Recruiting minorities into teaching careers." *Teacher Education Quarterly* 14, no. 4: 107–9.

Educational Research Service. 1995. *Demographic factors in American education*. Arlington, VA: Author.

Educational Testing Service. 1991. *The state of inequality*. Princeton, NJ: Author.

———. 1994. *NAEP 1992 trends in academic progress*. Washington, DC: National Center for Education Statistics, Government Printing Office.

Education Commission of the States. 1990. "ECS cites problems with current minority teacher efforts." *Black Issues in Higher Education* 7, no. 8: 9.

Education Trust. 1996. *Education watch: The 1996 Education Trust state and national data book.* Washington, D. C.: Author.

Ekstrom, R. B., and A. M. Villegas. 1991. "Ability grouping in middle grades mathematics: Processes and consequences." *Research in Middle Level Education* 15, no. 1: 1–20.

Epstein, J. L. 1991. "Effects on student achievement of teachers' practices of parent involvement." In S. B. Silvern (ed.), *Advances in reading/language research: Vol. 5. Literacy through family, community, and school interaction,* pp. 261–76. Greenwich, CT: JAI.

Erickson, F. 1975. "Gatekeeping and the melting pot: Interaction in counseling encounters." *Harvard Educational Review* 45, no. 1: 44–70.

Farber, K. S. 1995. "Teaching about diversity through reflectivity: Sites of uncertainty, risk, and possibility." In R. J. Martin (ed.), *Practicing what we teach: Confronting diversity in teacher education,* pp. 49–63. Albany: SUNY Press.

Farber, K. S., and W. D. Armaline. 1994. "Examining cultural conflict in urban field experiences through the use of reflective thinking." *Teacher Education Quarterly* 21, no. 2: 59–76.

Feagin, J. R., H. Vera, and N. Imani. 1996. *The agony of education: Black students at white colleges and universities.* New York: Routledge.

Federal Interagency Forum on Child and Family Statistics. 1999. *America's children: Key national indicators of well-being.* Washington, DC: U.S. Government Printing Office.

Feiman-Nemser, S. 1990. "Teacher preparation: Structural and conceptual alternatives." In W. R. Houston, M. Haberman, and J. Sikula (eds.), *Handbook of research in teacher education,* pp. 212–33. New York: Macmillan.

Feiman-Nemser, S., and J. Remillard. 1996. "Perspectives on learning to teach." In F. Murray (ed.), *The teacher educator's handbook: Building a knowledge base for the preparation of teachers,* pp. 63–91. Washington, DC: American Association of Colleges for Teacher Education.

Feiman-Nemser, S., and S. Melnick. 1992. "Introducing teaching." In S. Feiman-Nemser and H. Featherstone (eds.), *Exploring teaching: Reinventing an introductory course,* pp. 1–17. New York: Teachers College Press.

Fernández-Balboa, J.-M. 1999a. "Critical pedagogy in action: Principles, purposes, and procedures." Paper presented at the annual meeting of the American Educational Research Association, Montreal, Canada.

———. 1999b. "Dialogical pedagogy, teacher education, and democracy." Paper presented at the annual conference of the American Association of Colleges for Teacher Education, Washington, DC.

Fernández-Balboa, J.-M., and J. P. Marshall. 1994. "Dialogical pedagogy in teacher education: Toward an education for democracy." *Journal of Teacher Education* 45, no. 3: 172–82.

Feuerstein, R. 1979. *The dynamic assessment of retarded performers—The learning potential assessment device: Theory, instruments and techniques.* Baltimore: University Park Press.

Finn, J. D., and C. M. Achilles. 1990. "Answers and questions about class size: A statewide experiment." *American Educational Research Journal* 27, no. 3: 557–77.

Firestone, W. A., and J. R. Pennell. 1993. "Teacher commitment, working conditions, and differential incentive policies." *Review of Educational Research* 63, no. 4: 489–525.

Firestone, W. A., S. Rosenblum, and A. Webb. 1990. *Student and teacher commitment: One key to school effectiveness: A study and recommendations.* Philadelphia: Research for Better Schools.

Fleischman, H. L., and P. J. Hopstock. 1993. *Descriptive study of services to limited English proficient students. Volume 1: Summary of findings and conclusions.* Arlington, VA: Development Associates, Inc.

Floden, R. F. 1991. "What teachers need to know about learning." In M. Kennedy (ed.), *Teaching academic subjects to diverse learners*, pp. 181–202. New York: Teachers College Press.

Fordham, S., and J. Ogbu. 1987. "Black students' school success: Coping with the burden of 'acting white.'" *Urban Review* 18, no. 3: 1–31.

Foster, M. 1989. "'It's cookin' now': A performance analysis of the speech event of a black teacher in an urban community college." *Language in Society* 18, no. 1: 1–29.

———. 1993. "Educating for competence in community and culture: Exploring the views of exemplary African American teachers." *Urban Education* 27, no. 4: 370–94.

Franklin, J. H. 1987. "The desperate need for black teachers." *Change* 19, no. 3: 44–45.

Freeman, R. B. 1999. *The new inequality: Creating solutions for poor America.* Boston: Beacon.

Freire, P. 1968. *Pedagogy of the oppressed.* Translated by M. B. Ramos. New York: Seabury Press.

———. 1985. *The politics of education: Culture, power, and liberation.* New York: Bergin and Garvey.

Freire, P., and D. Macedo. 1987. *Literacy: Reading the word and the world.* Granby, MA: Bergin and Garvey.

Frierson, H. T. 1990. "The situation of black education researchers: Continuation of a crisis." *Educational Researcher* 19, no. 2: 12–17.

Fullan, M. 1993. *Change forces: Probing the depths of educational reform.* London: Falmer.

———. 1999. *Change forces: The sequel.* London: Falmer.

Fuller, M. L. 1992. "Monocultural teachers and multicultural students: A demographic clash." *Teaching Education* 4, no. 2: 87–93.

Gándara, P. 1995. *Over the ivy walls: The educational mobility of low-income Chicanos.* Albany: SUNY Press.

García, E. E. 1988. "Attributes of effective schools for language minority students." *Education and Urban Society* 20, no. 4: 387–98.

———. 1995. "Educating Mexican American students: Past treatment and recent developments in theory, research, policy, and practice." In J. Banks and C. A. M. Banks (eds.), *Handbook of research on multicultural education*, pp. 372–87. New York: Macmillan.

———. 1999. *Student cultural diversity: Understanding and meeting the challenge.* Boston: Houghton Mifflin.

Gardner, H. 1983. *Frames of mind: The theory of multiple intelligences.* New York: Basic.

———. 1988. "Beyond IQ: Education and human development." *Harvard Educational Review* 57, no. 2: 187–93.

Gares, D., and E. A. Delco. 1991. "Ten steps to successful minority hiring and retention." *New Directions for Community Colleges* 74, Summer: 103–8.

Garibaldi, A. M. 1986. "Sustaining black educational progress: Challenges for the 1990s." *Journal of Negro Education* 55, no. 3: 386–96.

———. 1992. "Preparing teachers for culturally diverse classrooms." In M. E. Dilworth (ed.), *Diversity in teacher education: New expectations,* pp. 23–39. San Francisco: Jossey-Bass.

———. 1993. "Building cultural bridges: A bold proposal for teacher education." *Education and Urban Society* 25, no. 3: 285–99.

Garza, H. 1993. "Second class academics: Chicano/Latino faculty in U.S. universities." *New Directions for Teaching and Learning* 53: 33–41.

Gay, G. 1988. "Designing relevant curricula for diverse learners." *Education and Urban Society* 20, no. 4: 327–40.

Gibson, M. A. 1987. "The school performance of immigrant minorities: A comparative view." *Anthropology and Education Quarterly* 18, no. 4: 262–75.

Giroux, H. 1989. *Teachers as intellectuals.* Granby, MA: Bergin and Garvey.

Giroux, H., and P. McLaren. 1986. "Teacher education and the politics of engagement: The case for democratic schooling." *Harvard Educational Review* 56, no. 3: 213–38.

Glasersfeld, E. von. 1995. *Radical constructivism: A way of knowing and learning.* London: Falmer.

Gollnick, D. M., and P. C. Chinn. 1986. *Multicultural education in a pluralistic society,* 2nd ed. Columbus, OH: Merrill.

Gomez, M. L. 1994. "Teacher education reform and prospective teachers' perspectives on teaching other people's children." *Teaching and Teacher Education* 10, no. 3: 319–34.

———. 1996. "Prospective teachers' perspectives on teaching 'other people's children.'" In K. Zeichner, S. Melnick, and M. L. Gomez (eds.), *Currents of reform in preservice teacher education,* pp. 109–32. New York: Teachers College Press.

Gonzalez, N. 1995. "Processual approaches to multicultural education." *Journal of Applied Behavioral Science* 31, no. 2: 234–44.

Gonzalez, N., and C. Amanti. 1997. "Teaching anthropological methods to teachers: The transformation of knowledge." In C. Kottak, J. White, R. Furlow, and P. Rice (eds.), *The teaching of anthropology: Problems, issues, and decisions,* pp. 353–59. Mountain View, CA: Mayfield.

Goodlad, J. I. 1990a. "Better teachers for our nation's schools." *Phi Delta Kappan* 72: 185–94.

———. 1990b. *Teachers for our nation's schools.* San Francisco: Jossey-Bass.

———. 1994. *Educational renewal: Better teachers, better schools.* San Francisco: Jossey-Bass.

Goodwin, A. L. 1994. "Making the transition from self to other: What do preservice teachers really think about multicultural education? *Journal of Teacher Education* 45, no. 2: 119–31.

———. 1997a. "Historical and contemporary perspectives on multicultural teacher education." In J. King, E. Hollins, and W. Hayman (eds.), *Preparing teachers for cultural diversity*, pp. 5–22. New York: Teachers College Press.

———. 1997b. "Introduction." In A. L. Goodwin (ed.), *Assessment for equity and inclusion: Embracing all our children*, pp. xiii–xvi. New York: Routledge.

Goodwin, A. L., and M. B. Macdonald. 1997. "Educating the rainbow: Authentic assessment and authentic practice for diverse classrooms." In A. L. Goodwin (ed.), *Assessment for equity and inclusion: Embracing all our children*, pp. 229–40. New York: Routledge.

Gordon, J. A. 1994. "Preparing future teachers for diversity." *The Urban Review* 26, no. 1: 25–34.

Gould, S. J. 1994. "Curveball." *The New Yorker* (November 28), pp. 139–49.

Graham, P. A. 1987. "Black teachers: A drastically scarce resource." *Phi Delta Kappan* 68, no. 3: 598–605.

Granger, M. W. 1993. "A review of the literature on the status of women and minorities in higher education." *Journal of School Leadership* 3: 121–35.

Grant, C. A. 1991. "Culture and teaching: What do teachers need to know?" In M. Kennedy (ed.), *Teaching academic subjects to diverse learners*, pp. 237–56. New York: Teachers College Press.

———. 1994a. "Best practices in teacher preparation for urban schools: Lessons from the multicultural teacher education literature." *Action in Teacher Education* 16, no. 3: 1–18.

———. 1994b. "The multicultural preparation of U.S. teachers: Some hard truths." In G. K. Verma (ed.), *Inequality and teacher education: An international perspective*, pp. 41–57. London, England: Falmer.

———. 1997. "Critical knowledge, skills, and experiences for the instruction of culturally diverse students: A perspective for the preparation of preservice teachers." In J. J. Irvine (ed.), *Critical knowledge for diverse teachers and learners*, pp. 1–26. Washington, DC: American Association of Colleges for Teacher Education.

Grant, C. A., and W. G. Secada. 1990. "Preparing teachers for diversity." In R. W. Houston, M. Haberman, and J. Sikula (eds.), *Handbook of research on teacher education*, pp. 403–22. New York: Macmillan.

Greenbaum, P. E., and S. D. Greenbaum. 1983. "Cultural differences, nonverbal regulation and classroom interaction: Sociolinguistic interference in American Indian education." *Peabody Journal of Education* 61, no. 1: 16–33.

Greenwald, R., L. V. Hedges, and R. D. Laine. 1996. "The effect of school resources on student achievement." *Review of Educational Research* 66, no. 3: 361–96.

Griffin, P. 1997a. "Facilitating social justice education courses." In M. Adams, L. A. Bell, and P. Griffin (eds.), *Teaching for diversity and social justice: A sourcebook*, pp. 279–98. New York: Routledge.

———. 1997b. "Introductory module for the single issue courses." In M. Adams, L. A. Bell, and P. Griffin (eds.), *Teaching for diversity and social justice: A sourcebook*, pp. 61–81. New York: Routledge.

Griffin, P., and B. Harro. 1997. "Heterosexism curriculum design." In M. Adams, L. A. Bell, and P. Griffin (eds.), *Teaching for diversity and social justice: A sourcebook*, pp. 141–69. New York: Routledge.

Grognet, A., J. Nutta, and I. Canton. 1999. "The University of South Florida/Center for Applied Linguistics experiment in teaching pre-service teachers about English language learners via videoconferencing and e-mail." Paper presented at a U. S. Department of Education conference, Improving the Education of English Language Learners: Best Practices, July, Washington, DC.

Gross, J. S. 1993. "Teaching and teacher education: An institutional challenge and commitment." In M. J. Guy (ed.), *Teachers and teacher education: Essays on the National Education Goals*, pp. 61–73. Washington, DC: ERIC Clearinghouse on Teacher Education and American Association of Colleges for Teacher Education.

Grossman, P. 1992. "Teaching and learning with cases: Unanswered questions." In J. Shulman (ed.), *Case methods in teacher education*, pp. 227–39. New York: Teachers College Press.

Guillaume, A., C. Zuniga, and I. Yee. 1998. "What difference does preparation make? Educating preservice teachers for learner diversity." In M. E. Dilworth (ed.), *Being responsive to cultural differences*, pp. 143–59. Thousand Oaks, CA: Corwin Press.

Haberman, M. 1987. *The urban teacher selection interview*. Milwaukee: School of Education, University of Wisconsin-Milwaukee.

———. 1988. *Proposals for recruiting minority teachers: Promising practices and attractive detours*. University of Wisconsin-Milwaukee School of Education. (ERIC Document Reproduction Service No. ED 292 760.)

———. 1989. "More minority teachers." *Phi Delta Kappan* 70: 771–76.

———. 1991. "The rationale for training adults as teachers." In C. Sleeter (ed.), *Empowerment through multicultural education*, pp. 275–86. Albany: SUNY Press.

Haberman, M., and L. Post. 1998. "Teachers for multicultural schools: The power of selection." *Theory into Practice* 37, no. 2: 96–104.

Habermas, J. 1971. *Knowledge and human interest*. Boston: Beacon.

Haley, A. 1965. *The autobiography of Malcolm X*. New York: Ballantine.

Haney, W., C. Madaus, and X. Krietzer. 1987. "Charms talismanic: Testing teachers for improvement of American education." In E. Rothkopf (ed.), *Review of Research in Education 14*, pp. 169–238. Washington, DC: American Educational Research Association.

Hargreaves, A., and M. Fullan. 1998. *What's worth fighting for out there*. New York: Teachers College Press.

Harklau, L. 1994a. "ESL versus mainstream classes: Contrasting L2 learning environments." *TESOL Quarterly* 28, no. 2: 241–72.

———. 1994b. "'Jumping tracks': How language minority students negotiate evaluations of ability." *Anthropology and Education Quarterly* 25, no. 3: 347–63.

Haro, R. 1992. "Lessons from practice: What not to do." *Change* 24, no. 1: 54–58.

Harrington, H. L., and R. S. Hathaway. 1995. "Illuminating beliefs about diversity." *Journal of Teacher Education* 46, no. 4: 275–84.

Haselkorn, D., and E. Fideler. 1996. *Breaking the class ceiling: Paraeducator pathways to teaching.* Belmont, MA: Recruiting New Teachers.

Hawley, W. D. 1986. "Toward a comprehensive strategy for addressing the teacher shortage." *Phi Delta Kappan* 67: 712–18.

Hayden, J., and K. Cauthen (Producers). 1996. *Children in America's schools with Bill Moyers.* New York and Washington, DC: Public Broadcasting Service.

Heath, S. B. 1983a. "Questioning at home and at school: A comparative study." In G. Spindler (ed.), *Doing ethnography: Educational anthropology in action,* pp. 102–31. New York: Holt, Rinehart and Winston.

———. 1983b. *Ways with word: Language, life, and work in communities and classrooms.* London: Cambridge University Press.

Henze, R., and T. Lucas. 1993. "Shaping instruction to promote the success of language minority students: An analysis of four high school classes." *Peabody Journal of Education* 69, no. 1: 54–81.

Hernandez, J. S. 1995. "Teachers at-risk: Monolingual teachers and language minority children." Paper presented at the annual meeting of the American Educational Research Association, San Francisco.

Herrnstein, R. J. 1973. *IQ in the meritocracy.* Boston: Atlantic Little-Brown.

Herrnstein, R. J., and C. Murray. 1994. *The bell curve: Intelligence and class structure in American life.* New York: Free Press.

Hidalgo, F., and L. Huling-Austin. 1993. "Alternate teacher candidates: A rich source for Latino teachers in the future." In F. Hidalgo and L. Huling-Austin (ed.), *Reshaping teacher education in the Southwest-A forum: A response to the needs of Latino students and teachers,* pp. 13–34. Claremont, CA: Tomás Rivera Center.

Hill, P. J. 1991. "Multiculturalism: The crucial philosophical and organizational issues." *Change,* July/August: 38–47.

Hilliard, A. 1989. "Teachers and cultural styles in a pluralistic society." *NEA Today* 7: 65–69.

———. 1990. "Misunderstanding and testing intelligence." In J. Goodlad and P. Keating (eds.), *Access to knowledge: An agenda for the public schools,* pp. 145–57. New York: College Board.

Hollins, E. 1982. "The Marva Collins story revisited: Implications for regular classroom instruction." *Journal of Teacher Education* 33, no. 1: 37–40.

Holmes, N. (Producer and Director). n.d. *We all know why we're here.* [Film of Leslie Stein teaching second grade in Central Park East Elementary School]. Charlie/Pappa Productions.

The Holmes Group. 1990. *Tomorrow's schools: Principles for the design of professional development schools.* East Lansing, MI: Holmes Group.

Hood, S., and L. Parker. 1991. "Minority students informing the faculty: Implications for racial diversity and the future of teacher education." *Journal of Teacher Education* 45, no. 3: 164–71.

hooks, b. 1994. *Teaching to transgress: Education as the practice of freedom.* New York: Routledge.

Hoover-Dempsey, K. V., and H. M. Sandler. 1995. "Parental involvement in children's education: Why does it make a difference?" *Teachers College Record 95*, no. 3: 310–31.

———. 1997. "Why do parents become involved in their children's education?" *Review of Educational Research 67*, no. 1: 3–42.

Hopstock, P. J., and B. J. Bucaro. 1993. *A review and analysis of estimates of the LEP student population.* Arlington, VA: Development Associates, Inc.

Howard, G. R. 1999. *We can't teach what we don't know: White teachers, multiracial schools.* New York: Teachers College Press.

Howey, K. 1996. "Designing coherent and effective teacher education programs." In J. Sikula (ed.), *Handbook of research on teacher education,* 2nd ed., pp. 143–70. New York: Simon and Schuster Macmillan.

Huling-Austin, L., and E. Cuellar. 1991. "Defining an ethnically diverse teaching force." *Teacher Education and Practice 6*, no. 2: 9–12.

Humphreys, D. 1998. "Higher education, race and diversity: Views from the field." Washington, DC: Association of American Colleges and Universities. (ERIC Document Reproduction Service No. 423 778).

Humphreys, D., and C. G. Schneider. 1997. "Curricular change gains momentum: New requirements focus on diversity and social responsibility." *Diversity Digest,* Winter: 2–4.

Hunt, J. 1964. "The psychological basis for using pre-school environment as an antidote for cultural deprivation." *Merrill Palmer Quarterly 10:* 209–48.

Irvine, J. J. 1988. "An analysis of the problem of the disappearing black educator." *Elementary School Journal 88*, no. 5: 503–14.

———. 1990a. "Beyond role models: The influence of black teachers on black students' achievement." Paper presented at Educational Testing Service, Princeton, NJ.

———. 1990b. *Black students and school failure.* New York: Greenwood Press.

———. 1992. "Making teacher education culturally responsive." In M. E. Dilworth (ed.), *Diversity in teacher education: New expectations,* pp. 79–92. San Francisco: Jossey-Bass.

Jackson, S. 1995. "Autobiography: Pivot points for engaging lives in multicultural contexts." In J. M. Larkin and C. E. Sleeter (eds.), *Developing multicultural teacher education curricula,* pp. 31–44. Albany: SUNY Press.

Jacob, E., and C. Jordan. 1987. "Explaining the school performance of minority students" [Special issue]. *Anthropology and Education Quarterly 18*, no 4.

Jacobowitz, T. 1994. "Admission to teacher education programs: Goodlad's sixth postulate." *Journal of Teacher Education 45*, no. 1: 46–52.

Jacobowitz, T., and N. Michelli. 1999. "Montclair State University and the New Jersey Network for Educational Renewal." In W. F. Smith and G. D. Fenstermacher (eds.), *Leadership for educational renewal: Developing a cadre of leaders,* pp. 233–51. San Francisco: Jossey-Bass.

Jensen, A. R. 1969. "How much can we boost I.Q. and scholastic achievement?" *Harvard Educational Review 39*, no. 1: 1–123.

Joy, M. F., and B. A. Bruschi. 1995. "Bringing teacher assistants into teacher education programs." In A. M. Villegas, B. C. Clewell, B. T. Anderson, M.

E. Goertz, M. F. Joy, B. A. Bruschi, and J. J. Irvine, *Teaching for diversity: Models for expanding the supply of minority teachers*, pp. 72–100. Princeton, NJ: Educational Testing Service.

Kagan, D. M. 1992. "Implications of research on teacher belief." *Educational Psychologist* 27: 65–90.

Kantor, H., and B. Brenzel. 1992. "Urban education and the 'truly disadvantaged': The historical roots of the contemporary crisis." *Teachers College Record* 94, no. 2: 278–314.

Kennedy, M. M. 1991. "Merging subjects and students into teaching knowledge." In M. Kennedy (ed.), *Teaching academic subjects to diverse learners*, pp. 273–84. New York: Teachers College Press.

———. 1998. *Learning to teach writing: Does teacher education make a difference?* New York: Teachers College Press.

Kilborn, P. T. 1996. "The welfare overhaul: A special report." *New York Times* (November 30), pp. 1, 10.

King, J. 1991. "Dysconscious racism: Ideology, identity, and the miseducation of teachers." *The Journal of Negro Education* 60, no. 2: 133–46.

King, S. H. 1993. "The limited presence of African-American teachers." *Review of Educational Research* 63, no. 2: 115–49.

Kingston, M. H. 1976. *The woman warrior: Memoirs of a girlhood*. New York: Knopf.

Kirby, S. N., and L. Hudson. 1993. "Black teachers in Indiana: A potential shortage?" *Educational Evaluation and Policy Analysis* 15, no. 2: 181–94.

Kleinfeld, J. S. 1989. *Teaching taboo topics: The special virtues of the case method*. Fairbanks: College of Rural Alaska.

———. 1992. "Learning to think like a teacher: The study of cases." In J. Shulman (ed.), *Case methods in teacher education*, pp. 33–49. New York: Teachers College Press.

———. 1998. "The use of case studies in preparing teachers for cultural diversity." *Theory into Practice* 37, no. 2: 140–47.

Koppelman, K., and R. Richardson. 1995. "What's in it for me? Persuading nonminority teacher education students to become advocates for multicultural education." In R. J. Martin (ed.), *Practicing what we teach: Confronting diversity in teacher education*, pp. 145–59. Albany: SUNY Press.

Korthagen, F. A., and J. Kessels. 1999. "Linking theory and practice: Changing the pedagogy of teacher education." *Educational Researcher* 28, no. 4: 4–17.

Kozol, J. 1991. *Savage inequalities: Children in America's schools*. New York: Crown.

Kraemer, B. A. 1997. "The academic and social integration of Hispanic students into college." *Review of Higher Education* 20, no. 2: 163–79.

Kuhn, T. 1970. *The structure of scientific revolutions*, 2nd ed. Chicago: University of Chicago Press.

Labaree, D. F. 1997. "Public goods, private goods: The American struggle over educational goals." *American Educational Research Journal* 34, no. 1: 39–81.

Labov, W. 1973. "The logic of non-standard Negro English." In N. Keddie (ed.), *The myth of cultural deprivation*, pp. 21–66. Harmondsworth, England: Penguin.

Ladson-Billings, G. 1990. "Culturally relevant teaching." *The College Board Review* 155: 20–25.

———. 1991. "When difference means disaster: Reflections on a teacher education strategy for countering student resistance to diversity." Paper presented at the annual meeting of the American Educational Research Association, Chicago.

———. 1992. "Liberatory consequences of literacy: A case of culturally relevant instruction for African American students." *Journal of Negro Education* 61, no. 3: 378–91.

———. 1994. *The dreamkeepers: Successful teachers of African American children.* San Francisco: Jossey-Bass.

———. 1995. "Multicultural teacher education: Research, practice, and policy." In J. A. Banks and C. A. M. Banks (eds.), *Handbook of research on multicultural education*, pp. 747–59. New York: Macmillan.

Ladson-Billings, G., and A. Henry. 1990. "Blurring the borders: Voices of African liberatory pedagogy in the United States and Canada." *Journal of Education* 172, no. 2: 72–88.

Lang, M. P. 1995. "Preparing teachers for multicultural science integration." In J. M. Larkin and C. E. Sleeter (eds.), *Developing multicultural teacher education curricula*, pp. 171–85. Albany: SUNY Press.

Larke, P. J. 1990. "Cultural diversity awareness inventory: Assessing the sensitivity of preservice teachers." *Action in Teacher Education* 12, no. 3: 23–30.

Larkin, J. M. 1995. "Curriculum themes and issues in multicultural teacher education programs." In J. M. Larkin and C. E. Sleeter (eds.), *Developing multicultural teacher education curricula*, pp. 1–16. Albany: SUNY Press.

Larkin, J. M., and C. E. Sleeter. 1995. "Introduction." In J. M. Larkin and C. E. Sleeter (eds.), *Developing multicultural teacher education curricula*, pp. vii–xi. Albany: SUNY Press.

Lave, J., and E. Wegner. 1991. *Situated learning: Legitimate peripheral participation.* Cambridge, England: Cambridge University Press.

Lee, O., and S. H. Fradd. 1998. "Science for all, including students from non-English-language backgrounds." *Educational Researcher* 27, no. 4: 12–21.

Levine, M. 1996. "Educating teachers for restructured schools." In F. B. Murray (ed.), *The teacher educator's handbook: Building a knowledge base for the preparation of teachers*, pp. 620–47. San Francisco: Jossey-Bass.

Lightfoot, S. L. 1994. *I've known rivers: Lives of loss and liberation.* Reading, MA: Addison-Wesley.

Linthicum. D. S. 1989. *The dry pipeline: Increasing the flow of minority faculty.* Report prepared for the National Council of State Directors of Community/Junior Colleges. (ERIC Document Reproduction Service No. 307 950).

Lipka, J. 1991. "Toward a culturally based pedagogy: A case study of one Yup'ik Eskimo teacher." *Anthropology and Education Quarterly* 22, no. 2: 203–23.

Lipman, M. 1997. "Thinking in community." *Inquiry: Critical Thinking Across the Disciplines* 16, no. 4: 6–21.

Liston, D. P., and K. M. Zeichner. 1991. *Teacher education and the social conditions of school.* New York: Routledge.

Loo, C. M., and G. Rolison. 1986. "Alienation of ethnic minority students at a predominantly white university." *Journal of Higher Education* 57: 58–77.

Lortie, D. C. 1975. *Schoolteacher: A sociological study.* Chicago: University of Chicago Press.

Lucas, T. 1991. "Individual variation in students' engagement in classroom personal journal writing." *The CATESOL Journal* 4, no. 1: 7–39.

———. 1992. "Diversity among individuals: Eight students making sense of classroom journal writing." In D. Murray (ed.), *Diversity as resource: Redefining cultural literacy* pp. 202–32. Washington, DC: TESOL.

———. 1997. *Into, through, and beyond secondary school: Critical transitions for immigrant youths.* Washington, DC and McHenry, IL: Center for Applied Linguistics and Delta Systems.

———. 2000, June. *Teaching and Learning in Community: Montclair State University America Reads and Service Learning Programs, 1999–2000. Year Three Final Report.* Upper Montclair, NJ: Montclair State University.

Lucas, T., and A. M. Villegas. 1996. "Changing conceptions of educational excellence: Dynamics of reform in a diverse suburban school district." Paper presented at the annual meeting of the American Anthropological Association, November, San Francisco.

Lucas, T., R. Henze, and R. Donato. 1990. "Promoting the success of Latino language minority students: An exploratory study of six high schools." *Harvard Educational Review* 60, no. 3: 315–40.

Lucas, T., and S. Wagner. 2000. "Facilitating secondary English language learners' transition into the mainstream." *TESOL Journal* 8, no. 4: 6–13.

Mannheim, K. 1936. *Ideology and utopia.* New York/London: Hartcourt Brace Jovanovich.

Martin, R. 1995a. "Deconstructing myth, reconstructing reality: Transcending the crisis in teacher education." In R. J. Martin (ed.), *Practicing what we teach: Confronting diversity in teacher education*, pp. 65–77. Albany: SUNY Press.

———. 1995b. "Introduction." In R. Martin (ed.), *Practicing what we preach: Confronting diversity in teacher education*, pp. xi–xxii. Albany: SUNY Press.

Matcznski, T. J., and E. A. Joseph. 1989. "Minority teacher shortage: A proposal to counter the lack of activity." *Action in Teacher Education* 11, no. 2: 42–46.

McArthur, E. 1993. *Language schooling in the United States, a changing picture: 1979 and 1989.* Washington, DC: National Center for Educational Statistics.

McCullun, P. 1989. "Turn-allocation in lessons with North American and Puerto Rican students." *Anthropology and Education Quarterly* 20, no. 2: 133–56.

McDermott, R. P. 1977. "Social relations as contexts for learning in school." *Harvard Educational Review* 47, no. 2: 198–213.

McDiarmid, G. W. 1990a. "Challenging prospective teachers' beliefs during early field experience: A quixotic undertaking." *Journal of Teacher Education* 41, no. 3: 12–20.

———. 1990b. *What to do about differences? A study of multicultural education for teacher trainees in the Los Angeles Unified School District.* East Lansing, MI: National Center for Research on Teacher Learning.

————. 1991. "What teachers need to know about cultural diversity: Restoring subject matter to the picture." In M. Kennedy (ed.), *Teaching academic subjects to diverse learners*, pp. 257–69. New York: Teachers College Press.

————. 1992. "Tilting the webs of belief: Field experiences as a means of breaking with experience." In S. Feiman-Nemser and H. Featherstone (eds.), *Exploring teaching: Reinventing an introductory course*, pp. 34–58. New York: Teachers College Press.

McDiarmid, G. W., and J. Price. 1990. *Prospective teachers' views of diverse learners: A study of the participants in the ABCD Project*. East Lansing, MI: National Center for Research on Teacher Learning.

McGraw-Hill Primis. 1995. "Molly Clark." *Silverman-Welty-Lyon: Case studies for teacher problem solving*. Princeton, NJ: McGraw-Hill.

Mehan, H. 1979. *Learning lessons*. Cambridge, MA: Harvard University Press.

————. 1994. "The role of discourse in learning, schooling, and reform." In B. McLeod (ed.), *Language and learning: Educating linguistically diverse students*, pp. 71–96. Albany: SUNY Press.

Mehan, H. A., D. Lintz, D. Okamoto, and J. S. Wills. 1995. "Ethnographic studies of multicultural education in classrooms and schools." In J. Banks and C. McGee Banks (eds.), *Handbook of research on multicultural education*, pp. 129–44. New York: McMillan.

Meier, K. J., J. Stewart, and R. E. England. 1989. *Race, class and education: The politics of second-generation discrimination*. Madison: University of Wisconsin Press.

Melnick, S. L., and K. M. Zeichner. 1998. "Teacher education's responsibility to address diversity issues: Enhancing institutional capacity." *Theory into Practice* 37, no. 2: 88–95.

Mercer, W. A., and M. M. Mercer. 1986. "Standardized testing: Its impact on blacks in Florida's educational system." *Urban Educator* 8, no. 1: 105–13.

Merseth, K. K. 1991. *The case for cases in teacher education*. Washington, DC: American Association for Higher Education and American Association of Colleges for Teacher Education.

Michaels, S. 1981. "Sharing time: Children's narrative styles and differential access to literacy." *Language in Society* 10, no. 3: 423–42.

Mickelson, R. A., and M. L. Oliver. 1991. "Making the short list: Black candidates and the faculty recruitment process." In P. G. Altbach and K. Lomotey (eds.), *The racial crisis in American higher education*, pp. 149–66. Albany: SUNY Press.

Middleton, E. J., E. J. Mason, W. E. Stilwell, and W. C. Parker. 1988. "A model for recruitment and retention of minority students in teacher preparation programs." *Journal of Teacher Education* 39, no. 1: 10–13.

Milk, R., C. Mercado, and A. Sapiens. 1992. *Re-thinking the education of teachers of language minority children: Developing reflective teachers for changing schools*. Washington, DC: National Clearinghouse for Bilingual Education.

Miller, L. S. 1995. *An American imperative: Accelerating minority achievement*. New Haven, CT: Yale University Press.

Mills, R. J., and C. W. Buckley. 1992. "Accommodating the minority teacher candidate: Non-black students in predominantly black colleges." In M. E. Dilworth (ed.), *Diversity in teacher education: New expectations*, pp. 134–59. San Francisco: Jossey-Bass.

Mohatt, G., and F. Erickson. 1981. "Cultural differences in teaching styles in an Odawa school: A sociolinguistic approach." In H. Trueba, G. Guthrie, and K. Au (eds.), *Culture and the bilingual classroom*, pp. 105–19. Rowley, MA: Newbury House.

Moll, L. C. 1988. "Some key issues in teaching Latino students." *Language Arts* 65, no. 5: 465–72.

———. 1992. "Bilingual classroom and community analysis: Some recent trends." *Educational Researcher* 21, no. 2: 20–24.

Moll, L., C. Amanti, D. Neff, and N. Gonzalez. 1992. "Funds of knowledge for teaching: Using a qualitative approach to connect homes and classroom." *Theory into Practice* 31, no. 2: 132–41.

Moll, L. C., and N. Gonzalez. 1997. "Teachers as social scientists: Learning about culture from household research." In P. M. Hall (ed.), *Race, ethnicity, and multiculturalism: Policy and Practice*, pp. 89–114. New York: Garland.

Moll, L. C., and R. Diaz. 1987. "Teaching writing as communication: The use of ethnographic findings in classroom practice." In D. Bloome (ed.), *Literacy and schooling*, pp. 55–65. Norwood, NJ: Ablex.

Montecinos, C. 1995. "Multicultural teacher education for a culturally diverse teaching force." In R. J. Martin (ed.), *Practicing what we teach: Confronting diversity in teacher education*, pp. 97–116. Albany: SUNY Press.

Morine-Dershimer, G., and K. Leighfield. 1995. "Student teaching and field experiences." In L. W. Anderson (ed.), *International encyclopedia of teaching and teacher education*, pp. 588–93. Tarrytown, NY: Elsevier Science.

Moses, Y. 1990. "The challenge of diversity: Anthropological perspectives on university culture." *Education and Urban Society* 22, no. 4: 402–12.

Murray, D. E. 1992. "Unlimited resources: Tapping into learners' language, culture, and thought." In D. E. Murray (ed.), *Diversity as resource: Redefining cultural literacy*, pp. 259–74. Washington, DC: TESOL.

Murray, F. B. 1995. "Beyond natural teaching: The case for professional education." In F. B. Murray (ed.), *The teacher educator's handbook: Building a knowledge base for the preparation of teachers*, pp. 3–13. San Francisco: Jossey-Bass.

Murray, F. B., and A. Porter. 1996. "Pathway from the liberal arts curriculum to lessons in the schools." In F. B. Murray (ed.), *The teacher educator's handbook: Building a knowledge base for the preparation of teachers*, pp. 155–78. San Francisco: Jossey-Bass.

Murrell, P. C. 1991. "Cultural politics in teacher education: What is missing in the preparation of minority teachers?" In M. Foster (ed.), *Readings on equal education: Qualitative investigations into schools and schooling*, pp. 205–25. New York: AMS Press.

National Association of Independent Colleges and Universities. 1991. *Pluralism in the professoriate: Strategies for developing faculty diversity*. Washington, DC: Author.

National Center for Education Statistics. 1993a. *America's teachers: Profile of a profession.* Washington, DC: U. S. Government Printing Office.

———. 1993b. *Schools and staffing in the U.S.: A statistical profile 1990–91.* Washington, DC: U. S. Government Printing Office.

———. 1994. *Digest of educational statistics.* Washington, DC: U. S. Government Printing Office.

———. 1996a. *Digest of educational statistics.* Washington, DC: U. S. Government Printing Office.

———. 1996b. "Supplemental table 9–2: Among 1989–90 beginning students at community colleges, percentage distribution according to transfer status, by selected characteristics." *The condition of education 1996.* <www.nces.ed.gov/pubs/ce/c9609d02.html>.

———. 1996c. "Supplemental table 11–1: Percentage of college graduates completing a bachelor's degree within various years of starting college, by selected characteristics: 1993." *The condition of education 1996.* <www.nces.ed.gov/pubs/ce/c9611d01.html>.

———. 1997a. Common core of data. "Public Elementary/Secondary School Universe" survey, 1993–94, and "Public Elementary/ Secondary Education Agency Universe" survey, 1993–94. <www.ed.gov/NCES/pubs/96212bt.html>.

———. 1997b. *Digest of educational statistics.* Washington, DC: U. S. Government Printing Office.

———. 1997c. *NAEP 1996 mathematics report card for the nation and the states.* Washington, DC: U. S. Government Printing Office.

———. 1997d. *NAEP 1996 science report card for the nation and the states.* Washington, DC: U. S. Government Printing Office.

———. 1997e. *Projections of education statistics to 2007 (NCES 97–382).* Washington, DC: U. S. Government Printing Office.

———. 1998. *Data file: 1996–97 common core of data public elementary and secondary school universe.* Washington, DC: U. S. Government Printing Office.

———. 1999a. *Digest of educational statistics.* Washington, DC: U. S. Government Printing Office.

———. 1999b. "Dropout rates in the United States, 1996: Table 13—High school completion rates and method of completion of 18- through 25-year-olds not currently enrolled in high school or below, by race-ethnicity: October 1998 through October 1999." <www.nces.ed.gov/pubs98/dropout/ch06tl3a.html>.

———. 1999c. *NAEP 1998 reading report card for the nation.* Washington, DC: U. S. Government Printing Office.

———. 1999d. *Predicting the need for newly hired teachers in the United States to 2008–09.* Washington, DC: U. S. Government Printing Office.

———. 2000. *The condition of education, 2000.* Washington, DC: U. S. Government Printing Office.

National Center for Restructuring Education, Schools, and Teaching. 1995–96. *Images of practice: A series of professional development videotapes.* New York: Author.

National Clearinghouse for Bilingual Education. 1998. *Summary report of the survey of the states' limited English proficient students and available educational programs and services 1995–96.* Washington, DC: Author.

National Coalition of Advocates for Students. 1991. *New voices: Immigrant students in U. S. public schools.* Boston: Author.

National Coalition of Educational Equity Advocates (NCEEA). 1994. *Educate America: A call for equity in school reform.* Chevy Chase, MD: The Mid-Atlantic Equity Consortium.

National Commission on Teaching and America's Future. 1996. *What matters most: Teaching for America's future.* New York: Author.

National Education Goals Panel. 1994. *Data volume for the National Education Goals Report: Volume 1—National data.* Washington, DC: U. S. Government Printing Office.

National Latino Communications Center. 1997. *Chicano!* Los Angeles: Author. Videocassette.

Natriello, G., and K. Zumwalt. 1993. "New freedom for urban schools? The contribution of the provisional teacher program in New Jersey." *Education and Urban Society* 26, no. 1: 49–62.

Natriello, G., E. L. McDill, and A. M. Pallas. 1990. *Schooling disadvantaged children: Racing against catastrophe.* New York: Teachers College Press.

Nelson-Barber, S. S., and J. Mitchell. 1992. "Restructuring for diversity: Five regional portraits." In M. E. Dilworth (ed.), *Diversity in teacher education: New expectations,* pp. 229–62. San Francisco: Jossey-Bass.

Nelson-Le Gall, S. 1994. "Addressing the continuities and discontinuities between family and school for ethnic minority children." In F. L. Rivera-Batiz (ed.), *Reinventing urban education: Multiculturalism and the social context of schooling,* pp. 183–207. New York: IUME Press.

Nichols, P. C. 1992. "Language in the attic: Claiming our linguistic heritage." In D. E. Murray (ed.), *Diversity as resource: Redefining cultural literacy,* pp. 275–93. Washington, DC: TESOL.

Nieto, S. 1996. *Affirming diversity: The sociopolitical context of education.* White Plains, NY: Longman.

———. 1999. *The light in their eyes: Creating multicultural learning communities.* New York: Teachers College Press.

Nieto, S., and C. Rolón. 1997. "Preparation and professional development of teachers: A perspective from two Latinas." In. J. J. Irvine (ed.), *Critical knowledge for diverse teachers and learners,* pp. 89–123. Washington, DC: American Association of Colleges for Teacher Education.

Noel, J. R. 1995. "Multicultural teacher education: From awareness through emotions to action." *Journal of Teacher Education* 46, no. 4: 267–73.

Noordhoff, K., and J. Kleinfield. 1993. "Preparing teachers for multicultural classrooms." *Teaching and Teacher Education* 9, no. 1: 27–39.

Oakes, J. 1985. *Keeping track: How schools structure inequality.* New Haven, CT: Yale University Press.

———. 1990. *Multiplying inequalities: The effects of race, social class, and tracking on opportunities to learn mathematics and science.* Santa Monica, CA: RAND Corporation.

Oakes, J., and M. Lipton. 1994. "Tracking and ability grouping: A structural barrier to access and achievement." In J. Goodlad and P. Keating (eds.), *Access to knowledge: The continuing agenda for our nation's schools*, pp. 187–204. New York: College Board.

———. 1999. *Teaching to change the world*. Boston: McGraw-Hill.

Oakes, J., K. Welner, S. Yonezawn, and R. Allen. 1998. "Norms and politics of equity-minded change." In A. Hargreaves, A. Lieberman, M. Fullan, and D. Hopkins (eds.), *International handbook of educational change*, pp. 952–73. Dondrecht: Kluwer Academic Publishers.

Ogbu, J. 1995a. "Cultural problems in minority education: Their interpretations and consequences. Part one: Theoretical background." *The Urban Review* 27, no. 3: 189–205.

———. 1995b. "Cultural problems in minority education: Their interpretations and consequences. Part two: Case studies." *The Urban Review* 27, no. 4: 271–95.

Olmedo, I. 1997. "Challenging old assumptions: Preparing teachers for inner city schools." *Teaching and Teacher Education* 13, no. 3: 245–58.

Olsen, L., and N. A. Mullen. 1990. *Embracing diversity: Teachers' voices from California classrooms*. San Francisco: California Tomorrow.

Orfield, G. 1983. *Public school desegregation in the United States, 1968–1990*. Washington, DC: Joint Center for Policy Studies.

Ortiz, A. A., and E. Maldonado-Colon. 1986. "Reducing inappropriate referrals of language minority students in special education." In A. C. Willig and H. F. Greenberg (eds.), *Bilingualism and learning disabilities*, pp. 37–50. New York: American Library.

Osajima, K. 1995. "Creating classroom environments for change." In R. J. Martin (ed.), *Practicing what we teach: Confronting diversity in teacher education*, pp. 131–43. Albany: SUNY Press.

Padilla, A. M. 1994. "Ethnic minority scholars, research, and mentoring: Current and future issues." *Educational Researcher* 23, no. 4: 24–27.

Paine, L. 1989. *Orientations toward diversity: What do prospective teachers bring?* East Lansing, MI: National Center for Research on Teacher Education.

Pajares, F. 1993. "Preservice teachers' beliefs: A focus for teacher education." *Action in Teacher Education* 15, no. 2: 45–54.

Paley, V. 1981. *Wally's stories*. Cambridge, MA: Harvard University Press.

Pang, V. O., and V. A. Sablan. 1998. "Teacher efficacy: How do teachers feel about their abilities to teach African American students?" In M. E. Dilworth (ed.), *Being responsive to cultural differences*, pp. 39–58. Thousand Oaks, CA: Corwin.

Parker, M. B., and L. J. Tiezzi. 1992. "Exploring teaching with cases." In S. Feiman-Nemser and H. Featherstone (eds.), *Exploring teaching: Reinventing an introductory course*, pp. 86–105. New York: Teachers College Press.

Patterson, R. S., N. M. Michelli, and A. Pacheco. 1999. *Centers of pedagogy: New structures for educational renewal*. San Francisco: Jossey-Bass.

Payne, R. S. 1994. "The relationship between teachers' beliefs and sense of efficacy and their significance to urban LSES minority students." *Journal of Negro Education* 63, no. 3: 181–96.

Peters, W. 1987. *A class divided: Then and now*, expanded edition. New Haven, CT: Yale University Press.

Philips, S. 1972. "Participant structures and communicative competence: Warm Springs children in community and classroom." In C. Cazden, V. John, and D. Hymes (eds.), *Functions of language in the classroom*, pp. 370–94. New York: Teachers College Press.

———. 1983. *The invisible culture: Communication in classroom and community on the Warm Springs Indian Reservation*. New York: Longman.

Phillips, D. C. 1995. "The good, the bad, and the ugly: The many faces of constructivism." *Educational Researcher* 24, no. 7: 5–12.

Phillips, R. G. 1991. "Model programs in minority access." *New Directions for Community Colleges* 74, Summer: 23–30.

Piaget, J. 1977. *The development of thought: Equilibrium of cognitive structures*. Translated by A. Rosin. New York: Viking.

Piestrup, A. M. 1973. *Black dialect interference and accommodation of reading instruction in first grade*. (Monograph No. 4). Berkeley: Language Behavior Research Laboratory.

Post, L. M., and H. Woessner. 1987. "Developing a recruitment and retention support system for minority students in teacher education." *Journal of Negro Education* 56, no. 2: 203–11.

Powell, R. R. 1996. "The music is why I teach: Intuitive strategies of successful teachers in culturally diverse learning environments." *Teacher and Teacher Education* 12, no. 1: 49–61.

Price, J., and L. Valli. 1998. "Institutional support for diversity in preservice teacher education." *Theory into Practice* 37, No. 2: 114–20.

Pugach, M., and S. Pasch. 1994. "The challenge of creating urban professional development schools." In R. Yinger and K. Borman (eds.), *Restructuring education: Issues and strategies for schools, communities and universities*, pp. 129–56. Norwood, NJ: Ablex.

Ramirez, M., and A. Casteñeda. 1974. *Cultural democracy, by cognitive development, and education*. New York: Academic Press.

Reed, D. F. 1993. "Multicultural education for prospective teachers." *Action in Teacher Education* 15, no. 3: 27–34.

Reed, D. F., and D. J. Simon. 1991. "Preparing teachers for urban schools: Suggestions from historically black institutions." *Action in Teacher Education* 13, no. 2: 30–35.

Reich, R. B. 1999. "Forward." In R. B. Freeman, *The new inequality: Creating solutions for poor America*, pp. vii–xiii. Boston: Beacon.

Rendón, L. I., and R. O. Hope. 1996. "An educational system in crisis." In L. Rendón and R. Hope (eds.), *Educating a new majority: Transforming America's educational system for diversity*, pp. 1–32. San Francisco: Jossey-Bass.

Resnick, L. B. 1989. "Introduction." In L. B. Resnick (ed.), *Knowing, learning, and instruction: Essays in honor of Robert Glaser*, pp. 1–24. Hillsdale, NJ: Lawrence Erlbaum.

Reyes, M. de la Luz. 1992. "Challenging venerable assumptions: Literacy instruction for linguistically different students." *Harvard Educational Review* 62, no. 4: 427–46.

Reyes, M. de la Luz, and J. J. Halcon. 1991. "Practices of the academy: Barriers to access for Chicano academics." In P. G. Altbach and K. Lotomey (eds.), *The racial crisis in American higher education*, pp. 167–86. Albany: SUNY Press.

Reynolds, M. C. (ed). 1989. *Knowledge base for the beginning teacher*. Elmsford, New York: Pergamon.

Richardson, V. 1994. "Constructivist teaching and teacher education: Theory and practice." Paper presented at the annual meeting of the American Educational Research Association, New Orleans.

———. 1995. "The role of attitudes and beliefs in learning to teach." In J. Sikula, T. Buttery, and E. Guyton (eds.), *Handbook on research on teacher education*, 2nd ed., pp. 102–19. New York: Macmillan.

———. 1999. "Teacher education and the construction of meaning." In G. A. Griffin (ed.), *The education of teachers: Ninety-eighth yearbook of the National Society for the Study of Education*, pp. 145–66. Chicago: University of Chicago Press.

Richardson, V., U. Casanova, P. Placier, and K. Guilfoyle. 1989. *School children at risk*. London: Falmer.

Riessman, F. 1962. *The culturally deprived child*. New York: Harper and Row.

Rios, F. 1993. "Thinking in urban, multicultural classrooms: Four teachers' perspectives." *Urban Education* 28, no. 3: 245–66.

Rist, R. 1970. "Student social class and teacher expectations: The self-fulfilling prophecy in ghetto education." *Harvard Educational Review* 40, no. 3: 411–51.

Robertson, P. F., and T. Frier. 1994. "Recruitment and retention of minority faculty." *New Directions for Community Colleges* 22, no. 3: 65–71.

Rodriguez, R. 1982. *Hunger of memory: An autobiography. The education of Richard Rodriguez*. Toronto: Bantam Books.

Rodriguez, Y. E., and B. R. Sjostrom. 1995. "Culturally responsive teacher preparation evident in classroom approaches to cultural diversity: A novice and an experienced teacher." *Journal of Teacher Education* 46, no. 4: 304–16.

Rosebery, A. S., B. Warren, and F. R. Conant. 1992. "Appropriating scientific discourse: Findings from language minority classrooms." *The Journal of the Learning Sciences* 2, no. 1: 61–94.

Rosenberg, P. 1993. "The presence of an absence: Issues of race in teacher education at a predominantly white college campus." Paper presented at the annual meeting of the American Educational Research Association, Atlanta.

Rosenthal, R., and L. Jacobson. 1969. *Pygmalion in the classroom: Teacher expectations and pupils' intellectual achievement*. New York: Holt, Rinehart, and Winston.

Ross, D., and W. Smith. 1992. "Understanding preservice teachers' perspectives on diversity." *Journal of Teacher Education* 43, no. 2: 94–103.

Rosser, J. M. 1990. "The role of the university president in realizing the multicultural university." *American Behavioral Scientist* 34, no. 2: 223–31.

Russell, C. 1996. *The official guide to racial and ethnic diversity*. Ithaca, NY: New Strategist Publications.

Salomon, G., and D. N. Perkins. 1998. "Individual and social aspects of learning." In P. D. Pearson and A. Iran-Nejad (eds.), *Review of research in education 23*, pp. 1–24. Washington, DC: American Educational Research Association.

Schmidt, P. R. 1996. "One teacher's reflections: Implementing multicultural literacy learning." *Equity and Excellence in Education* 29, no. 2: 20–29.

Scott, R. A. 1992. "Developing diversity as a campus strength." Paper presented at the Annual Meeting of the Association of American Colleges, Washington, DC.

Sfard, A. 1998. "On two metaphors for learning and the dangers of choosing just one." *Educational Researcher* 27, no. 2: 4–13.

Shade, B. 1995. "Developing a multicultual focus in teacher education: One department's story." *Journal of Teacher Education* 46, no. 5: 375–80.

Sharp, A. M. 1991. "The community of inquiry: Education for democracy." *Thinking: The Journal of Philosophy for Children* 9, no. 2: 31–37.

Shaw, C. 1991. "Multicultural teacher education: A call for conceptual change." *Multicultural Education* 31(Winter): 342–49.

Shirts, R. G. 1969. *Star Power*. La Jolla, CA: Western Behavioral Sciences Institute.

———. 1977. *BaFa BaFa*. La Jolla, CA: Western Behavioral Sciences Institute.

Shulman, J. H. (ed.). 1992. *Case methods in teacher education*. New York: Teachers College Press.

Shulman, J. H., and A. Mesa-Bains (eds.). 1993. *Diversity in the classroom: A casebook for teachers and teacher educators*. Hillsdale, NJ: Lawrence Erlbaum.

Shulman, L. S. 1987. "Knowledge and teaching: Foundations of a new reform." *Harvard Educational Review* 57, no. 1: 1–22.

———. 1992. "Toward a pedagogy of cases." In J. Shulman (ed.), *Case methods in teacher education*, pp. 1–30. New York: Teachers College Press.

Sims, M. J. 1992. "Inquiry and urban classrooms: A female African-American teacher in search of truth." *Theory into Practice* 31, no. 4: 342–49.

Sleeter, C. 1992. *Keepers of the American dream: A study of staff development and multicultural education*. London: Falmer.

———. 1995a. "Teaching whites about racism." In R. Martin (ed.), *Practicing what we teach: Confronting diversity in teacher education*, pp. 117–30. Albany: SUNY Press.

———. 1995b. "White preservice students and multicultural education coursework." In J. M. Larkin and C. E. Sleeter (eds.), *Developing multicultural teacher education curricula*, pp. 17–29. Albany: SUNY Press.

Sleeter, C. E., and C. A. Grant. 1991. "Race, class, gender, and disability in current textbooks." In M. Apple and L. K. Christian-Smith (eds.), *The politics of the textbook*, pp. 78–110. New York: Routledge and Chapman Hall.

Smith, D. G. 1989. *The challenge of diversity: Involvement or alienation in the academy?* ASHE-ERIC Higher Education Report, No. 4. Washington, DC: School of Education and Human Development, George Washington University.

Smith, G. P. 1992. "Recruiting minority teachers." Paper presented at a Major Symposium of the Annual Meeting of the American Association for Teacher Education, New Orleans.

Smylie, M.A. 1990. "Teacher efficacy at work." In P. Reyes (ed.), *Teachers and their workplace: Commitment, performance, and productivity*, pp. 48–66. Newbury Park, CA: Sage.

Smylie, M. A., M. Bay, and S. E. Tozer. 1999. "Preparing teachers as agents of change." In G. A. Griffin (ed.), *The education of teachers: Ninety-eighth Yearbook of the National Society for the Study of Education*, pp. 29–62. Chicago: University of Chicago Press.

Snell, J., and J. Swanson. 2000. "Essential knowledge and skills of teacher leaders: A search for a conceptual framework." Paper presented at the Annual Meeting of the American Educational Research Association, New Orleans.

Spellman, S. O. 1988. "Recruitment of minority teachers: Issues, problems, facts, possible solutions." *Journal of Teacher Education* 39, no. 4: 58–63.

Stachowski, L. L., and J. M. Mahan. 1998. "Cross-cultural field placements: Student teachers learning from schools *and* communities." *Theory into Practice* 37, no. 2: 155–62.

Stalvey, L. 1988. *The education of a WASP*. Madison: University of Wisconsin Press.

Stanton-Salazar, R. D. 1997. "A social capital framework for understanding the socialization of racial minority children and youths." *Harvard Educational Review* 67, no. 1: 1–40.

Steel, C. M. 1997. "A threat in the air: How stereotypes shape intellectual identity and performance." *American Psychologist* 52, no. 6: 613–29.

Sternberg, R. J. 1986. *Applied intelligence*. Boston: Harcourt Brace Jovanovich.

———. 1996. "Myths, countermyths, and truths about intelligence." *Educational Researcher* 25, no. 2: 11–16.

Stewart, J., K. J. Meier, R. M. La Follette, and R. E. England. 1989. "In quest of role models: Change in black teacher representation in urban school districts 1968–86." *Journal of Negro Education* 58, no. 2: 140–52.

Sturm, S., and L. Guinier. 1996. "The future of affirmative action: Reclaiming the innovative ideal." *California Law Review* 84, no. 4: 953–1036.

Sutton, R. E. 1991. "Equity and computers in schools: A decade of research." *Review of Educational Research* 61, no. 4: 475–503.

Suzuki, B. H. 1984. "Curriculum transformation for multicultural education." *Education and Urban Society* 16, no. 3: 294–322.

Swanson, J. 2000. "What differentiates an excellent teacher from a teacher leader?" Paper presented at the Annual Meeting of the American Educational Research Association, New Orleans.

Sykes, G., and T. Bird. 1992. "Teacher education and the case idea." In C. Grant (ed.), *Review of Research in Education 18*. Washington, DC: American Educational Research Association.

Tabachnick, B., and K. Zeichner. 1993. "Preparing teachers for cultural diversity." *Journal of Education for Teaching* 19, no. 4/5: 113–24.

Tatto, M. T. 1996. "Examining values and beliefs about teaching diverse students: Understanding the challenges for teacher education." *Educational Evaluation and Policy Analysis* 18, no. 2: 155–80.

Tatum, B. 1992. "Talking about race, learning about racism: The application of racial identity development theory in the classroom." *Harvard Educational Review* 62, no. 1: 1–24.

Teitelbaum, K., and D. P. Britzman. 1991. "Reading and doing ethnography: Teacher education and reflective practice." In B. R. Tabachnick and K. Zeichner (eds.), *Issues and practices in inquiry-oriented teacher education*, pp. 186–202. Bristol, PA: Falmer.

Tellez, K., P. Hlebowitsh, M. Cohen, and P. Norwood. 1995. "Social service field experiences and teacher education statistics." In J. Larkin and C. E. Sleeter (eds.), *Developing multicultural teacher education curricula*, pp. 65–78. New York: SUNY Press.

Terzian, A. L. 1991. "A model in community college transfer programs." *New Directions for Community Colleges* 74, Summer: 87–92.

Thiagarajan, S. 1990. *Barnga: A simulation game on cultural clashes.* Yarmouth, ME: Intercultural.

Tiedt, I. M. 1993. "Collaborating to improve teacher education: A dean of education's perspective." In M. J. Guy (ed.), *Teachers and teacher education: Essays on the National Education Goals*, pp. 35–59. Washington, DC: ERIC Clearinghouse on Teacher Education and American Association of Colleges for Teacher Education.

Tierney, W. G., and E. M. Bensimon. 1996. *Promotion and tenure: Community and socialization in academe.* Albany: SUNY Press.

Tom, A. R. 1984. *Teaching as a moral craft.* New York: Longman.

———. 1997. *Redesigning teacher education.* Albany: SUNY Press.

Tomás Rivera Center. 1993. *Resolving a crisis in education: Latino teachers for tomorrow's classrooms.* Claremont, CA: Author.

Turner, C. S. V., and S. L. Myers. 2000. *Faculty of color in academe: Bittersweet success.* Boston: Allyn and Bacon.

U. S. Census Bureau. 1993. *Social and economic characteristics, 1990: United States.* Washington, DC: Author.

———. 1995. *Statistical brief: Health insurance coverage.* Washington, DC: Author.

———. 1999a. *Asset ownership of households: 1993.* Washington, D. C.: Author. <www.census.gov/hhes/www/wealth/wlth93f.html>.

———. 1999b. *Historical poverty tables—families.* Washington, DC: Author. <www.census.gov/hhes/poverty/histpov/hstpov4.html>.

U. S. Department of Commerce. 1996. *Current population reports: Population projections of the United States by age, sex, race, and Hispanic origin: 1995 to 2050.* Washington, DC: Author.

———. 1998. *Statistical abstract of the United States 1998: The national data book.* Washington, DC: Author.

U. S. Department of Health and Human Services. 1996. *Health, United States: 1995.* Hyattsville, MD: Author.

U. S. Department of Labor. 1997. *Median usual weekly earnings of full-time wage and salary workers by selected characteristics, annual averages.* Washington, DC: Author. <hhtt://stats.bls.gov/news.release/wkyeng.toc.htm>.

U. S. Immigration and Naturalization Services. 1995. *Statistical yearbook of the immigration and naturalization services*. Washington, DC: U.S. Government Printing Office.

Vaden-Kiernan, N. 1996. *Statistics in brief: Parents' reports of school practices to involve families*. Washington, DC: National Center for Education Statistics.

Valli, L. 1995. "The dilemma of race: Learning to be color blind and color conscious." *Journal of Teacher Education* 46, no. 2: 120–29.

Vanett, L., and D. Jurich. 1990. "A context for collaboration: Teachers and students writing together." In J. K. Peyton (ed.), *Students and teachers writing together*, pp. 49–62. Washington, DC: TESOL.

Vásquez, O. 1992. "A Mexicano perspective: Reading the world in a multicultural setting." In D. Murray (ed.), *Diversity as resource: Redefining cultural literacy*, pp. 113–34. Washington, DC: TESOL.

Villegas, A. M. 1988. "School failure and cultural mismatch: Another view." *The Urban Review* 20, no. 4: 253–65.

———. 1991. *Culturally responsive teaching for the 1990s and beyond*. Washington, DC: American Association of Colleges for Teacher Education.

———. 1995. "Restructuring teacher education for diversity: The innovative curriculum." In *Teaching for diversity: Models for expanding the supply of minority teachers*, pp. 48–71. Princeton, NJ: Educational Testing Service.

———. 1997. "Increasing the diversity of the U.S. teaching force." In B. Biddle, T. Good, and I. Goodson (eds.), *The international handbook of teachers and teaching*, pp. 297–336. The Netherlands: Kluwer Academic.

———. 1998. "Equity and excellence in education." Princeton, NJ: Educational Testing Service.

———. 1999, Winter. "Democracy's challenge: Creating culturally responsive schools." *Doubts and Uncertainties* 13, no. 1: 1–5.

Villegas, A. M., and B. C. Clewell. 1998a. "Increasing teacher diversity by tapping the paraprofessional pool." *Theory into Practice* 37, no. 2: 121–30.

———. 1998b. "Increasing the number of teachers of color for urban schools." *Education and Urban Society* 31, no. 1: 42–61.

Villegas, A. M., and J. W. Young. 1997. "Immigrant education in New Jersey: Policies and practices." In T. Espenshade (ed.), *The impact of immigration in New Jersey*, pp. 173–98. Washington, DC: The Urban Institute.

Vygotsky, L. 1978. *Mind in society*. Cambridge, England: Cambridge University Press.

Wade, R. C. 1997a. "Community service-learning: An overview." In R. C. Wade (ed.), *Community service learning: A guide to including services in the public school curriculum*, pp. 19–34. Albany: SUNY Press.

———. 1997b. "Service-learning in preservice teacher education." In R. C. Wade (ed.), *Community service learning: A guide to including services in the public school curriculum*, pp. 314–30. Albany: SUNY Press.

Wah, L. M. 1994. *The color of fear*. Produced by the Oakland Men's Project and Todos Institute. Videocassette.

Walker, A. 1983. *In search of our mothers' gardens: Womanist prose*. San Diego: Harcourt Brace Jovanovich.

———. 1996. *The same river twice: Honoring the difficult: A meditation on life, spirit, art, and the making of the film, The Color Purple, ten years later.* New York: Scribners.

Walters, K. 1992. "Whose culture? Whose literacy?" In D. E. Murray (ed.), *Diversity as resource: Redefining cultural literacy*, pp. 3–29. Washington, DC: TESOL.

Wasley, P. A. 1991. *Teachers who lead: The rhetoric of reform and the realities of practice.* New York: Teachers College Press.

Waters, M. M. 1989. "An agenda for educating black teachers." *The Educational Forum* 53, no. 3: 267–79.

Weiner, Lois. 1993. *Preparing teachers for urban schools: Lessons from thirty years of school reform.* New York: Teachers College Press.

Wells, A. S., and I. Serna. 1996. "The politics of culture: Understanding local political resistance to detracking in racially mixed schools." *Harvard Educational Review* 66, no. 1: 93–118.

Wenglinsky, H. 1997. *When money matters.* Princeton, NJ: Educational Testing Service.

Westat, Inc. 1992. *Reaching for college: Vol. 2. Case studies of college-school partnerships.* Rockville, MD: Author.

Wijeyesinghe, C. L., P. Griffin, and B. Love. 1997. "Racism curriculum design." In M. Adams, L. A. Bell, and P. Griffin (eds.), *Teaching for diversity and social justice: A sourcebook*, pp. 82–109. New York: Routledge.

Wilson, S. M. 1991. "Parades of facts, stories of the past: What do novice history teachers need to know?" In M. Kennedy (ed.), *Teaching academic subjects to diverse learners*, pp. 99–116. New York: Teachers College Press.

Wilson, W. J. 1996. *When work disappears: The world of the new urban poor.* New York: Vintage Books.

Wolfram, W., C. T. Adger, and D. Christian. 1999. *Dialects in schools and communities.* Mahwah, NJ: Lawrence Erlbaum.

Wolfram, W., and D. Christian. 1989. *Dialects and education: Issues and answers.* Englewood Cliffs, NJ: Prentice Hall.

Wong-Fillmore, L. 1990. *Now or later? Issues related to the early education of minority group students.* Unpublished paper from the Council of Chief State School Officers.

Yeskel, F., and B. Leondar-Wright. 1997. "Classism curriculum design." In M. Adams, L. A. Bell, and P. Griffin (eds.), *Teaching for diversity and social justice: A sourcebook*, pp. 231–60. New York: Routledge.

Young, L. S. J. 1998. "Care, community, and context in a teacher education classroom." *Theory into Practice* 37, no. 2: 105–13.

Zeichner, K. 1990a. "Changing directions in the practicum: Looking ahead to the 1990s." *Journal of Education for Teaching* 16, no. 2: 105–32.

———. 1990b. "Contradictions and tensions in the professionalization of teaching and the democratization of schools." Paper presented at the annual meeting of the American Educational Research Association, Boston.

———. 1992. *NCRTL special report: Educating teachers for cultural diversity.* East Lansing: Michigan State University, National Center for Research on Teacher Learning.

———. 1993. *Educating teachers for cultural diversity.* East Landsing, MI: National Center for Research on Teacher Learning Special Report.

———. 1996a. "Designing educative practicum experiences for prospective teachers." In K. Zeichner, S. Melnick, and M. L. Gomez (eds.), *Currents of reform in preservice teacher education,* pp. 215–34. New York: Teachers College Press.

———. 1996b. "Educating teachers for cultural diversity." In K. Zeichner, S. Melnick, and M. L. Gomez (eds.), *Currents of reform in preservice teacher education,* pp. 133–75. New York: Teachers College Press.

Zeichner, K., C. Grant, G. Gay, M. Gillette, L. Valli, and A. M. Villegas. 1998. "A research informed vision of good practice in multicultural teacher education: Design principles." *Theory into Practice* 37, no. 2: 163–71.

Zeichner, K., and K. Hoeft. 1996. "Teacher socialization for cultural diversity." In J. Sikula, T. Buttery, and E. Guyton (eds.), *Handbook on research on teacher education,* 2nd ed., pp. 525–47. New York: Macmillan.

Zeichner, K., and S. Melnick. 1995. "The role of community field experiences in preparing teachers for cultural diversity." Paper presented at the annual meeting of the American Association of Colleges for Teacher Education, Washington, DC.

———. 1996. "The role of community field experiences in preparing teachers for cultural diversity." In K. Zeichner, S. Melnick, and M. L. Gomez (eds.), *Currents of reform in preservice teacher education,* pp. 176–96. New York: Teachers College Press.

Zimpher, N. L. 1989. "The RATE Project: A profile of teacher education students." *Journal of Teacher Education* 40, no. 6: 27–31.

Zimpher, N. L., and E. A. Asburn. 1992. "Countering parochialism in teacher candidates." In M. E. Dilworth (ed.), *Diversity in teacher education: New expectations,* pp. 40–62. San Francisco: Jossey-Bass.

Zimpher, N. L., and S. Yessayan. 1987. "Recruitment and selection of minority populations into teaching." *Metropolitan Education* XX: 57–71.

Zlotkowski, E. 1999. "Pedagogy and engagement." In R. G. Bringle (ed.), *Colleges and universities as citizens,* pp. 96–120. Boston: Allyn and Bacon.

INDEX

achievement: cultural difference theory for gap in, 42–44; deficit theories for gap in, 1, 39–42; and race/ethnicity of students, 9–12, 203nn3, 4; and socioeconomic background of students, xi, 13, 14; of students of color, xi–xii, 1; teachers' expectations of, 19, 37–38, 169

action plans, 117

action research projects, 97

admissions (colleges/universities): criteria for, 159; information on, 155. *See also* recruitment; selection criteria (teacher education)

advising, of students of color in colleges/universities, 161

affirming perspective/orientation: attitude toward cultural diversity, 36, 37; attitude toward culturally different students, 36, 37, 38; attitude toward dominant culture, 36, 37; as characteristic of culturally responsive teachers, xiv, 121, 198; development of, 35–53; expectations of student achievement, 38

African Americans/blacks: accounts of successful teachers of, 133; decreasing number in teaching force, 20, 21; income and household wealth of, 28, 29; increasing population of, 2; school-age population of, 3–4, 5; use of term, 203n1. *See also* faculty of color; students of color

agents of change. *See* change agents

American Indian students: cultural diversity among, 6; differing

home/school communication patterns for, 42–43, 85; school-age population of, 4, 5. *See also* faculty of color; students of color

Armstrong Atlantic State University (AASU), career ladder program, 175–76

arts and sciences schools/colleges: collaboration among schools/colleges of education, school districts and, xiv, 184–91, 200–201; collaboration between faculty in education and, 177–81; courses relevant to multicultural society, 178–79; courses for understanding students' community life, 86–89; faculty modeling culturally responsive teaching, xv, 179–80

Asian students: cultural diversity among, 6; increasing number of, 4, 5; as LEP students, 8. *See also* faculty of color; students of color

assessment: in community of learners classroom, 120; using varied practices for, 105–7, 110

Associated Colleges of the Midwest, Urban Education Program, 139

assumptions, underlying authors' proposal for teacher education curriculum, xvii–xxi, 26, 199

attitudes: of affirming vs. deficit perspectives, 35–37; toward cultural diversity, 36, 37; toward culturally different students, 35–53, 169; toward dominant culture, 35, 36, 37